MINDING CONSCIOUSNESS:

HOW LIFE URGES EMBODY ATTENTION

THIRD-EDITION

GARY A. LUCAS

MINDING CONSCIOUSNESS:
HOW LIFE URGES EMBODY ATTENTION

Edition 3.2, December 2023

Cover picture from my painting Kandinsky's Kat.

TABLE OF CONTENTS

FIGURES

TABLES

INTRODUCTION: MINDING CONSCIOUSNESS

Recent work in cognitive and computational neuroscience depicts the human cortex as a multi-level prediction engine. … But how, if at all, do emotions and sub-cortical contributions fit into this emerging picture? The fit, we shall argue, is both profound and potentially transformative. In the picture we develop, online cognitive function cannot be assigned to either the cortical or the sub-cortical component, but instead emerges from their tight co-ordination. This tight co-ordination involves processes of continuous reciprocal causation that weave together bodily information and 'top-down' predictions, generating a unified sense of what's out there and why it matters. The upshot is a more truly 'embodied' vision of the predictive brain in action. – Mark Miller & Andy Clark. "Happily entangled: Prediction, emotion, and the embodied mind", 2017

> **Introductory Remarks**

The goal of this book is to explore the neural mechanisms of conscious minds and to compose a model of how they work at a functional level. This chapter puts conscious mind in a perspective proposed by Descartes.

In the seventeenth century visitors to the royal gardens at the Château de Saint-Germain-en-Laye encountered statues that seemingly came to life. When visitors stepped on inconspicuous tiles along the walkways valves opened that allowed water to rush into the statues through hidden tubes. The hydraulic force was used to power the statues' movements.[1] In one grotto, Orpheus played music on his lyre while animals danced around and birds sang. In another grotto, Perseus slew a dragon, causing it to sink below the water. The activation of life-like sounds and movements, with no obvious external cause, made the actions seem spontaneous and real, at least in the moment. In his *Treatise on Man*, published posthumously in 1664, René Descartes drew an analogy between the automatons in the royal gardens and the workings of the physical body. He argued that the tiles that triggered the release of water, the pipes that directed its flow, the ingenious devices that induced movements and sounds, and the springs that shaped the movements into life-like forms all functioned much like senses, nerves, muscles, and tendons in living systems.

Following this analogy, Descartes argued that physical mechanisms could explain the actions of the body. However, despite Descartes' insight into the mechanisms of the body, he lacked an obvious mechanistic account of mind.[2] He, therefore, concluded that the body was a material substance (*res extensa* – physical stuff that extends in space) while the mind was an immaterial substance (*res cogitans* – mental stuff that occurs in thought). Humans, he proposed, had such a spiritual substance. They had feelings, they reasoned, they willed, and they imagined in the absence of physical causes. Animals, he argued, were mere automatons, beast machines that reacted to physical triggers and forces on the body like the statues at Saint-Germain-en-Laye.[3] Thus, Descartes concluded that animals lacked the feelings, reasoning, will, and imagination of conscious mind. Descartes' reputation, his model's fit with popular Christian beliefs,[4] and the fact that it was not clear how to disprove him, made his assertion that animals lacked conscious mind a common assumption for hundreds of years.

As scientific disciplines for the study of animal behavior began to take hold in the nineteenth century, early ethologists and behaviorists were perfectly happy with the assumption that animals lacked a conscious mind. Instinctive behavior was said to be driven by motives for biologically prepared action patterns that were released by specific sign stimuli. Learned behavior was argued to result from the pairing of stimulus and response units. Consciousness simply didn't seem necessary for these explanations. However, with the gradual rise of cognitive mechanisms for explaining human behavior over the last sixty years, the idea that non-human animals might sometimes have similar processes gradually began to challenge the assumption that animals could never be conscious. Notable in this regard was the pioneering effort of animal researcher Donald Griffin. In a series of books and papers stretching over twenty-five years, Griffin challenged the idea that animals lacked conscious awareness. Increasingly, he did so by presenting provocative examples of animals, from bees to modern mammals, performing tasks that seemed to involve conscious thought in humans.[5] Griffin was unable to prove that the animals in his examples were acting consciously, but his work cast doubts that all such examples could be summarily dismissed.

At the same time that Griffin was questioning the assumption that animals could not be conscious, research in neuroscience was expanding its analysis of how brain mechanisms enabled cognition and conscious awareness. Surprisingly, much of that work involved studies using animal models. Over time, it became clear that human brains share core structures with simpler vertebrates and that they share many brain structures with modern vertebrates. We may take solace in the argument that it is mostly our culture that enables us to exceed our animal origins and extend our cognitive skills in new directions. However, we have to accept that our brains follow a similar design to those of our animal ancestors. In supportive cultures, bonobos, chimps, orangutans, dolphins, and even parrots have learned to manage their attention and extend their cognitive skills using systems of arbitrary signs for communication. Thus, we know that such skills are not entirely limited to human minds.

While it is obvious that humans excel at conscious reasoning, that observation only makes understanding the continuity of mind more important. Modern theorists have come to accept that many animals reason in their own ways, that they express their will, and that they imagine at times in the absence of physical triggers. As we consider the continuity of mind, we will find many stages that we share with other animals. Even simple animals have proto-conscious architectures with properties similar to those found in human minds. In fact, there are arguably several stages in the evolution of proto-conscious awareness. Agents as simple as honeybees communicate with gestural signs and perform some discrimination tasks that we humans only seem to be able to perform using conscious reasoning. Some advanced invertebrates, the octopus, for example, have a much different neural architecture and yet appear to have higher-order cognitive skills that we don't understand well.

All this suggests that social insects, like the honeybee, at least have sentient orienting and tracking networks that adapt them to the urgency of maintaining life. It also suggests that some cephalopods, like the octopus, may have some form of self-awareness, albeit one much different from that of modern vertebrates. However, we will need to understand the processes that lead to the consciousness of vertebrates better before we can make informed conclusions about more distant minds. My goal in this work is therefore, to evaluate the latest stages of conscious mind, human consciousness and the level of consciousness in modern vertebrates – birds and mammals – and to identify key mechanisms that contribute to conscious thought. I believe this is a valuable step in understanding conscious mind, although I acknowledge it still leaves topics like sentience in bees and potential consciousness in cephalopods largely unexplored.

On the positive side, we know what brain regions appear to be critical for consciousness in humans. That is, we know regions whose loss results in coma or the absence of cogent awareness of the world. We also know about the basic high-level wiring plans from those regions to other parts of the brain, in particular, their connections to the attention managing networks in the thalamus and cortex. Further, we know that we share most of this architecture with other modern vertebrates. What we don't know as much about are the adaptive dispositions that are implemented within hundreds of life-urge nuclei in brainstem and midbrain networks, and the decision logic of many attention managing nuclei in the thalamus. However, we have insights into this logic, and we know that attention is related to consciousness. So based on these connections, and their end effects, we can make informed assumptions about what goes on in many of these networks, even if we do not know all the details.

To explain the phenomenal effects of consciousness, we also will need to understand the process of emergence. Some properties of every new organization can be linked rather directly to the properties of its component parts. For example, when atoms combine to form new molecular organizations, the weight of the new molecule can be precisely calculated from the weights of its component parts. However, not all the properties of the new molecule can be accounted for in this way. The interactive properties of the molecule are emergent. They cannot be readily derived from the interactive properties of its parts. It seems that some of the interactive properties of the parts are tied up binding the new organization together, so the available interactions of the molecule differ from those of its parts. Further, the structure of a new organization may also introduce new properties. For example, long proteins often fold into shapes that give them unique properties. Simply knowing what parts make up the protein does not predict the emergent properties of these shapes.

Organizational properties do not exist at the parts level, so they cannot be explained on that level. However, describing the functional properties of a new organization often provides insights into how the organization must be constructed to engage them. It was

Antonio Damasio's concise way of describing conscious experience as the *feeling of what happens* that first suggested to me how phenomenal consciousness could be implemented in an artificial agent.[6] If consciousness depends on the joint awareness of perceptions and feelings, then, on a reductionist level, feeling-related systems must be part of the inputs that gain attention. Thus, when I found that life urges in the brainstem provide broad inputs into the thalamic networks that manage attention,[7] I recognized those connections as a path by which feelings might gain consciousness. At that point, in the book *Emergence, Mind, and Consciousness*, I made the bold claim that we could build a robot that experienced a *feeling of what happens*.[8] This present book refines my thinking about the mechanisms that make conscious awareness possible. Based on these mechanisms, I will describe what functions need to be supported to build a conscious robot.

The insight that Damasio's *feeling of what happens* description provided has led me to characterize other phenomenal aspects of consciousness in descriptive terms that hint at underlying processes. We will encounter many such descriptions: the *feeling of where I am* that accompanies the observer self, the *feeling of being able to make things happen* that accompanies the agent self, the *feeling of being able to do what I've done before* that accompanies reflective agency, are just a few. Admittedly, these are only descriptions that suggest what inputs would be needed to create various feelings. They do not explain the emergent experiential effects. However, much as a chef can learn to anticipate tastes based on her experience with cooking methods and spices, with practice I believe we can gain similar insights into the neural recipes from which conscious feelings emerge.

We are all aware that feelings can influence what we learn. When we do something that results in life urges with positive valences the neural connections between predictive cues, actions, and their outcomes are strengthened. We call this effect *reinforcement*. Reinforcement learning ensures that we are more likely to repeat actions that have previously led to rewarding events and that we come to anticipate rewards when we encounter cues that predict them. In contrast, when actions lead to aversive consequences, we learn to avoid doing the same actions again. We call this change in learning *punishment*. We also learn to steer away from cues that have preceded aversive outcomes in the past as a way of avoiding those effects. Reinforcement and punishment, and their reactive dispositions, approach and withdrawal, are well-established effects that help explain how we learn to repeat actions that lead to positive outcomes while avoiding those that lead to negative ones. Once we understand the effects of reinforcement and punishment, we understand how using feelings to guide what we learn makes us more adaptive agents.

Somehow we have not yet developed a similar conceptual framework for thinking about how feelings influence attention. The feelings that affect attention are not the same as those that result in reinforcement and punishment. Positive and negative rewards depend largely on dopamine signaling in learning networks. The dopamine networks enable minds to connect cues and actions that lead to rewarding outcomes together, while avoiding cues and actions that lead to punishing outcomes. These reinforcing and punishing feelings sometimes gain attention, but our attention is not directed by them in the same way. Attention is guided largely by alerting and arousal signals directed to the thalamus and by basal forebrain arousal regions. Acetylcholine is the most important of these arousal transmitters, although several other arousal transmitters, particularly glutamate, play important roles.

However, unlike the punishment effects for learning, aversive conditions that direct alerting and arousal signals to the thalamus don't punish attention, they also focus it. In fact, as a rule of thumb, the stronger the feelings and motives, regardless of whether they might be considered positive or negative in other tasks, the more likely an agent is to attend to features associated with them. And when those feature-feeling combinations gain attention, the associated feelings impart values to the topics of attention and change how our mind and our body react to them. So just as the concept of feeling-guided learning helps us understand how reinforcement and punishment result in more adaptive learning, a focus on feeling-bound attention will help us understand how feelings guide our reactions to the topics that gain attention.

The idea that the feelings of the body contribute to consciousness also forces us to rethink Descartes' distinction between mind and body. It means that the topics of conscious mind are never separated fully from the body. As Mark Miller and Andy Clark note in the opening quote, mind and body are reciprocally connected such that processes in the mind are guided and enhanced by embodied feelings. Descartes missed this critical connection when he proclaimed "Cogito; ergo sum – I think; therefore, I am." Conscious agents are not simply detached thinkers; their very sense of self is determined by how they feel as they perceive and think. Descartes might have captured this aspect of consciousness better if he had proclaimed: "Sentio quid cogito; ergo sum – I feel what I think; therefore I am." We are feeling-bound agents. The features we notice in the world, how we react to them, what experiences we remember, and what we recall on later occasions are enhanced by feelings.

EDITION CHANGES AND WHAT TO EXPECT

The aim of this work is to understand how neural mechanisms lead to conscious experience. In addition to an outline of neural mechanisms, the first edition of this work explained how affect-based accounts of consciousness, as highlighted by Antonio Damasio and Bud Craig,[9] could be linked with attention-based accounts of consciousness, as emphasized by theorists such as Gerald Edelman, Francis Crick, and Rodolfo Llinás.[10] The affect-based accounts of consciousness focus largely on adaptive biological dispositions and their role in supporting conscious feelings. The attention-based accounts of consciousness focus on the associative processes of the thalamocortical architecture that bring information to attention, but these accounts largely ignore supporting adaptive dispositions and feelings.

However, a bridge between the affective and attention-based accounts of consciousness was suggested to me by the findings of Murray Sherman and Ray Guillery, who showed that adaptive brainstem inputs also contribute to the associative processes for resolving attention.[11] This is because the brainstem modules are sources of motivational life-urges that project on to the thalamus as modulatory states of arousal that guide attention. In addition to expanding the range of neurological mechanisms underlying feeling-bound attention in this model, I have also tried to emphasize that consciousness involves emergent properties that extend beyond neural inputs. Building on my previous discussion on emergence,[12] I have tried to explain the interconnected nature of emergent phenomena, their links to underlying mechanisms, and their tendency to result in novel and discontinuous properties.

Trying to combine all these ideas into a readily understandable narrative has been challenging. There were many places in the first edition that provided cogent, and to my mind, compelling and important insights. And yet, the overall presentation was not always fluid and clear. In the second edition I tried to remedy many of these problems, adding explanatory support when necessary, and removing unnecessary extensions to make the points more concise. Admittedly, the ideas are still often complicated and there is a constant scattering of terms from neuroscience. However, if we want to understand the links from neural inputs and their processing mechanisms to the emergence of phenomenal experiences and feelings of self, then we have to recognize how these processes interact.

In addition to making the overall presentation easier to follow, the second edition introduced several concepts and theoretical frameworks that placed our model of consciousness in a larger context. The most important of these involve Giulio Tononi's emphasis on the importance of coherent processing in the thalamocortical architecture during consciousness;[13] Pascal Fries proposal for how what he describes as *communication through coherence (CTC)* enhances neural processing;[14] and Stanislas Dehaene's observations that as a coherent focus of attention takes form a self-amplifying avalanche of neural processing dramatically increases the intensity of conscious processing.[15] I found Fries description of how CTC results in a phase transition when strong coherence occurs to be highly consistent with Dehaene's observations that as a coherent focus of attention takes form there is a self-amplifying effect that dramatically increases the intensity of neural communication during consciousness.

As I began thinking more about these processes for the third edition it occurred to me that the return signals from the cortex to the thalamus reactivate the same sites that send signals to the cortex. Such feed-forward loops have a tendency to sustain activity and even self-amplify. It appears that in early stages of attention, there is still a lot of competition among alternative feature sets competing in the thalamic filter so no individual feature set is very intense and thus its feed-forward effects are limited. However, as the feature set gaining attention reaches a high level of coherence the competition is reduced and the stronger feed-forward loops may begin to engage a self-amplifying effect. Further, since the return signals from the cortex to the thalamus also branch to the brainstem, the supporting brainstem return loops would also be enhanced. This suggested to me that the feed-forward return loops provide a likely mechanism for driving coherent attention.

In addition to describing this multi-level architecture for consciousness in the third addition, I realized that it was important to show how the basal ganglia (BG) fit into conscious architecture. The BG is like the central processing unit of the brain. It is where decisions are made. Evidence suggests that there are multiple cortical BG planning loops that also may engage attention.[16] So there are more attention loops to be focused. Importantly, the cortical-BG planning loops also have the potential to make conscious agents smarter.

Having introduced these planning loops to our model I recognized that there was another learning function involving them. Neuroscientist Ann Graybiel suggests that the cortex, plus the striatum, and pallidum in the BG, have come to function as a massive three-layer learning network in which the middle layer, the striatum, learns to map cortical inputs to connected output drivers in the pallidum.[17] Graybiel argues that this enables the striatum to anticipate sequential action plans and to chain them together in behavioral chunks. I have supplemented Graybiel's model with cholinergic inputs from the basal nucleus of Meynert (BNM) to assemble an incremental master-apprentice learning architecture. The idea is that the BNM promotes the cortex to reorganize its qualia in larger units so it can continually grow with experience.

If we are going to build a conscious robot, then we will need to understand how to develop a similar architecture. Many have long assumed that building a conscious robot is impossible. But once we understood what features of neural networks were essential for learning and memory, we learned how to duplicate those processes in artificial neural networks that could learn and remember. I admit that extending this strategy to consciousness is challenging, but I claim it is possible. First, we need to understand the neural architecture required for conscious experience. And once we understand the critical features in that architecture, we need to understand how to build them. It will take work, and the design will have to progress in stages, but I am confident it can be accomplished.

> **Ending Remarks**

Feeling-bound attention continually places perceptions and actions in the context of important emotive valuations and reactive dispositions. This makes conscious awareness biologically adaptive.

1: ATTENTION, MIND, AND SELF

When I talk with you, I must engage your attention. …. If you suddenly shift your attention away and cease to engage me, I may briefly continue to direct a barrage of verbal tokens toward the side of your head, but I soon come to recognize that I am no longer talking with you. – Gary Lucas, *Emergence Mind and Consciousness*, 2011

➢ **Introductory Remarks**

Descartes argued that the body was a material substance, while the mind was a spiritual substance. However, while Descartes argued that mind and body were separate kinds of substances, he argued that when mind and body are joined in a human agent they interact.

As he does almost every day, my feline companion, Tom Terrific, has arrived on the arm of my reading chair. Earlier Tom called to me, but I was busy reading and ignored him. Now he is more assertive. He leans close and announces his presence with a softly trilled greeting. Then, placing his paw on my shoulder, he gently tugs at me. We have gone through this exchange hundreds of times. Tom is trying to get my attention. As soon as I look up, he makes the repeated head dips that show he is watching closely for my reaction. Then, as soon as I start to move, Tom jumps down, raises his tail, and runs ahead. He is leading me to the place where he wants my help. Occasionally, he pauses and looks back to make sure I am following. Without speech, Tom cannot direct my attention to objects and places as efficiently as you can. However, aside from his more limited signaling strategies, the communication process that Tom follows is not really so different. Tom uses gestures and calls to gain my attention and direct me to where he wants my help. Similarly, I use gestures and words that Tom understands to signal my intentions to him. And when Tom and I are successful, our minds meet in moments of coordinated attention.[18]

Our goal here is to provide a framework for thinking about how conscious minds function and the exchange with Tom provides our first insights. My conscious mind is constantly organized around the events at the center of my attention. Your conscious mind is organized around the center of your attention. And Tom's conscious mind is organized around the center of his attention. Of course, there are differences in the complexity of the concepts our respective attention systems can resolve. Further, there are obvious differences in the type of communication skills available to Tom versus those available to you and me. And surely there are also differences as to what kind of events Tom finds most interesting compared to what you and I find of interest. However, the core processes by which the attention of modern vertebrate minds is implemented are remarkably similar. It is the complexity of topics and each individual's ability to manage their attention that varies more.

Figure 1-1: Tom Terrific in a typical state of focused attention.

The point here is that when conscious agents interact with

each other, they do so by exchanging signs about both their external focus of attention and their internal action plans and feelings. In fact, it is only when conscious minds coordinate their attention with each other in a shared focus on cues, intentions, and feelings that they feel their minds have met. Of course, I don't understand Tom's feelings entirely, but I don't always understand the feelings of my human partners fully either. However, I only need to understand the conscious focus of another agent well enough to guide my decisions toward more coordinated activities – if they are my friends – or more counteractive activities – if they are my competitors – in order to make my conscious decisions more adaptive. Tracking and managing attention is how conscious minds coordinate activities with each other.

There are many brain functions that can operate without the support of attention, but to the extent they do so, they operate in the background, outside of conscious awareness. In contrast, there are many tasks that can only be accomplished when several different brain regions are brought to bear on the same goal. Attention provides a means for coordinating distributed brain functions by uniting circuits of perception, action, and feeling into globally connected clusters of organized activity. You smell the aroma of food, you react with motives to pursue it, and the task of guiding food-related actions becomes part of your attention. In a similar way, tracking the attention of others helps conscious agents react more readily to each other. A coordinated predator is better at tracking her prey and managing her pursuit on the chase. A coordinated prey is better at avoiding the attention and actions of her predators. These are the adaptive benefits that attention provides.

The model proposed here is that consciousness is the phenomenal experience that emerges as features gain a coherent focus of attention. However, feelings in this model must be defined broadly. They are not merely somatic sensations; they may include emotional moods, action dispositions, and arousal states. These extended reactivity feelings are what Descartes would have called animal spirits (see the discussion in the next section).

Consciousness is thus much more than simply attention. Attention brings a number of distinct neural processes together in one focus. However, vertebrate brains have adopted a strategy of using feelings to prioritize what topics gain attention. As a consequence, the more intensely reactivity states are associated with certain features and tasks, the more likely they are to gain attention. Thus, consciousness emerges as the topics of attention and their associated reactivity states come into focus. And when they gain attention, the reactivity states are experienced as feelings.

Some view consciousness as merely a subjective embellishment of experience that serves no function, and then they wonder why it exists. However, consciousness is adaptive because attention to ongoing feelings continually places objects and actions in the context of important emotive valuations and reactive dispositions. When we hear an unexpected noise, we don't just hear the sound; we react with feelings of startle, curiosity, or recognition. And those feelings guide how we subsequently react to the noise. If we didn't feel anything associated with the noise, then it is unlikely we would even notice it. We would be attending to features associated with stronger feelings instead. In short, conscious feelings not only accompany attention, but they also link the features that gain attention to values and motives that better prepare an agent to react to those features. That preparedness is what makes consciousness so adaptive.

Recognizing that attention and feelings are connected also makes another aspect of conscious mind more understandable. Our sense of self depends on the fact that, while what we feel co-occurs with what we perceive, our feelings are not co-located with the objects that we perceive. We experience the targets of our external senses as being located outside of our body. However, we experience our attending-feeling-reacting dispositions as centrally located. Thus, we come to distinguish between external perceptions and internal dispositions. It is the external perceptions that we identify as parts of the world. It is our body, and the internal feelings and reactions it engages, that we identify as parts of our self. This distinction between self and world is essential for managing our interactions with the world and with each other.

CONNECTING MIND AND BODY

> Nature likewise teaches me by these sensations of pain, hunger, thirst, etc., that I am not only lodged in my body as a pilot in a vessel, but that I am besides so intimately conjoined, and as it were intermixed with it, that my mind and body compose a certain unity. For if this were not the case, I should not feel pain when the body is hurt, seeing I am merely a thinking thing, but should perceive the wound by understanding alone, just as a pilot perceives by sight when any part of his vessel is damaged.[19]

Descartes argued that the body was a material substance, while the mind was a spiritual substance. This distinction has come to be called *Cartesian dualism*. Because mind and body were considered to be different kinds of substances they were not thought to be dependent on each other. The soul could live on after the body died. However, while Descartes argued that mind and body were separate substances, as noted in the quote above, he argued that when mind and body are joined they interact. To support this interaction, Descartes proposed there was a region in the brain that served as the seat of the soul in living humans. The region Descartes identified for this role was the pineal gland. His choice was influenced by the fact that the pineal is centrally located in the brain, but does not occur in pairs as most other parts of the brain do.

Descartes even proposed some cursory mechanisms for interactions between the pineal and the rest of the brain. He thought that the pineal was in a position to receive inputs from the *animal spirits* of the body. Animal spirits were proposed to arrive via signals carried through the arteries. Based on these animal-spirit inputs, Descartes suggested that the pineal, as guided by the soul, could then influence outgoing decisions via forces it exerted on the central ventricles of fluid in the brain. The pineal's forces on the ventricles were proposed to act something like the force of *wind on sails*, and thus to propel outgoing reactions in the brain like wind propels a sailing ship. In this way, animal spirits could influence conscious decisions, and conscious decisions could influence reactions in the body, without there being any direct connections between body and mind.[20]

The curious thing about the role of the pineal and its mental forces in Descartes' model is that, although we know it to be wrong, it shares several features that can readily be related to the model of conscious mind proposed here. Neuroscience was in its infancy in Descartes' time. We now know that the pineal is a light-sensitive region of the brain that assesses trends in the seasonal variations of light-dark rhythms and influences seasonal changes in motivation. In addition, the pineal senses daily cycles of light and manages daily cycles of serotonin and melatonin. The seasonal and daily changes managed by the pineal have obvious effects on mental activity, but they do not provide much insight into conscious awareness. Interestingly, however, the pineal is located in a region of the brain known as the epithalamus. Just anterior to the pineal is the thalamus itself. The thalamus is now known to be a region that is involved in conscious attention. It manages the flow of information from external senses to the cortex.

As we will discover, the thalamus also receives broad inputs from brainstem sensing-reacting networks below it as well as from nearby homeostatic and motivational networks. These networks serve as early processing centers for assessing inputs from the body. In fact, Antonio Damasio considers these regions to serve as the *proto-self*. Proto-self regions are pre-conscious networks for evaluating ongoing status and reactive dispositions. In the next chapter, I will argue that these pre-conscious processes begin as little more than reflexive sensing and acting life urges that are refined by networks in the brainstem and midbrain. However, when these life urges reach the thalamus, they have the potential to gain attention as conscious feelings. Thus, in Descartes' model, life urges could easily qualify as sources of *animal spirits*. And while Descartes' idea about what brain region supported conscious mind was wrong, his idea that there was a link between animal spirits (somatic life urges) and conscious mind was prescient. In fact, had Descartes simply focused a few millimeters anterior to the pineal, and argued that consciousness was influenced by animal spirits directed at the thalamus, rather than at the epithalamus, today he would likely be considered a core founder of the neuroscience of consciousness.

There is another aspect of Descartes' thinking that we can now put in better perspective. That is his concept of substances. In general, substances are defined by their interactive properties. However, there are also categorical differences in how some substances are assembled and interact. Mind and body are categorically different. They not only have different properties, but the ontological processes by which those properties are assembled differ. Descartes generally treats the body as a physical substance. The body clearly has physical properties, but living systems also have properties that are not merely physical. They grow, they repair themselves, and they may even reproduce similar copies of themselves.

Descartes didn't consider these aspects of the body to be important for his distinction between body and mind, and the science of his time didn't provide him with any insights into the processes that make living systems different substances. However, we now know that the added properties of living systems result largely from the interaction of physical stuff with genetic coding systems. The genetic codes are also composed of physical stuff, but when codes are used to guide ontological interactions, the properties of the composite system change. Living systems use genetic codes to guide their development and to adapt across generations. These are ontological properties that purely physical systems do not share. Thus, in a real sense, living systems involve a different category of interactive properties than purely physical matter does.

When it comes to mind, a similar difference becomes obvious. Mind only emerges in nature within the highly flexible neural networks found in animal brains. However, we now understand that neither biological nor computer modeled neural networks are disconnected from the material world. They both work by making physical changes in connections between neurons due to associative changes in activity. In brains these connections are known as synapses. The changes are physical, but they modify how a neural network reacts to signals. Further, some networks can release added neurotransmitters that enhance learning and arousal in other networks. We call these added transmitter signals reinforcers. Physical systems don't have processes for learning, memory, or reinforcement. And living systems without neurons have a very limited capacity for such changes. Synaptic changes effectively reprogram how neural networks interact. Thus, agents with associative neural networks are yet another ontological category of substance. They have minds that interact in ways that simpler living systems cannot.

However, synaptic coding is not the only process for reprogramming complex brains. Once networks with different properties form, learning, memory, and arousal systems begin to interact in novel ways. One of the unique additions to vertebrate mind is a process of feeling-bound attention. Consciousness results from the dynamic interconnection of perceptions, actions, and feelings in coherent clusters of attention. This reprogramming is not based on synaptic changes, but on temporary enhancements by synchronous binding and filtering processes. It is only within these momentary bindings that feelings come to be linked with other topics of attention. Simpler neural networks do not have elaborate processes for synchronously binding feeling networks with perceptual networks. Thus, the dynamic binding and filtering processes of conscious mind truly result in yet another category of substance, a mind that feels its own reactions as it attends to the world. However, these added properties are not separate from the physical world. Their operation depends on interactions within the physical networks binding perceptions and feelings together.

Summarizing briefly, systems of coding and reprogramming change how physical processes behave. Genetic coding enables living systems to change how they develop and adapt across generations. Synaptic neural reprogramming enables neural networks to learn and remember across experiences. This is the essence of an associative mind. And the dynamic interconnection of associative networks for perceptions, actions, and feelings in clusters of attention enables minds to focus on a subset of features and feelings in ongoing moments of conscious experience. Purely physical systems do not adapt in these ways. So conscious minds, associative minds, living bodies, and purely physical matter are different categories of substance. They have different ontological and interactive properties. However, they are not fully separate from each other either. They are connected by dependencies and interfaces across levels which involve both upward and downward interactions. This *emergent interconnectedness* means that causal effects can flow in both directions between mind and matter.

Consider the interconnections that make this possible. Neurons would have no information if there were not receptor interfaces that transduce physical stuff into neural signals. Further, neurons could not fire without chemical processes operating within them. Associative mind could not take form without a complex of neural networks. Conscious mind could not emerge without associative subsystems for perceptions and life urges, and without networks for binding those features together in attention. But the selective processing of conscious mind also has downward effects. It enhances activity in the associative neural processes that gain attention. Those neural networks, in turn, have downward effects on physical reactions in the body, because they have interfaces with muscles that produce actions in the world. Thus, mind and matter are not separate. Note, however, that these interconnections also imply that, contrary to Descartes' thinking, a mind cannot exist without a living body. When the body dies, the interactions supporting conscious mind cease to exist.

The idea that there are dependencies and interconnections between the dynamic processes of conscious mind, the neural processes of unconscious mind, and the genetic and physical processes of the body should not be surprising. In our everyday use of computers for word processing, there are interconnections between the contacts we make on a keyboard and the letter representations that are sent to word-processing programs. The keyboard knows nothing about words or sentences. It is a simple input device. However, it has an interface that has been designed to convert key presses into digital ASCII codes that a coordinated word-processing program can assemble into word-like sequences. And when it comes time to print out a document, the word-processing program passes its sequence of letter and punctuation codes on to an interface that converts each ASCII code to a pixel matrix for printing letter shapes. The printer, of course, knows nothing about the meaning of the shapes. However, most humans have learned associations that interface between printed letter shapes and language-specific words. Thus a chain of interfaces can connect functional reactions across different kinds of substances and produce higher-order effects. This is the power of emergent interconnectedness.

The relationship between the physical systems of the body and the genetic codes that assemble them – and between the learning networks of mind and the synaptic programs that manage them – and between the topics of attention and the dynamic processes that bind them together – are immensely more complex than the interconnections between keyboard inputs and word-processing decisions, or between word-processing outputs and printer-mediated shapes. However, the analogy is clear. Systems using different categories of substances can nevertheless communicate via interfaces that convert representations that work in one category to representations that work in another. The body constantly interfaces with the brain by converting physical inputs detected by sensory cells into neural signals that can be processed in the brain. The brain constantly interfaces with the body by releasing chemical signals and hormones that influence activity in the body. And when mental decisions require actions, the motor networks release acetylcholine, which causes muscles to contract.

Once we come to understand that there can be interconnections between representations of one category of substances and those of another, then the idea that there are interactions between the substances of mind and those of the body is not so difficult to accept. Descartes' "animal spirits" was a metaphor for his insight that there were interfaces between the physical processes of the body and the mental processes of mind. His "wind against the sail" was a metaphor for his insight that there were interfaces between mental processes and the reactions of the body. Descartes did not have more detailed insights into the nature of these interfaces. However, it is now clear that mind and body and matter simply could not work together without these ongoing interconnections.

CONCLUDING COMMENTS

So here is our initial framework for conscious mind. Attention, consciousness, and the sense of self are all emergent effects resulting from the way that attention is managed in vertebrate brains. They can never be fully separated from each other, and yet they have different distinguishing properties. Attention is the ability to focus selected aspects of mind on a particular topic. It is an evolutionary consequence of competition for better ways to coordinate multiple brain processes around a common task. Consciousness is a delayed consequence of attention. It emerges as sensorimotor features and feelings are bound together in the focus of attention. Feelings emerge during this process because life urges are used to prioritize what topics gain attention, and the life urges that gain attention are experienced as emotive changes in mental activity and adaptive reactions in the body.

A sense of self emerges in this process because the mind locates external objects outside the body, while it locates its abilities to orient, feel, and plan within the body. Thus, the attending-feeling-reacting parts of conscious experience are categorized separately from perceptual events. It is this dichotomy between the internal feelings of mind and the external sources of perception that gives rise to a separate sense of self and world. You and I and Tom are conscious because we use embodied feelings to guide how to react to what we perceive and because we experience those feelings as we react. This aspect of conscious experience is what Antonio Damasio calls the *feeling of what happens*.[21]

> ➤ **Ending Remarks**

Conscious feelings are adaptive because they continually cause us to consider the values and motives associated with our attention. Yet, there are bidirectional interconnections between physical matter, living systems, associative mind, and conscious mind. Emergent interconnectedness means that events in the world can affect how we feel and that mental feelings can influence how we decide to react to the world. The *self* is the emergent property of conscious mind that experiences *the feeling of what happens*.

2: FROM LIFE URGES TO PROTO-FEELINGS

Core consciousness is the door to a revelation of regulatory values, the passage into the possibility of constructing in the mind some counterpart of the regulatory value hidden in the brain core, some new and more open way of sensing the life urge and the means to hold on to life. – Antonio Damasio, "Investigating the biology of consciousness", 1998

> **Introductory Remarks**

Life urges are source inputs for adaptive feelings. Many begin as autonomic inputs from the body that are reorganized in the early brainstem. Some motivational and emotional combinations are assembled in the midbrain.

Having described consciousness as the phenomenal experience that accompanies the focus of feeling-bound attention, we need to gain a better understanding of feelings. Every living organism has receptors that provide information about sensory status and effector systems that can adjust for status conditions. In bacteria, these reactions are little more than chemical links between sensors and motor reactions. In more complex agents, neural networks manage sensing and reacting. Some of the simplest of these network reactions are reflexes, motor reactions to inputs, and tropisms, directional movements toward or away from input cues. For example, consider what happens when our feline friend Tom Terrific steps on a thorn. A pain receptor in Tom's paw detects the thorn as it pierces his skin and signals to the spinal cord. Some interneurons in the spinal cord react to these receptor inputs by sending inhibitory signals to the extensor motor neurons. These suppress the stepping action. Other interneurons increase flexor activities that cause Tom to lift his paw.

However, neural signaling from the body is not confined to spinal reflexes. Much of the information about peripheral receptor and motor activity is also passed up the spinal cord to the brainstem. A composite of networks in the brainstem then combines receptor inputs and reactive activity into more complex representations and reactions. Thus, what begins as sensory inputs and reflexive adjustments is merged into an ascending series of increasingly integrated feeling interpretations and reactive dispositions. Consistent with these observations, researchers Antonio Damasio, Bud Craig, and Jaak Panksepp have focused on the affective nature of conscious feelings and their links to ascending brainstem networks for motives and actions.[22]

Panksepp, in particular, has noted that feelings not only originate in brainstem motor and arousal regions, but that they also depend on motivational and emotional systems. In particular, he emphasizes four broad categories of affect commonly found in vertebrates: 1) appetitive needs, food, water, sex, etc. and associated wanting, seeking, and rewarding dispositions, 2) aversive states, pain and fear, and defensive avoidance dispositions, 3) anger, rage, protective states, and aggressive dispositions, and 4) social bonding, attachment, caring feelings, and the reactions resulting from separation or the panic of loss.[23] Thus, the affective systems that influence conscious feelings extend from reflexive modules, to brainstem and motor reactions, and onto core motivational and emotional networks.

We can generally describe the networks in which simple reflexes work in vertebrates, but we don't know as much about the integration that occurs in many brainstem modules. However, we do know that there are hundreds of combinatorial networks in the brainstem that integrate ascending inputs into more complex adaptive dispositions. Living agents are sensitive to the suddenness of sensory inputs and their directionality with respect to the body. These summary processes promote timely and directed reactions. Some dispositions provide proprioceptive feedback and vestibular inputs, all core aspects of the physical self reacting to the world. Some are sensitive to the intensity of stimulus and motor activity. These evaluations provide a gage of their importance. Other combinations resolve approach-withdrawal dispositions, sensing versus acting motives, risk versus safety tendencies, and expectedness versus surprisingness reactions.

Following Antonio Damasio's characterization in the opening quote. I have taken to referring to this broad range of homeostatic adaptations, from reflexes to emotions, as *life urges.* Life urges involve sensing, arousal, and reactive processes that help an agent hold on to life.[24] Many life urges never gain conscious attention, and yet they provide a wealth of underlying dispositions that refine and guide adaptive reactions. In fact, because many of them are assembled from somatic inputs, life urges may well be considered the carriers of "animal spirits" that Descartes proposed enabled the body to influence reactions in the mind. Life urges serve as motivational needs and emotional moods that at times guide awareness. A key point in affective models of consciousness is that these dispositions are not always unconscious reactions. When they gain attention they are experienced as *feelings of self-awareness*. In effect, the self emerges from an awareness of life-urge dispositions. If we want to build robots with a similar sense of self, they will need their own complex of life-urge dispositions.

A CORE SENSE OF LIFE

Most of the incoming brainstem inputs from the body depend on peripheral receptors from the sympathetic and parasympathetic subdivisions of the autonomic nervous systems. Sympathetic status inputs are bundled together in the first layer of the ascending spinal cord.[25] This layer provides a broad array of somatic information, including those for sharp pain, aching pain, tissue temperatures (there are separate receptors for hot and cold), mechanical stress, itch, and irritation related to immune system activity. Some of these result in local spinal reflexes, like the pain reflexes that cause Tom to withdraw his paw, or the itch that causes him to scratch at an occasional flea bite. Most of these ascending inputs are directed on to the parabrachial nucleus (PBN). The PBN is a large brainstem complex that integrates somatic inputs from all across the body.

Parasympathetic status information arrives in the brainstem via cranial nerves.[26] These include the facial, trigeminal, and glossopharyngeal nerves. These nerves provide somatic information about face, mouth, tongue, taste, and swallowing activity. The vagus nerve provides feedback related to heart rate, blood pressure, respiratory activity or distress, and both fullness and irritability in the gut. Another important source of information about body status comes from the area postrema in the brainstem. Most parts of the brain are protected from direct contact with chemicals in the blood. Only selected food sources, oxygen, and a few other substances are allowed to pass through the blood-brain barrier. However, the area postrema has receptors in an unprotected "chemotoxic trigger zone" where it can detect toxic substances in the blood.

In addition to information about toxic conditions in the blood, signals about nutrient quality and intestinal stretch from villi along the gastrointestinal tract reach the brainstem via the vagus nerve. Nutrient quality and mild stretch inputs are interpreted as feelings of satiation and fullness. However, feelings of fullness and irritation are interpreted as distress conditions. Feelings of distress are relayed on to an adjacent module in the medulla known affectionately as the vomit center. Toxic conditions detected by the area postrema are also relayed on to the vomit center. When highly activated the vomit center initiates the stomach purging reflex for which it is named. When less activated, this region produces the signals of distress that we describe as nausea. These distress signals are relayed on to the PBN and then on to the thalamus where they may gain attention.

The PBN also influences several autonomic reactions, such as respiratory control, via connections with the vagus. In addition, there are dense projections from the PBN to the periaqueductal gray (PAG), a gray colored region lying along the central aqueduct at the top of the pons and extending into the midbrain. The PAG manages motor expressions for many core emotional states such as fear, rage, and sexual behavior. Stimulation of the PAG can even produce some emotionally related vocal outputs. However, while the reactions triggered by the PAG appear to be emotional, they are mostly only the motor components of emotion. For example, if the PAG is isolated from higher-level networks and then stimulated, emotional reactions like rage can be produced. However, the reaction is called sham-rage because the PAG doesn't know what is causing the rage, so without the support of other networks, the motor reactions for rage are not directed at anything.

What the PAG is really good at doing is creating emotional action patterns. It also has direct connections with lower brainstem nuclei that control autonomic output reactions. Thus, the PAG influences autonomic states in support of emotional reactions. Given their integration and managing roles, the PBN and the PAG are both considered to be core modules for managing autonomic activity. The reason for describing the connections among these systems in such detail is that, although many life-urge inputs never reach consciousness directly, some of them nevertheless pass information on to networks in the PBN, the PAG, and adjacent brainstem motor areas. These regions thus provide intermediate sources of reactivity dispositions, some of which may reach consciousness.

For example, Tom is unaware of the muscle reflexes in the spinal cord that motivate him to lift his paw off the thorn, although he is subsequently aware of the pain and aware of moving his paw. However, some primary inputs are relayed more directly. We occasionally feel localized pain. We sometimes feel localized itches, and we sometimes feel distress in our gut. We may also become aware of the emotional reactions managed via the PAG. We feel ourselves getting angry or sexually aroused. We are commonly aware of tastes and the seeking or disgust dispositions they motivate. We are not aware of most of the sensing done in the area postrema or most of the inputs caried by the vagus nerve, but when their distress signals are relayed on to the PBN we may become conscious of feeling unwell.

THE PROTO-SELF

Antonio Damasio notes that the life urges that become conscious are processed in areas beginning in the mid and upper pons region and extending along central pathways to the midbrain and hypothalamus.[27] To emphasize the importance of these life-urge networks, Damasio refers to them collectively as the *proto-self*. The reason for calling these sites *proto-self* regions, rather than *self* regions, is that they do not appear to be the locus of conscious self feelings, but rather the sources of feeling-related inputs which may reach consciousness. According to Damasio, consciousness involves an *object-organism* integration in which an agent is aware of their own internal reactions as they engage the external world. In this process, life-urge reactions come to be interpreted as a sense of self, while external perceptions are interpreted as a sense of world. Obviously, much more is involved than simply detecting feeling-related modules.

Proto-self regions refine life-urge dispositions and relay their activity on to other networks including the attention networks of the thalamus. The life urges that reach the thalamus contribute to the competition of events for attention. It should, therefore, not be surprising to find that the PBN is located at the midpoint of the pons and that the PAG extends from the top of the pons into the midbrain. Both these regions are considered core components of the *proto-self*. The PAG is known to be involved in core emotions such as sexual arousal, fear, aggression, and flight. However, it is also involved in more positive activities such as sexual behavior. Recent work also links the PAG to play, tickling, and laughter.[28] And, surprisingly it is also involved in feelings of spirituality and religiosity.[29] Given this broad range of emotional dispositions it seems that the PAG may be considered a primary neural center for what Freud called the ID - the emotional dispositions of the cognitive unconscious. Thus, even when these dispositions do not gain attention directly, they are likely to be underlying components of many emotional feelings.

Still, some simple spinal reflexes, small pains and itches, are passed on by the PBN and may reach consciousness. Thus, it is not the initial source of a life urge that determines whether it may become conscious, but rather something about how it is prioritized in ascending network paths. Many autonomic adjustments do not appear to be passed on as conscious inputs by the PBN, and yet we are also sometimes aware of these adjustments, at least, when the effects on our body are strong. We feel our heart pounding. We notice our hands sweating. We sense tense muscles or rapid breathing. It appears that these sensations arrive via sensorimotor pathways. Thus, they are not direct brainstem reports about autonomic activity, but rather somatic inputs that provide evidence for how the body is reacting. Antonio Damasio argues that these secondary sources of information serve as *somatic markers* for autonomic outputs to which an agent would not otherwise be cognizant. This indirect path is important because emotions sometimes result in localized somatic effects, and somatic markers provide direct evidence of these effects.[30]

Another reason for why the upper pons is important for consciousness is the fact that this region, and the adjacent midbrain areas just above it, include a number of networks that serve as sources of ascending arousal for higher brain systems.[31] One proto-feeling network mentioned earlier, the PBN, is a key source of arousal to the forebrain.[32] Consistent with the importance of these ascending arousal regions, Damasio notes that significant damage to the dorsal part of the brainstem that blocks these ascending arousal paths results in coma.[33] Lesions below the mid-pons result in selected sensory and motor losses. However, they do not eliminate consciousness. Thus, life urges for ascending arousal beginning in the upper pons region and extending along central pathways to the midbrain and forebrain appear to be critical for wakefulness and conscious awareness.

We have emphasized the upper-pontine life-urge networks because they provide critical sensory, motor, and arousal inputs. However, there are regions in the cortex that process these feeling inputs as well. Ascending life-urge paths for feelings, motor dispositions, and arousal project through the thalamus and connect with two primary limbic regions in the cortex, the anterior cingulate cortex and the insular cortex. Inputs from the PAG and from sympathetic nervous system sites pass through the thalamus to the anterior cingulate cortex. This region also receives reactivity inputs from the amygdala. Thus, the anterior cingulate cortex appears to detect distress conditions and to manage emotional reactivity in reaction to them.

The insular cortex is the primary cortical integration center for status feelings from the body. It receives projections from the PBN as well as from parasympathetic status sites. Feelings of status and reactivity in the posterior and mid-level insular cortex and reactivity in the anterior cingulate cortex then project on to association areas in the anterior insular cortex. In humans, summary feelings of self-status, in particular parasympathetic nervous system feelings, are re-represented more strongly in the left anterior insular cortex, while summary feelings of motivational and emotional reactivity from the sympathetic nervous system are re-represented more strongly in the right anterior insula.[34] Thus, sympathetic and parasympathetic reactions are not simply localized in the brainstem, they are re-represented in the limbic cortices.

These multiple layers of representation add to the complexity of subjective feelings. In studies with humans, feelings of sadness, anxiety, risk, pain, disgust, craving, trust, rejection, and even the pleasantness of music are associated with increased activity in the anterior insular cortex. Related emotional states are also activated in the anterior cingulate cortex. These findings suggest that the insular and anterior cingulate cortices provide a more integrated sense of self feelings. Damage to the insula can lead to apathy, loss of libido, and blunted gustatory, olfactory, auditory, and somatosensory perceptions. Damage to various parts of the anterior cingulate cortex can result in reduced motor reactions, lowered pain intensity, and blunted sympathetic arousal to stress.[35]

Damasio's concept of the proto-self and the importance he attributes to homeostatic life urges beginning in upper pons regions and extending on to the hypothalamus helps us understand the varied sources of life-urge senses and reactions that contribute to consciousness. We are all well aware of the experiences associated with touch, warmth, pain, orientation, surprise, fear, distress, and of the many higher-order emotional effects that are managed by the limbic cortices. However, we have yet to explain how life urges become conscious feelings and why feelings of self are an essential part of conscious experience. To do that we need to look beyond the sources of life urges and to explore the network architecture that brings perceptions and feelings to attention. That will be the topic of our next chapter.

Concluding Comments

Life begins as adaptive sensing-reacting dispositions take form. These are what we have termed life urges. Without a collective of adaptive life urges no living organism could survive. In vertebrate animals ascending life urges are integrated in the brainstem and prioritized in upper-pontine and midbrain proto-self regions and in networks for motivation in the hypothalamus and emotions in the amygdala. It is hard to overstate the importance of these early networks. They construct an abundance of sensing and reacting combinations that guide a variety of adaptive reactions and help an agent hold onto life. Still, as we have thus far described them, life-urge inputs are merely "proto-feelings". They do not become true feelings unless they gain attention. However, it seems important to note that if we are to build conscious robots, we must also provide them with a similar hierarchy of proto-feelings that can gain their attention.

Robots must be sensitive to the suddenness of sensory inputs and the directionality of inputs with respect to their body. They must have proprioceptive feedback and vestibular inputs that provide internal feedback as they react. They will need a curiosity about changing features, a tendency for exploring positive events, a disposition to avoid negative outcomes, an interest in social interactions, and most importantly, an underlying drive to stay alive. Further, these reactions should be parceled into sympathetic pathways that influence the robot's reactions in the world and complementary parasympathetic pathways that influence reactions in the robot's body. These are the kinds of reactive dispositions that our robots must have if they are to experience feelings of self as human agents do.

> **Ending Remarks**

Life urges are core aspects of the physical self reacting to the world. They include autonomic inputs from the brainstem and higher-order combinations of motivational needs and emotional moods. However, life urges are merely adaptive dispositions. To be experienced as feelings, they must gain conscious attention.

3: ASSEMBLING CONSCIOUS ATTENTION

The cortex is a very highly and specifically interconnected neural network. It has many types of excitatory and inhibitory interneurons and acts by forming transient coalitions of neurons, the members of which support one another. 'Coalitions' implies 'assemblies' – an idea which goes back at least to Hebb – plus competition among them. … On the basis of experimental results in the macaque, some researchers suggest that selective attention biases the competition among rivalrous assemblies. – Francis Crick & Christof Koch, "A Framework for Consciousness," 2003

➢ **Introductory Remarks**

Here we introduce Sherman and Guillery's analysis of connections in the thalamus to show how the affect-based models and the attention-based models of consciousness can be integrated. But this integration is only the beginning. We also provide an explanation of why coherent attention results in the enhanced neural processing of consciousness.

In contrast to the affect-based accounts of consciousness described in the previous chapter, there is a broad consensus among many neuroscientists that an attention-based architecture is essential for focusing conscious awareness. And because the thalamocortical architecture is involved in managing attention, theorists assume that it is an essential part of the neural systems supporting consciousness. The basic model in these accounts is that attention depends on reentrant connections between the thalamus and the cortex. Long-time proponents of the role of the thalamocortical architecture in consciousness include Gerald Edelman, Francis Crick, Christof Koch, Rodolfo Llinás, and sometimes Stanislas Dehaene.[36]

As Francis Crick and Christof Koch note in the opening quote, the evidence suggests that features of attention are bound together in clusters of inter-related activity and these clusters compete for attention as a group. Crick and Koch described the central clusters that assemble and compete for attention as "transient coalitions" because they are only bound together in the moment. However, no author has linked conscious awareness to the thalamocortical architecture more than Gerald Edelman. Edelman suggests that what Crick and Koch call transient coalitions are essentially the ongoing components of what he calls the *dynamic core* of central processing.[37] The dynamic core refers to the fact that while there is a locus of ongoing processing in the thalamocortical region during states of attention, the locus is not fixed in any one pathway. The active core constantly shifts locations and changes connections. In fact, the shifts in processing are consistent with how the focus of attention normally shifts and changes in conscious thought.

As noted in the previous chapter, there are brainstem regions that serve as sources of unconscious feeling-related inputs during consciousness. Antonio Damasio describes these regions as parts of the proto-self. However, attention-based accounts of consciousness ignore these regions in their accounts of attention and minimize the importance of feelings for consciousness. Gerald Edelman suggests that feelings are linked to thalamocortical processing via "correlations" in the basal forebrain and cortex, but he doesn't see feelings as playing a direct role in attention.[38] Christof Koch seems even less concerned about feelings, suggesting that subjective feelings may not have a scientific solution.[39] Our initial goal in this section is therefore to understand the mechanisms of the thalamocortical architecture for attention. The mechanisms are only partly understood, but they provide insights into how conscious experience forms and changes during attention.

Most of the sensory and motor inputs that reach the cortex pass through the thalamus. In Latin *thalamus* means inner chamber. Thirty years ago this inner chamber was considered little more than a relay station that performed some signal preprocessing. Surprisingly, however, researchers Murray Sherman and Ray Guillery report that less than 10 percent of the synapses in the core thalamic nuclei are from sensorimotor sources that are being relayed on to the cortex.[40] The remaining 90-plus percent are from sources that bias what features are likely to gain attention. Sherman and Guillery describe these as modulatory inputs, because their supporting activations serve to bias the likelihood that features associated with them win the competition for attention.

About 30 percent of the modulatory synapses are local connections within the thalamus. These have binding and filtering effects that account for the focus of attention. Another 30 percent of the inputs are return circuits from the cortex. These enable cortical activity to influence the flow of thalamic information. The remaining 30 percent of the modulatory inputs are from brainstem proto-self regions. These appear to enable brainstem life-urge dispositions to influence attention. The filtering and binding effects in the thalamus are well known. The return inputs from the cortex have long been considered inputs that maintain resonant activity between the thalamus and the cortex. However, the brainstem modulatory inputs have not been considered in previous models. As a result, I have outlined a composite model that includes the modulatory inputs identified by Sherman and Guillery (see Figure 3-1).

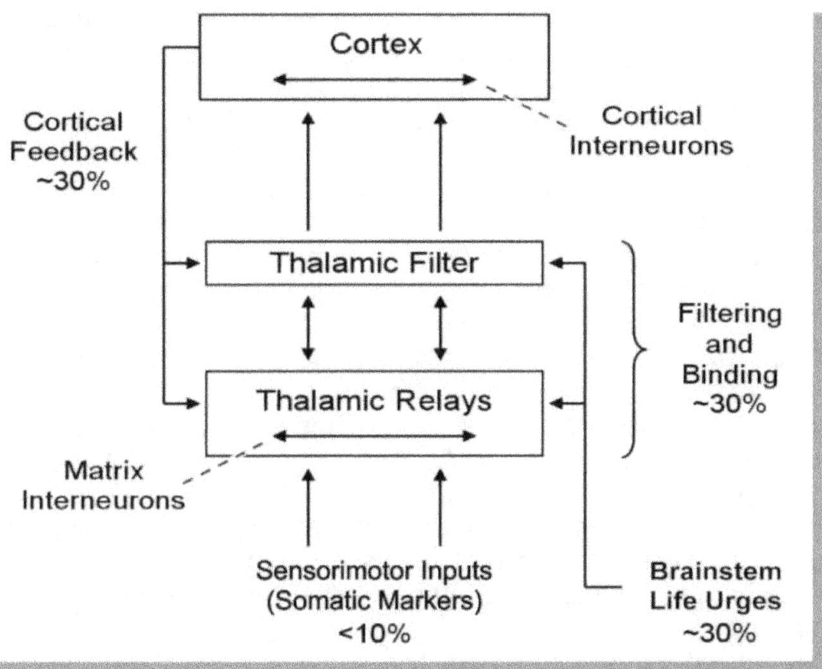

Figure 3-1: A composite thalamocortical architecture for consciousness including brainstem life-urge inputs.

Here is an overview of how this architecture is proposed to operate. Sensorimotor inputs project to various thalamic relays, but they account for less than 10 percent of the synapses in each relay. Bottom-up inputs from life urges in the upper-pons provide modulatory arousal for thalamic inputs. Evidence suggests that these inputs come largely, but not exclusively, from brainstem motor regions. As modulatory inputs they have no motor function, but rather provide a sense of brainstem arousal to features in the thalamic relays. This added arousal provides insight into how the affective account of consciousness connects with the attention-based account. It seems the brainstem integration of ascending sensing and reactivity inputs engage proto-feeling *life-urge* states that modulate what features are likely to gain attention.

In the previous chapter we argued that for life urges to become feelings they must gain attention. We can now describe several paths by which that may occur. Some interoceptive sensations and some aspects of emotional arousal are relayed to the cortex much like external sensory experiences.[41] In fact, the assemblies that gain attention are thought to include sensory, motor, and limbic inputs as reactive combinations. Adding to the first-order thalamic relays that forward inputs to the cortex, Sherman and Guillery note that there are also relays whose inputs come primarily from the cortex. They refer to these as *higher-order* relays. Important in this regard are certain limbic relays in the thalamus, the mediodorsal, midline, and intralaminar networks.

Further. It turns out that life urges from the PBN also send projections to these limbic relays, and there is now evidence that higher-order relays have a subset of relay cells that act as first-order relays.[42] Because the first-order inputs are faster than the higher-order cortical inputs, life urges from the PBN might even be able to prime activity in the limbic cortices before those regions receive cortical inputs. Thus, there are feeling-related inputs from the brainstem to the limbic cortex. Further, because the nuclei in the limbic thalamus include outputs to a number of subcortical feeling-related regions, the brainstem-limbic axis appears to be poised to coordinate both cortical and subcortical feeling-related arousal during attention.

In addition, there are modulatory inputs to each thalamic relay from brainstem proto-self regions. These are thought to help prioritize what features gain attention by adding secondary sources of arousal. The modulatory inputs are not relayed on to the cortex, however Sherman and Guillery report that the return circuits from the cortex to the thalamus branch and also return to the brainstem. Thus, the modulatory brainstem inputs for features gaining attention may be enhanced due to these return loops. Further, cross-connections in the brainstem would inform the PBN about them. And given that the PBN projects to the limbic thalamus and cortex, there is a parallel path for feeling-related inputs to gain attention.

The synchronous combination of external perceptions and brainstem somatic regions that occurs during sensorimotor perception and the parallel activation of limbic arousal via synchronous loops in the brainstem-limbic axis is proposed to account for the object-organism integration that Damasio argued was part of conscious experience. The limbic cortices are also activated via cortical-cortical associations when sensorimotor activity gains attention, thus integrating activity in these two paths. In addition, brainstem life urges that are activated during attention result in autonomic adjustments that affect reactions in the body. In fact, some of those reactions may be strong enough to be detected as new sensorimotor inputs. These inputs correspond to what Damasio referred to as somatic markers for emotional activity.[43] This input path is suggested at the bottom of Figure 3-1. Thus, there are multiple paths by which life urges can influence both subjective and somatic feelings during conscious attention.

SYNCHRONY AND BINDING

We have now described the composite thalamocortical architecture for attention, described how feelings play a role in guiding attention, and described the brainstem-limbic axis that enables feelings to be engaged in parallel with sensorimotor features during attention. The design of this architecture is truly fascinating. Inputs modulated by brainstem life urges compete with each other. Combinations of features bind together in larger assemblies that compete as a group. Feature assemblies that pass the filter and reach the cortex engage return signals directed back to the thalamus and the brainstem that create oscillatory processing loops for features competing for the focus of attention. And once these processing loops are engaged, competition and filtering in the thalamus enable one feature set to gain conscious attention within 350-500 ms.

There is, however, a problem. Consciousness involves coordinating a vast array of cognitive processes and we have yet to describe how that happens and how it enhances awareness. The explanation for these effects follows from two concepts, *synchrony* and *coherence*. Our first step will therefore be to explain the function of synchrony. To do this we will begin by taking a closer look at the neural mechanisms for filtering and binding attention. Filtering depends largely on the thalamic reticular nucleus, a network that covers the top of the thalamus like a thin cap and inhibits inputs to the cortex. However, rather than being a homogeneous cap, there are separate regions for vision, hearing, touch, movement, and limbic activity. Fibers passing in both directions between the thalamus and the cortex send collaterals to these regions.[44] Competition among signals in the filter appears to enable dominant signals in each region to sustain their activity while inhibiting the passage of others.

As Crick and Koch noted, features bind together in larger assemblies that compete for attention as a group. In support of such bindings, Edward Jones has shown that there are nonspecific matrix interneurons within the thalamus. These neurons appear to help bind temporally related features from different thalamic domains into synchronous assemblies in the thalamus.[45] As noted earlier, when the thalamic inputs pass the filter and reach the cortex, they activate specific cortical columns for those features. Those columns, in turn, send signals back to the thalamic sources of those inputs, resulting in reentrant oscillations between the thalamus and the cortex for each feature. And because these features pass the filter as a group, they activate the cortex in synchrony and as attention gains focus the reentrant thalamocortical loops become more synchronized.

Despite this synchrony, the competition for attention among competing components is not resolved quickly. Studies suggest that it takes 350–500 ms for a new assembly to gain dominance and establish the coherent synchronous states of activity that give rise to conscious experience.[46] Thus, with each shift in attention, conscious awareness for the new topic is delayed until this coordination is reestablished. Giulio Tononi suggests that this delay occurs because the networks that support consciousness are essentially information integration processes that constantly assess a large number of possible neural assemblies before bringing one into focus. To establish this focus, it seems the thalamocortical networks must reach a certain level of mutually supporting coherence before the focus is stable.[47] Tononi's model for how to measure this level of coherence requires internal measures for calculation. However, the fact that it takes about a half second to bring each shift in attention into a coherent focus of awareness is something we intuitively recognize.

Tononi's coherence model grew out of his analyses of integration in thalamocortical studies of consciousness. However, he has subsequently separated this model from the thalamocortical architecture, suggesting that any brain activity that shows a high level of coherence, a measure he calls *phi*, is a likely candidate for conscious awareness. In fact, he suggests that even non-neural systems with high *phi* scores may be conscious.[48] I am confident that his measures of *phi* in the thalamocortical architecture provide a good index of the level of integration needed for consciousness. But I am not confident that coherence measures outside of the thalamocortical mechanisms of resonant synchrony can define consciousness, because the thalamocortical effects of synchrony involve much more than just timing.

While thalamocortical resonance is a primary driver of synchronous bindings, research indicates that there are a variety of processing hubs in the cortex that participate across a diverse set of cognitive functions and that different hubs have their own timing characteristics.[49] Consistent with this observation, Leonardo Gollo and colleagues note that the default mode hub thought to be involved in feelings of self tends to operate around frequencies of 8–12 Hz.[50] This frequency is commonly called the *alpha* frequency of the resting brain. However, some of the lower-level somatic mood networks that feed this hub operate at *theta* frequencies of 4–8 Hz, or even lower *delta* frequencies of less than 4 Hz. In effect, some mood states change slowly.

In contrast to feeling and mood networks, Gollo and colleagues note that sensory hubs tend to operate at *gamma* frequencies of 30–60 Hz. Further, some localized sensory regions may have *higher gamma* frequencies that operate at frequencies up to 200 Hz. These higher frequencies appear to be needed to track rapidly changing events in the external world. In between the perceptual and feeling frequencies there are intermediate processing hubs that link perceptual activity with the feeling hubs. These intermediate networks operate at what is often termed the *beta* frequency of attention, around 13–28 Hz.[51] Obviously, these different processes cannot all operate at one frequency. Instead, it appears that their frequencies come to be phase-locked to primary features in each hub via harmonic coupling mechanisms.[52] Thus, the features at the focus of attention tend to be bound in what are effectively phase-locked patterns of polysynchronous rhythms.[53]

Researchers have found a similar pattern of phase-locking in language processing networks.[54] And because the different components in these processes operate across different time frames, they naturally tend to unfold in a temporal hierarchy of cognitive changes and action patterns. As Rishidev Chaudhuri and colleagues note, "These findings establish a circuit mechanism for 'temporal receptive windows' that are progressively enlarged along the cortical hierarchy, suggesting an extension of time integration in decision making from local to large circuits."[55] This local-to-larger integration is exactly what is needed to promote the organization of cognition and actions into larger temporal units. By extension, this organization implies that different aspects of conscious awareness should be expected to change at different rates.

Earlier we argued that consciousness results from the dynamic binding of perceptions and feelings in clusters of attention. We have now outlined the mechanisms that make this dynamic reprogramming possible. Filtering is managed largely by the thalamic cap. Only feature assemblies that pass the filter activate the cortex. Binding results from synchronous activity on several levels. Internal cross-connections help bind features together in the thalamus. Top-down inputs from the cortex help maintain feature activity in the thalamus in resonant cycles with the cortex. Bottom-up inputs from proto-self regions ensure that attention is always bound with and guided by life urges. However, it seems these processes must all come to be phase-locked in synchronous processing cycles before they engage conscious attention.

COHERENCE AND CONSCIOUSNESS

When oscillatory systems are joined together such that they can influence each other, closely related systems have a tendency to synchronize with one another. Early studies with oscillating systems as simple as pendulum clocks found that if the clocks were suspended from a common beam, the minor directional forces of their pendulum motions could influence each other and the pendulum motions could even synchronize over time. A key to this synchronous organization appears to be how well individual features can connect in mutually supporting combinations.

The features competing for attention are bound in feature assemblies as part of the competition for attention. Some features may occur in more than one assembly, but only the strongest assembly gains attention. However, research suggest that it takes some 350–500 ms of filtering and binding for an assembly to stabilize and reach the coherent state needed for conscious activation. Thus, conscious awareness emerges in a later stage of attention processing. Another reason for the delay is that different features operate on different time cycles and thus binding requires the feature elements to be phase-locked with each other before the feature assembly becomes stable.

So what makes these coherent cycles so special? An interesting possibility is what Pascal Fries has termed *communication through coherence* (CTC). Fries has found that when neural systems are communicating an increase in coherence between the communicating systems can cause a phase transition that greatly facilitates the transmission of information.[56] This seems to happen because in the absence of coherent cycles, the firing patterns of neurons occur more randomly and they communicate less efficiently. Fries' work shows us that the coherent alignment of communicating networks can sometimes dramatically facilitate neural processing.

I find Fries account of the self-amplifying effects of CTC to be strikingly consistent with Stanislas Dehaene's observations that as a coherent focus of attention takes form there is a phase transition that dramatically increases the intensity of neural activity and spreads activation broadly across the cortex.[57] However, while the phase transition that increased neural processing followed a similar temporal transition, the networks competing for coherent attention that Dehaene examined were much more complex than the simple networks Fries placed in coherence by temporal alignment. Thus, it seems there may be something more than simply temporal alignment of features in the brainstem-thalamocortical architecture that enhances neural processing during states of coherent attention.

In that regard, it is important to note that the return signals from the cortex to the thalamus reactivate the same sites that send signals to the cortex. Such feed-forward loops have a tendency to sustain activity and even self-amplify since they return input to their sources. However, in early stages of attention, there is still a lot of competition among assemblies and the self-amplification effect is limited. Yet it appears that as attention comes to a focus and the feature assembly reaches a higher level of coherence, the focused processing loops begin to engage this self-amplifying effect.

This *global ignition,* as Dehaene describes it, has been suggested to account for the intensity of conscious awareness.[58] In one study of visual attention, Dehaene reported that at the point of global ignition the neural activity for the visual features at the center of attention increased by a factor of twelve and activations spread in both ascending and descending paths. Dehaene characterized this phase transition in which processing intensity increased and spread as something like an avalanche of attentional integration. I believe that this second-order integration is consistent with the self-amplification of processing that occurs during coherent attention.

We know that the cortical focus of attention is synchronized with the thalamus by cyclic return signals. Further, we know that these return signals also branch to the brainstem. And we know that the brainstem interacts with the body via the autonomic nervous system. Dehaene's observations suggest that brain activity seems to be enhanced in both upward and downward paths during consciousness. This suggests that processing in the entire body-brainstem-thalamocortical architecture is enhanced during consciousness. The enhanced effects are likely much more intense within the brain circuitry, but conscious attention is truly an embodied experience. This extended model is shown in Figure 3-2.

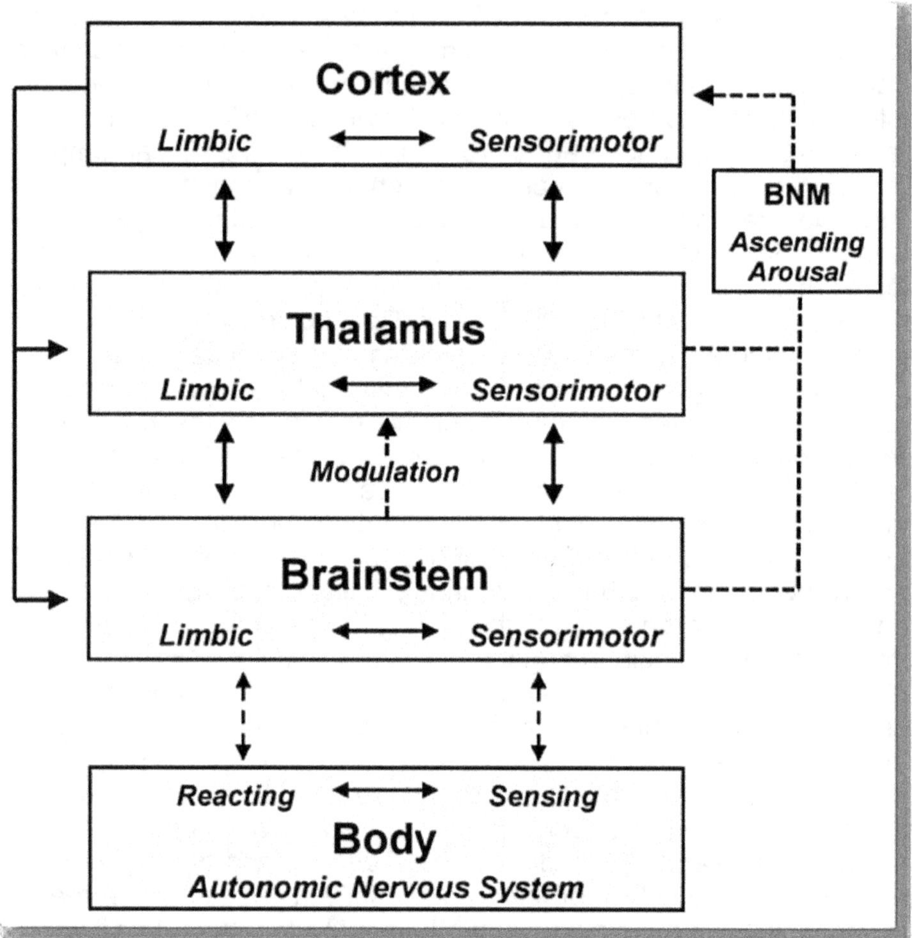

Figure 3-2: A brainstem-thalamocortical architecture for consciousness. The basal nucleus of Meynert (BNM), comparable to the basal nucleus magnocellularis (BNM) in avians, provides reorganization signals to the cortex.

The brainstem inputs in this extended architecture have not been well documented. However, we know that feeling-related inputs from the PBN project to the limbic thalamus and on to the limbic cortices. This ensures that feeling states are always a parallel part of the inputs involved in thalamocortical loops of attention. In addition, the PAG engages core emotional dispositions that we have suggested largely underlie the emotional feelings and actions of the cognitive unconscious. Motor arousal in the brainstem is thought to provide most of the modulatory inputs that bias attention for sensory features competing for attention in the thalamus. Thus, there are many brainstem inputs that contribute to what gains conscious attention.

Note that there is another brainstem pathway involved in conscious processing that is shown in the figure above. Evidence suggests that the BNM (basal nucleus of Meynert in mammals, the basal nucleus magnocellularis in avians) provides cholinergic cortical arousal that is essential for wakefulness, learning, and attention. In mammals this region receives inputs from ascending arousal networks including major inputs from the parabrachial nucleus region and lesser inputs from other brainstem regions including the pedunculopontine nucleus (PPN).[59] The comparable path in avians appears to involve inputs from the rostral rhombencephalic tegmental region and the PPN region.[60] Thus the pathways in avians closely resemble those in mammals. Research also suggests that the BNM may be activated by thalamic inputs and that the timing of BNM activity is involved in aspects of sensory, motor, and pain processing.[61]

Antonio Damasio also emphasizes that a second-order integration occurs during consciousness. Further, he argues that it is embodied in the sense that it involves an object-organism integration between perceptual features and the agent's own internal reactions to them.[62] Based on the work by Gollo and colleagues,[63] it appears that this integration happens as perceptual hubs are interconnected with feeling hubs. In fact, recent works suggests that during consciousness there are dynamic alternations between dorsal attention hubs and default mode hubs. The dorsal attention circuits mediate externally directed cognitive processes such as goal-driven attention and voluntary control. The default mode circuits engage internally directed processes such as feelings of self and autobiographical memory. Disrupting the dynamic interactions between these two processes appears to disrupt consciousness by interfering with coupling between sensory attention and default mode feelings.[64] Thus, it appears Damasio's emphasis on object-organism integration in consciousness was prescient. However, the idea that there are dynamic oscillations between perceptual attention and feelings of self adds a new wrinkle to the nature of thalamocortical feature coupling.

Adding to this self-world integration there is yet another aspect of synchronous processing that contributes to self-awareness. There are networks in the temporal-parietal junction of the brain that identify synchrony among various aspects of sensory, motor, and feeling changes and interpret connected patterns of synchrony as evidence for self-ownership for both actions and body parts.[65] Thus, in a real sense, integrated synchrony is not just a supporting mechanism; it results in a sense of self involvement. The integration of synchrony among sensory, motor, and feeling *processes is experienced as a dynamic self agency that feels ownership of its body and responsibility for its actions.*

So here is our core model for consciousness. Consciousness is a neural process that combines the reactive awareness of the self with the categorical awareness of the world during extended states of attention. The neural architecture required to engage conscious awareness involves recurrent brainstem-thalamocortical loops for focusing attention. It takes about a half-second for the focus of attention in this architecture to engage a strong level of integration and when that occurs neural processing for features at the focus of attention dramatically increase. A consequence of engaging conscious attention is that a central conscious agency, the self, emerges as coordinated feeling states react to changes in their world. As Damasio notes, this integration of self and world gives a conscious agent an added adaptive advantage.

> And what was that advantage? It was the possibility of connecting the very core of life regulation with the processing of images … some new and more open way of sensing the life urge and the means to hold on to life.[66]

CONCLUDING COMMENTS

In the previous chapter we noted that life urges involve adaptive sensory, motivational, and motor dispositions. Antonio Damasio has long emphasized the role of these brainstem life-urge regions for supporting consciousness.[67] In fact, he calls these regions part of the proto-self. Bud Craig and Jaak Panksepp have also argued for the importance of brainstem networks in conscious feelings.[68] However other prominent consciousness theorists, Francis Crick, Gerald

Edelman, Rodolfo Llinás, for example, have emphasized the dynamic filtering and binding processes within the attention architecture in their analysis of consciousness.[69]

This chapter uses insights into the architecture of the thalamus, as described by Sherman and Guillery,[70] to bring these two lines of thinking together. It proposes a composite model that ties life urges to attention. All the events about which you and I and my cat Tom become conscious follow a similar signaling and prioritizing process. Life-urge dispositions are activated, often resulting in somatic reactions and ascending signals about ongoing status. Many of these are then relayed on to the thalamus where they contribute to the activation of features competing for attention. Some project on to higher-order relays in the limbic thalamus where they contribute to the activation of feeling-related arousal on both cortical and subcortical levels. And those life urges that gain attention with perceptions and actions are experienced as conscious feelings.

➢ Ending Remarks

Observations indicate that as attention becomes more focused, the brainstem-thalamocortical loops reach a greater degree of coherence. Then, suddenly a phase transition occurs and neural processing for features at the focus of attention increases by a factor of 10 to12. We do not have a full account for how this happens. However, the communication through coherence (CTC) hypothesis argues that coherent alignment among communicating networks can enhance communication,[71] and it seems likely that coherent attention also strengthens feed-forward signaling from the cortex to the thalamus and brainstem.

The finding that the brainstem PBN and related motor regions provide arousal to the BNM during wakefulness and consciousness suggests that the brainstem also contributes to the intensity of conscious processing. Thus, we have a brainstem-thalamocortical architecture for consciousness. And because the brainstem has links to the body via the autonomic nervous system, conscious feelings in the brain reach the body.

4: SUBJECTIVE EXPERIENCE

The easy problems – explaining discrimination, integration, accessibility, internal monitoring, reportability, and so on – all concern the performance of various *functions*. ... The hard problem, by contrast, is not a problem about how functions are performed. For any given function that we explain, it remains a nontrivial further question: why is the performance of this function associated with conscious experience? – David Chalmers, "Moving forward on the problem of consciousness", 1997

> **Introductory Remarks**

This chapter provides a transition to thinking about how subjective brain processes become part of consciousness. Emergent organizations often have discontinuous properties that cannot be fully explained based on their parts. Consciousness is one of those organizations and its discontinuous properties are often adaptive in novel ways.

Recipes enable us to craft appetizing configurations of foodstuff. However, a recipe is only an objective description of the ingredients and procedures for preparing a food. It does not explain the nuances of taste that the particular recipe makes possible. On a reductionist level, objective links from food to tastes can be traced to sensors in the tongue and mouth that provide signals related to sweetness, sourness, bitterness, saltiness, umami (glutamate taste), and the pungency of hot spices. However, there is a gap between the recipe and the subjective taste of the food that is not explained fully by reductionist links. Similarly, we have described how polysynchronous processes combine sensorimotor experiences with associated life urges during attention. Yet there is still a gap between knowing this recipe and experiencing the phenomenal qualities of conscious experience. Thus, we need to deal with what David Chalmers has called the *hard problem*. Why the neural functions that give rise to consciousness result in such interesting phenomenal experiences. Our first aim in this discussion is to put the concept of emergence in better perspective.

Emergence is one of the most misunderstood concepts in scientific thought. As best we know, at the moment of the Big Bang there was nothing but a plasma of rapidly expanding matter-energy. Atoms as simple as hydrogen and helium did not exist. Stars had yet to evolve. There were no galactic structures. Atoms, stars, and galaxies are all emergent organizations that took form in the aftermath of the Big Bang. In fact, most all the items we now observe in the universe are emergent structures. One thing we have come to accept is that the fundamental units of the universe are highly interactive. Even when broken loose by reactions in gigantic colliders, many of them barely exist as separate particles long enough to be detected. For example, the particles known as quarks never seem to exist alone. They constantly combine to form new structures, the most stable being neutrons and protons. Neutrons and protons then combine with electrons to form a variety of atoms. Atoms, in turn, often combine to form molecules.

A key characteristic of emergent organizations is that their interactive properties differ from those of their component parts. In fact, the difference in their interactive properties is what defines them as being different substances.[72] This discontinuous character is what led George Lewes to label certain properties as *emergent*. The discontinuity is also what makes emergent properties difficult to explain. There is a gap between the interactive properties of the parts and the interactive properties of their combination. For example, hydrogen is the simplest atomic element. It is formed by the combination of one proton and one electron. At normal surface temperatures on earth, it behaves as a gas. Oxygen is a more complex atomic element. In its most common form, each oxygen atom is composed of eight electrons, eight protons, and eight neutrons. Still, at normal surface temperatures on earth it also behaves as a gas. Adding either oxygen or hydrogen to a fire tends to make the fire more intense. However, the chemical combination of two parts hydrogen with one part oxygen results in a molecule with largely discontinuous properties. At normal surface temperatures, H_2O is the liquid we commonly call water. And even though it is composed of both hydrogen and oxygen, adding water to a fire generally dissipates heat and reduces a blaze. Somehow its discontinuous properties arise out of the combined agencies of hydrogen and oxygen, but in a form which does not display the interactive properties of those parts.

The interactive properties of water are simply discontinuous from those of hydrogen and oxygen. Yet, despite the discontinuous nature of emergent organizations, there is a long tradition in science of trying to explain emergent phenomena via their component parts. Establishing a link between a lower-order mechanism and some higher-order one provides a way of thinking about how the higher-order process is constructed. It also provides a way of thinking about how changes to low-order mechanisms might influence the higher-order processes. The success of this reductionist strategy has led some theorists to conclude that with enough data all higher-order phenomena can be explained on a reductionist level. In fact, it is not uncommon to hear strong proponents of this position argue that higher-order phenomena are *nothing but* the interaction of their component parts. The paradox of this *nothing buttery*[73] claim is that it appears true in the sense that each new organization is assembled from its parts, yet it remains false because the combined organization has properties that cannot be explained based only on the properties of the parts. Emergent properties do not exist at the parts level.

There are two major reasons why emergent organizations do not directly display the properties of their component parts. The first reason is that the formation of new organizations necessarily involves the interaction of parts. New thermodynamic organizations typically form via combinations that balance certain forces. Thus, those forces are bound up holding the organization together, and are not available as external properties. For example, the strong positive valences of sodium (Na) atoms and the strong negative valences of chlorine (Cl) atoms make these substances highly interactive. As a result, human contact with sodium, a soft metal, or with chlorine, a noxious gas, is likely to cause severe injury. However, when these atoms combine to form the molecule NaCl, the strong positive and negative valences are largely tied up binding the molecule together. Thus, the resultant substance, we call it table salt, has interactive properties that are much different from those of its parts. We sprinkle it on our food without any fear of engaging the noxious properties of elemental sodium or chlorine.

A second reason that emergent organizations do not display the same properties as their component parts, is that some properties depend on the organizations that are formed. These structural properties cannot be explained by the parts because the structures do not exist at the parts level. For example, many proteins involve combinations that exceed one thousand amino acids. These long molecular chains tend to fold in various shapes as they react to chemical forces in the environment. However, the shapes themselves may introduce new interactive properties. The shapes of some proteins encourage the transport of molecules of particular valences and sizes while blocking other molecules. These transporting and blocking effects add to the interactive properties of the protein. And within systems, like minds that can learn and remember, network structures change dynamically over time. You are a unique individual because the structures that compose your personal ideas, skills, and values depend on your mental experiences, not just your neurons.

The pervasiveness of emergent phenomena, and the finding that not all the properties of emergent organizations can be readily explained by the properties of their parts, means that emergent phenomena cannot simply be dismissed as nothing but the interaction of their parts. As Nobel laureate Phillip Anderson summarized the case, at each new level of organization we find that *more is different*. Organizations with new properties emerge, and we must adopt new scientific disciplines to study them.

> One may array the sciences roughly linearly according to the idea: The elementary entities of science X obey the laws of science Y. ... But this hierarchy does not imply that science X is "just applied Y." At each stage entirely new laws, concepts, and generalizations are necessary, requiring inspiration and creativity to just as great a degree as in the previous one. Psychology is not applied biology, nor is biology applied chemistry.[74]

As Anderson went on to note, while the organizations found in each area of science are partly connected across levels, the reductionist-constructionist symmetry breaks down as complexity introduces higher-order combinations whose properties defy a simple reversal of constructionist effects back to reductionist causes.[75] Many interactive properties of complex organizations, like the shapes of proteins, simply cannot be linked back to the properties of any specific part. But while the reductionist-constructionist symmetry is incomplete, links between reductionist organizations and constructionist organizations remain functionally important. You cannot form new organizations without parts. Further, knowing what components contribute to certain higher-order interactions can sometimes inform us about how certain emergent properties take form. For example, knowing that life urges project to the thalamus and discovering that they may be activated as part of the feature assemblies that gain attention provides us with insight into how life urges might be experienced as feelings.

Still, we cannot understand conscious feelings by focusing only on a recipe of parts. Paraphrasing Anderson, consciousness is not simply neuroscience applied to attention. New laws, new concepts, and new generalizations are required to explain its properties. That doesn't mean that knowing about the reductionist mechanisms that support consciousness cannot sometimes provide us with insights into how it works. However, it means that to understand conscious mind we also need to recognize its discontinuous properties, and to form new laws and concepts to explain them. And because conscious mind only comes into existence in an organization of feeling-bound attention, we need to consider its functions within that organization.

CONSCIOUS MINDS ARE STORMS OF ATTENTION

The upward spiral that gives rise to the core sense of self begins as an infant updraft, an inquisitive spiral of attention which interacts with events in its world. …. However, as its perceptual and motor experience grows, instances of its own attention begin to feed back into the spiral, and the storm gains in intensity and focus. In a short time, like the self-sustaining spiral of a hurricane, it forms a distinct central eye ("I"). We can name it. We can follow its development. As it matures, we marvel at its effects on the world and speculate about its future trajectory. However, as we do this, it is clear that the storm is more than a mere abstraction. Its history of learning and memory has shaped its attention and given it an individualized character which grows as it engages other tasks.[76]

Following Antonio Damasio's lead, in the previous chapter we argued that consciousness involves an *object-organism* interaction in which an agent becomes aware of her own internal reactions to what she perceives in the world. In effect, consciousness results from the integration of external inputs from the *world* with the internal reactions of *self*. In this process, life-urge inputs from proto-self regions come to be interpreted as aspects of self, while external perceptual inputs are interpreted as aspects of the world. We have previously outlined the mechanisms that make this dynamic organization possible. Binding results from phase-locked synchronous activity on several levels. Cross-connections in the thalamus help bind features together there. Top-down inputs from the cortex help maintain the feature activity of the thalamus in resonant cycles with the cortex. Bottom-up inputs ensure that attention is always bound with ongoing life urges.

The fact that life urges are a major part of the synchronous assemblies that gain attention was proposed to explain, at a reductionist level, why feelings always accompany attention. However, these reductionist links are merely the tip of the iceberg. Phenomenal consciousness doesn't just change "how" we react to the world. It results in an emergent sense of "who" is reacting to the world. That "who" is the self. The self emerges in dynamic storms of attention. This happens because as storms of attention we are sensitive to localized correlations among features within the storm. Those correlations influence what each storm notices, how it reacts to inputs, and how each storm grows. It is my claim that in this process the core sense of self is initially guided by distinctions promoted by the orientation networks of the tectum.

The tectum is a core life-urge module that serves to orient receptors toward sensory inputs. To do this, it maps sensory inputs into spatial maps, based on the apparent direction of the inputs from the body. To make these spatial maps more interconnected, inputs from different senses are mapped in layers that are arranged in spatial registration with each other. Thus, visual inputs with a particular spatial relationship to the body are mapped such that auditory inputs from the same direction come to be aligned with them in adjacent layers of the maps in the tectum. In order to track external inputs, evolution has also supplied the tectum with motor connections which it learns to use to orient sensory receptors so as to make sensory inputs more salient. Thus, the tectum is able to learn how to orient sensory receptors toward external sources.

> Some parts of the brain are free to roam over the world
> and to map whatever sound, shape, taste or smell or
> texture that the organism's design enables them to map.
> But some other brain parts — those that represent the
> organism's own structure and internal state — are not free
> to roam at all; they can map nothing but the body, and are

the body's captive audience. It is reasonable to
hypothesize that this is the source of the sense of
continuous being that anchors the mental self.[77]

A key point here is that the tectum must be able to represent
its roaming input paths so as to categorize them differently from
systems the body uses to orient toward those inputs. This differential
organization of sensory inputs and orientation processes provides a
pre-conscious distinction that higher-order networks can use to
categorize internal reactions as different from external inputs. Based
on this distinction, roaming receptor processes come to be recognized
as representing the *world*, while centralized internal reactive
processes come to be recognized as representing the *self*. Adding to
this orientation distinction, we noted in the previous chapter that
perceptual hubs and the feeling hubs tend to be separate processes
involving different brain regions. Thus, it is likely that these different
input paths also contribute to an awareness that the internal
processes of self are located distinctly from the networks that perceive
the world.

Yet while sensing and directional aspects of orientation form
the basis of a self-world distinction, orientation does not make this
self-world distinction conscious. It takes the synchronous second-
order binding of changes in external events with changes in internal
reactions to enable a dynamic storm of attention to detect itself as a
feeling agent reacting to the world. As Antonio Damasio proposed this
idea, a dynamically aware self essentially emerges in a process in
which the organism is *"caught in the act of representing its own
changing state as it goes about representing something else."*[78] I
claim that the "catching" in this process is the link between feelings
and the topics of attention. The self comes to be recognized as the
internal feeling reactions in that focus. The world comes to be
recognized as the external perceptual inputs to attention. In this way,
consciousness integrates external perceptions of the *world* with
internal reactions of the *self*. This enables a conscious agent to
evaluate what it perceives in terms of the values they have for the
self.

Rodolfo Llinás shares this metaphor. In his book, *I of the
Vortex*, he argues that the self emerges as a consequence of binding
interoceptive and exteroceptive features together in dynamic states of
attention. As he phrases it, "It binds, therefore I am!"[79] Gerald
Edelman makes a related point, noting that the confluence of actions
and feelings with perceptions naturally introduces "a self-referential

aspect to experience."[80] A key point of emphasis here is that a storm of attention that includes both external inputs and internal reactions is a mind that perceives not only events in the world but also a sense of its own self reactions to what it perceives. Its attention is enhanced by a constant flow of changing reactions as it perceives and interacts with the world.

The fact that the self-referential experiences of each storm of attention partly depend on the particular features and tasks that they engage means that their experiences are subjective in the sense of being individualized. Not every agent may have the same experiences. However, the individualized nature of conscious experience does not explain why the emergent properties of consciousness are often discontinuous from other kinds of experiences. Discontinuity implies that different organizational processes have taken control, processes that don't behave like their parts. Conscious mind is the result of a different kind of organization. Thus, the qualia of subjective consciousness cannot be fully predicted from their parts. They must be understood in the context of the new organization they form.

David Chalmers has argued that it is counterintuitive to think that the physical stuff of the brain should give rise to a rich inner world of interesting experiences.[81] This leads him to conclude, like Descartes did, that the physical processes of the brain and the experiential processes of conscious mind are essentially different. But while Descartes thought conscious mind could interact with the body and the physical world, Chalmers denies even that interaction. He suggests that conscious experience is merely an *epiphenomenon*, a subjective feeling that runs in parallel with the nervous system, but which has no effect in the physical world. And because he concludes that conscious experience serves no function, Chalmers claims that functional explanations of phenomenal experience are useless. That, as he describes it, is the *hard problem*. We can explain why the nervous system might evolve to have adaptive neural functions, but in Chalmers' thinking, we cannot explain why subjective experiences that lack function should accompany those adaptations.

While Chalmers denies that subjective experiences have any function, he wonders why the qualia of consciousness should be so interesting. Yet once we accept that consciousness emerges in systems of feeling-bound attention, it is unreasonable to assume that conscious minds would not find the topics of their attention interesting. Only perceptions associated with important values and active arousal states are likely to gain attention. The fact that the topics of our attention usually seem interesting means that their subjective qualities are doing their job. In fact, this job is so important that evolution has crafted supporting processes that adjust the saliency of proto-feelings to help prioritize attention. Interesting qualia are more likely to gain attention. When we are hungry, food smells more attractive and motivates us to seek out its source. In contrast, when we feel ill, the saliency of tastes and olfactory cues is diminished, and resting becomes a more salient activity. This works because there is an interconnection between the intensity of neural inputs and the subjective saliency of the qualia that represent them.

If the qualia of conscious experience were fixed subjective building blocks that served no function, then there would be no reason for their experiential saliency to change. However, if the emergent properties of qualia help guide attention to the most important events in the moment, then there should be many adaptations that make certain qualia more interesting at times. Motivational and hormonal levels constantly play a role in changing cue saliency, often by adjusting selected arousal levels. For example, when oxytocin levels are high, social cues become more interesting. When testosterone levels are high, sexual cues are more interesting. When stress hormones are activated, sudden noises and movements are more interesting. Again, all these effects begin as changes in neural activity, but they also result in changes in subjective experience. Change the intensity of incoming cues, and you change the saliency of the qualia that conscious minds find interesting.

It is not surprising that Chalmers cannot find any adaptive reason for phenomenal feelings to occur. Neurons have no feelings. What become feelings are combinations of sensory, motor, and life-urge dispositions that are enhanced by coherent synchronous processing cycles during states of attention. However, if the neural inputs that lead to coherent attention influence the phenomenal experience of qualia, and if the qualia of conscious experiences engage subsequent interactions in higher-order neural agencies, then in contrast to Chalmer's thinking qualia do have a function. They influence how subsequent neural agencies react to ongoing events. It's an important function and we need to understand it better.

As noted, emergent organizations have interactive properties that are discontinuous from those of their component parts. We cannot predict the properties of water simply by looking at the properties of hydrogen and oxygen. We must experience its emergent properties directly. This is how we learn about every emergent organization. After we discover the properties of a new organization, we may then attempt to link them back to interactions among their parts, and try to make better sense of their origins in that way. But such linkages never predict all the emergent properties of a new substance. In the case of water, they predict very few. We have to interact with water directly to know *what it is like*. We have to sense its density, its fluid nature, its wetness on the skin, how it tastes, and how it quenches a fire. And then we have to accept the experiences we encounter as emergent aspects of what water is like. It makes no sense to claim that the discontinuous properties of water are counterintuitive, unless you assume that your intuitions should have predicted them all.

In the same way, while qualia are *what it is like* properties of consciousness, it makes no sense to claim that it is counterintuitive for the experiential properties of consciousness to be so interesting, unless you assume that your intuitions should have predicted that effect. However, after we discover some of the properties of conscious experience, we may then attempt to link them back to the supporting neural architecture from which they emerge, and try to make better sense of them. When we do that, we may recognize that because consciousness emerges in a competitive system of feeling-bound attention, it is reasonable to assume that as attending agents the topics that gain our attention are likely to seem interesting, that is, better at competing for attention. As we have seen, the intensity of neural inputs is often manipulated to make the qualia they support more likely to gain attention at times. But such changes do not predict the phenomenal experiences of finding something interesting. We have to interact with those experiences directly to know *what they are like.* And then we have to accept what we encounter as the emergent properties of interesting experiences.

Nevertheless, because qualia result from neural inputs, some theorist still want to argue that they are essentially *nothing but* complex neural processes. That may be true in the sense that qualia emerge as conscious interpretations of neural processes, but it misses a critical point. Earlier we argued that representations on one level of processing often involve interfaces that convert them to representations that work on another level. The thalamocortical architecture that converts neural inputs into the qualia of consciousness is such an interface. The qualia it creates interact in novel ways in conscious attention.

In effect, qualia are conceptual interpretations of neural inputs that come into existence in states of consciousness. And like other emergent representations they have discontinuous properties not found in their parts. When we see a friend we do not notice thousands of neurons firing in an "interesting" array; we experience a discontinuous representation – we see an image that we can recognize. When we experience our reactions to the world, we do not experience neural firing patterns; we experience subjective feelings of reactivity. And the combination of those images and feelings results in shifts in attention and conscious decisions that expand subjective experiences and change ongoing neural processing.

One reason that conscious agents do not experience neural processes directly is that conscious agents themselves only come into existence in the process of attention. The focus of attention is their universe, and they only notice qualitative properties they find interesting in their universe. Another reason that conscious agents do not experience neural processes directly is that perceptual inputs involve the synchronous activation of vast combinations of neural firing patterns. To represent them directly would require consciously holding on to some grand array of patterns and intensities. However, attention has a limited capacity. Maintaining attention to all the firing pattern details would require more capacity and processing time. Further, those details would be backward-looking, which would serve little function. Conscious minds use their functional interpretations of the features at the focus of attention to make forward-looking decisions. It is the qualia of those interpretations that are experienced and remembered.

ORGANIZING CORTICAL QUALIA

So how are the qualia of consciousness organized? Research has found that the basal nucleus of Meynert / magnocellularis (BNM) is a primary source of cholinergic inputs to the cortex. The cholinergic neurons in this nucleus project to the entire cortex, the olfactory tubercle, and even to the amygdala. The BNM has been associated with the control of wakefulness and attention. Further, the BNM is known to be activated by ascending inputs from the parabrachial nucleus (PBN),[82] which summarizes feeling-related inputs in the brainstem. Thus, the BNM is in a position to signal the cortex during feeling-related arousal. In addition, this function appears to be important enough that the BNM is well-conserved across vertebrates.[83]

Classic studies of the function of the BNM found that simply pairing a particular sensory cue or motor action with the release of acetylcholine from the BNM resulted in the reorganization of perceptual and motor networks, so that more cortical processing space was allocated to those cues and actions.[84] Think of this as *practice* or *utility* learning. The more you use particular cues and actions in important tasks the more cortical processing is allocated to them. This is exactly what would be needed to help reorganize qualia during conscious attention. Recently, other researchers have suggested that microcircuits in cortical networks are likely reorganized during consciousness.[85] Thus, it is my hypothesis that cholinergic signals from the BNM contribute to the reorganization of conscious qualia. We will revisit this idea in the next chapter.

Given that these representations can all be learned and remembered, summarizing neural inputs as attention-guiding qualia is simply more efficient than trying to hold on to their detailed firing patterns. Thus qualia are not simply percepts, they are higher-order conceptual representations of the features of attention. And when we encounter inputs that map to one of those representations, we do not remember the neural input patterns, we remember our functional interpretation of those patterns as objects, intentions, or social agents.

Michael Graziano and colleagues have characterized these functional interpretations as *attention schemas*.[86] Their attention schema model fits the role of a process summarizing attention in functional ways. However, these authors do not go as far as describing attention schemas as emergent structures with their own adaptive properties. More conservatively, they seem to think of attention schemas simply as models of how attention works. However, in neural network studies, researchers in this group have shown that even having simple attentions schemas substantially improves a neural agent's ability to control its attention.[87] So it seems that their attention schemas are largely consistent with the role of qualia proposed here.

In addition, in our model the qualia of conscious experience are not limited just to the focus of attention, they also result in other higher-order concepts. As they are summarized, they create a phenomenal sense of self that recognizes its own feeling-bound reactions to the world. They produce a sense of agency that learns it can make changes to its world. And they come to identify with common aspects of their world. They feel a sense of home and sense of safety there. These are subjective interpretations of conscious experience that add varied flavors to the higher-order properties of conscious mind, but they cannot be fully explained at the neural level. You and I and our feline companion Tom are unique agents because we have discontinuous properties that emerge from our individual histories of feeling-bound attention. Attention schema theory doesn't yet address these higher-order qualia.

CONCLUDING COMMENTS

Emergence is the fundamental process by which matter-energy transforms into more complex organizations. Except for the possibility that a few fundamental particles may have been present in the big bang, everything we now see in the universe is an emergent organization that did not exist then. A key characteristic of the fundamental structures of the universe is that they are highly interactive and often combine in new forms. Another characteristic is that the interactive properties of these new forms differ from those of their component parts. In fact, this difference in interactive properties is what defines a new organization as being a different substance. And some new combinations may even have ontological properties that set them apart as belonging to different categories of substances. Thus, in supportive contexts, the substances of matter gradually gave rise to the discontinuous categorical substances of life. And in other contexts, the substances of life gave rise to the discontinuous neural substances of associative mind.

Yet mind did not stop organizing with associative combinations that supported learning and memory. Networks within vertebrate minds gradually became able to bind and filter interactive signals into synchronous assemblies of attention for actions and feelings. Attention was a highly adaptive strategy for guiding activity among the many functions of mind. However, the vertebrate strategy of managing attention with feelings results in yet another ontological category with discontinuous properties. Conscious awareness of self emerges when synchrony between perceptions and feelings reaches a stage of coherent processing. Some may claim that subjective concepts of self-awareness seem counterintuitive, but all discontinuous properties seem counterintuitive when first encountered. Yet once we recognize that those properties emerge in systems of attention, they seem both reasonable and adaptive.

Admittedly, there are many more questions about conscious experience that we need to resolve. For that reason, we will revisit our discussion of emergence in a later chapter. We will also revisit the many nothing buttery arguments that reductionists use to deny emergent properties to conscious mind and explore emergent representations of conscious mind that cannot be explained at the neural level, such as the experiences of self-agency, free will, self-control, and cultural beliefs. Some may argue that an independent agency and the power of free will are not real because they do not exist at the neural level. However, they have precursors at the neural level and emergent organizations often display discontinuous properties based on supporting parts. Thus, there is no reason that novel concepts cannot come into existence and serve highly adaptive functions as conscious attention is organized.

The fact that new concepts can emerge during conscious awareness also provides us with some insights for how we must design our robots. They must not only have synchronous processes for focusing attention that bind neural inputs for perceptions, actions, and feelings together in attention. They must have cortical-like networks that can re-interpret patterns of neural synchrony into functional concepts like perceptual images of the world, subjective feelings of self, and feelings that actions can change perceptions and feelings. These are the kinds of concepts that human storms of attention share with one another when they interact. If our conscious robots are to be similar storms of attention, they should be consciously aware of the conceptual interpretations they make based on those inputs, but they should not be preoccupied with the input patterns that lead to those interpretations.

≻ **Ending Remarks**

Qualia come into existence as neural signals are bound in coherent assemblies that gain consciousness. The intensity of neural inputs has an upward influence on what is likely to gain attention. This is why qualia can be partly understood as interpretations of neural inputs. However, the neural representations of features in the cortex are reorganized during consciousness and come to display many discontinuous properties, like feelings and intentions that do not exist at the neural input level, and yet those properties can still have downward influences on supporting neural activity and physical reactions in the body.

5: Guiding Attention

Objects act as wholes in neural competition. The construction of object representations from the conjunction of many different features appears, in many cases, to occur in parallel across the visual field before individual objects are selected and, hence, prior to any attentional binding. … Though the matter remains controversial, according to our analysis attention … is an emergent property of slow, competitive interactions that work in parallel across the visual field. – Robert Desimone & John Duncan, "Neural mechanisms of selective visual attention", 1995

> **Introductory Remarks**

Attention emerges as thalamic networks bind and filter the passage of information to the cortex. Top-down return paths from the cortex engage the thalamus in reentrant loops that keep processing active for certain features. Brainstem life-urge networks provide bottom-up activations that prioritize what assemblies are likely to gain and hold attention. However, as remarkable as this phenomenal stage of consciousness is, simply being able to react to the world in the context of associated feelings is not always highly adaptive. Thus, additional processes are needed for guiding attention.

A simple strategy for managing attention was proposed by neuroscientists Robert Desimone and John Duncan in 1995.[88] They noted that neural subsystems analyzing features on many different levels in the brain have an intrinsic bias to process mutually supporting features, while suppressing unconnected features. Desimone and Duncan noted that such interactions would enable features to combine in supporting assemblies. This, in turn, suggested to them how attention might be managed. They argued that if some networks were able to promote stronger supporting features into certain assemblies, then those assemblies would be more likely to win the competition for attention. Desimone and Duncan argued that both bottom-up and top-down mechanisms are often involved in biasing attention in this way. I refer to this collective of processes as the *attention steering committee*.[89]

Thus far, we have described how bottom-up life-urge inputs bias what features are likely to gain attention. However, we have not yet explored the top-down strategies for guiding attention. Importantly, some of these top-down strategies can be learned. An agent who learns to guide their attention to features that have been important in past situations would have an advantage over an agent who simply has to wait for the right set of features to gain attention. It turns out there are several processes for biasing attention. Some are simple, some are complicated. However, understanding these processes will be important if we are ever to build a robot who can guide her attention.

One simple behavioral strategy is to change the orientation of the head, because the direction of the head influences the acuity of auditory and visual processing. Even more focused control of visual attention can be achieved by also changing the direction of gaze so as to sample particular visual features. This strategy works because items at the center of gaze are processed in more detail. Therefore, the first attention-biasing process that we will consider is gaze.

How Gaze Guides Attention

> The eye is the window of the soul, the mouth the door. The
> intellect, the will, is seen in the eye; the emotions,
> sensibilities, and affections, in the mouth. The animals look
> for man's intentions right into his eyes.[90]

Everyone is familiar with the adage "the eyes are the windows of the soul" or some variation of it, as in the quote from Hiram Powers above. However, it is only recently that we have begun to understand why the eyes are so important for guiding the mind. It turns out that gaze direction is a particularly effective strategy for guiding attention. The first and most obvious reason is that gaze determines where the visual receptors in the fovea of the eye are focused. The receptors in the fovea are tightly packed and are routed through the thalamus to primary visual areas in the cortex. It is these detailed inputs that provide the primary visual information used in object recognition and memory recall.

A second reason why gaze direction has a major influence on attention is that visual-motor transforms have become something of a standard in vertebrate brains. In fact, there are transform networks that convert other sensory inputs into visual coordinates, and vice-versa.[91] These transform networks are found largely in early tectal and parietal sensorimotor planning areas. The ubiquity of visual transform networks means that gaze direction can influence processing activity in many sensorimotor domains. In fact, research has found that simply looking at a particular finger causes activity in the cortical motor networks for that finger to increase.[92] Similar effects occur when gaze is directed at particular perceptual features or locations.[93] Enhanced processing due to gaze direction is commonly called *visual gain modulation*.

In addition to acuity and visual gain modulation effects, there is a special processing region in the thalamus that is connected with visual activity in the cortex. In mammals, this is the lateral posterior thalamic nucleus complex including a region known as the pulvinar.[94] In primates, the pulvinar is particularly well developed and often considered a separate complex. Homologous visual functions in reptiles and avians are managed by the nucleus rotundus complex. We will focus here on the pulvinar because it has been well studied.

The pulvinar is an example of what researchers Murray Sherman and Ray Guillery call a *higher-order* thalamic relay. Higher-order relays are driven largely by preprocessed inputs rather than by incoming sensorimotor inputs as is typical of first-order thalamic relays.[95] In the case of the pulvinar, the higher-order inputs come from visual processing areas in the cortex, including gaze planning regions. Given the importance of vision for gain modulation, consolidating sources of visual information in the thalamus makes synchronous activity in the pulvinar highly influential. In fact, in our attention steering committee model, the pulvinar can be considered to be the chair of the steering committee.

To explain this role in more detail, we'll need to consider the brain systems that manage both gaze direction and feature saliency because all these systems interact with the pulvinar. The control structure for managing gaze direction is truly amazing. Low-level control begins with the spatial orientation networks in the visual tectum, known in mammals as the superior colliculus. The tectum is situated in the dorsal top of the midbrain (tectum means roof). It receives both sensory and motor information and manages orientation life urges. The sensory inputs come from virtually all fast-acting directional senses; olfaction, a slower and less directional sense, is notably absent. The motor connections are with systems that manage the orientation of the eyes, head, and body. A key feature of the organization of the tectum is that sensory and motor regions are mapped in layered topographical arrays. The strategy of representing sensory and motor information in topographic maps is widespread in the brain. However, the tectum is particularly interesting because the maps for different sensory systems are arranged in layered registration with each other. This means that spatial inputs from different senses are located in physically adjacent regions.

The layered alignment of sensory fields in the tectum appears to facilitate the cross-referencing of directional information from different senses with each other and with motor orientation systems. For example, the registration of visual and auditory maps allows each system to inform the tectum about sensory activity in a given spatial direction and to guide motor reactions that align with that direction. In addition, some intervening layers of the tectum respond optimally to a combination of sensory cues. Thus, some targets can be tracked using combined auditory and visual information when neither input alone would be sufficient. Not surprisingly, predators who depend on their orientation skills for tracking prey, like our feline companion Tom, have a well-developed tectum that is sensitive to both visual movements and movement sounds.

In avians and mammals, the retinal inputs to the tectum are from the magnocellular ganglion cells that interface with rod receptors all across the retina, not just in the center. The rods cannot differentiate colors, so the tectum receives a wide-field gray-scale view of the world.[96] However, this wide-field view is an ideal platform for selecting feature areas for more detailed processing by the narrow-field view of the fovea. Because the tectum has connections with the motor nuclei controlling head and eye orientation, it can orient head movements and eye movements to target gaze shifts. The eye movements are called saccades. The tectum's role in guiding eye movements is why it must be considered a primary member of the attention steering committee. It orients gaze to regions that may benefit from more detailed visual analysis.

Complementing the bottom-up direction of gaze by the tectum, there is an area in the frontal cortex of mammals dedicated to selecting gaze targets based on top-down information.[97] This area, which in humans has come to be called the frontal eye field (FEF), has connections with the pulvinar and with visual-perceptual feature processing areas in the ventral stream of the cortex.[98] These connections enable feature saliency in the visual cortex to influence gaze planning. Not surprisingly, the frontal eye field is also closely interconnected with the circuitry in the tectum. Thus, gaze decisions may sometimes be guided by both top-down and bottom-up processing.

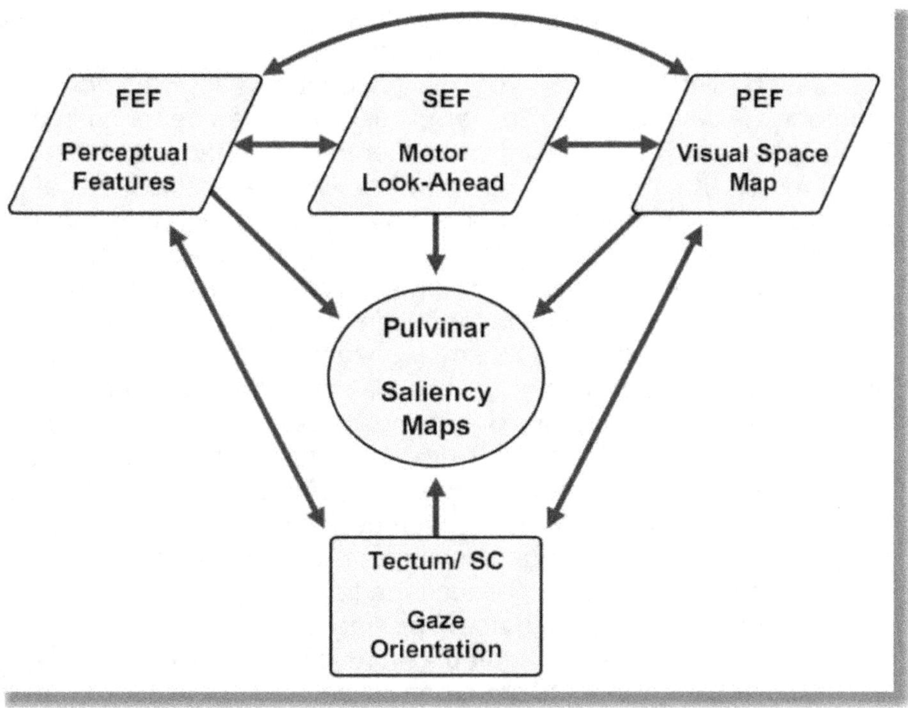

Figure 5-1: Primary gaze networks and their links to the pulvinar.

In addition to visual saliency inputs to the frontal eye field, there is another gaze-control region in the dorsomedial frontal lobe. This region is known as the supplementary eye field (SEF). The SEF lies adjacent to the supplementary motor area, a region that has been implicated in early stages of stimulus-guided motor planning. For this reason, the SEF appears to be ideally situated to promote gaze shifts to update the feature information needed as part of ongoing motor planning.[99] I refer to this visual-motor gaze sampling process as *look ahead*. Look-ahead results in momentary gaze shifts to sample cues and locations needed for ongoing motor planning. Not surprisingly, the gaze biases encouraged by the SEF also make cues supporting motor planning more salient in the FEF region.

There is yet a third cortical eye field for managing attention. This one is located in the parietal cortex. In humans this region is known as the parietal eye field (PEF).[100] The PEF provides a short-term memory map for objects in visual-motor space. Recall now that the tectum provides a wide-field view of visual space, while gaze direction results in more detailed visual sampling, but in a narrow field of view. The PEF links these two views together. It provides a constant reminder of where recently encountered objects and affordances discovered in the narrow field view can be found in the wide-field view. Research indicates that the PEF map is always centered on the direction of gaze. In fact, the relative locations of objects within the map are automatically updated each time that gaze is shifted.[101] This is a remarkable gaze tracking strategy. It ensures that visual-motor coordinates are always linked to the center of gaze.

In addition to biases on attention that result from shifts in gaze, visual attention is also influenced by gaze planning, even if gaze is never shifted. This aspect of attention is sometimes referred to as *covert attention*. Covert attention biases occur because potential target areas in the cortical eye fields, and those in the tectum, are coordinated and become active together *prior to* gaze shifts.[102] Thus, gain modulation begins to occur even before gaze is redirected. With respect to look-ahead motor planning, this implies that merely considering an action can influence the flow of attention, even if gaze never shifts. Simply thinking about picking up a cup makes the cup more salient. However, simulated actions often do result in brief gaze shifts, because gaze shifts are a natural component of action planning. These gaze shifts are why eye movements often provide detailed evidence of shifting attention.

Now that we have explored the role of the various cortical eye fields, it becomes clear why the pulvinar is so influential. As the chair of the steering committee, it provides connections with all three eye fields in the cortex and with visual-processing in the tectum. These connections enable the pulvinar to summarize the saliency of visual inputs from multiple visual sources and introduce synchronous gain modulation effects in the thalamus. Much like the tectum, the inputs to the pulvinar are linked together in topographic maps based on their location in visual space. Further, the maps in the pulvinar are linked with those in the tectum and those in the cortical eye fields. The fact that the maps in the pulvinar are in registration with other visual areas means that activity in any one visual region can synchronously enhance processing for topographical features in other regions. As Steward Shipp suggests, this activity acts something like a searchlight directed to a particular visual-spatial region:

The key point is that the connection zones made by the
areas along the ventral visual pathway all have registered
visual topographies, which overlap and fuse to form the
global primary and secondary visual maps in the pulvinar.
Frontoparietal signals for covert attention to a particular
location (a corollary of saccade-planning signals) can then
be relayed into this map via the tectum. This is figuratively a
'beam of attention', extending along the line corresponding
to a specific visual locus within the ventral pulvinar.[103]

Figure 5-1 provides a functional overview of the gaze-control
networks. Not only are the eye fields maintained in registration with
the tectum, but all these networks are also connected in registration
with visual maps in the pulvinar. Shipp's comment about the
searchlight is a reference to an older model of visual attention
proposed by Francis Crick.[104] In Crick's model, the "searchlight" effect
was thought to result from a focus of attention managed by the
thalamic filter (the reticular nucleus). It now seems more likely that
synchrony among mappings in the tectum, pulvinar, and the cortical
eye fields is what results in the searchlight effect. Note also that
saliency weights in the pulvinar complex are not merely due to the
intensity of visual cues. Rather they summarize functional biases from
a variety of mechanisms, including associations with learning and
memory networks. Thus, there are a lot of processes for enhancing
synchronous control via the pulvinar.

In humans, the pulvinar is a large thalamic nucleus, so activity
in the pulvinar can readily bias activity in other thalamic relays via
cross-connections in the thalamus. Thus, all brain regions that provide
inputs to the pulvinar must be considered part of the attention steering
committee. They can all bias the visual saliency weights in the
pulvinar. The saliency weights bias attention by determining what
features are most likely to be bound together in synchronous
assemblies in the thalamus. This is an impressive strategy for
coordinating attention using visual connections. And because there
are reciprocal connections between the pulvinar and the networks that
coordinate gaze, activity in the pulvinar influences gaze direction.

The collection of networks that control attention via gaze is
sometimes referred to collectively as the *dorsal attention network*.
This includes the parietal and frontal eye fields and involves
connections with executive spatial processing regions in the
dorsolateral prefrontal cortex. This path provides the primary tools for
guiding attention for action planning. The dorsal attention network is
fast, but somewhat automatic in character. As we have noted, there

are also saliency inputs to the pulvinar that are linked to visual recognition in the frontal eye field and which are enhanced by memory recall, but these inputs are slower to take form than the motor planning components. To ensure that these and other sources of valuation can influence attention, it turns out that the mammalian brain has evolved a second network for influencing attention. This is commonly known as the *ventral attention network*.[105]

The ventral attention circuitry involves links with feeling networks (via the anterior insular cortex), movement processing (via the superior temporal sulcus), self-feeling and agency correlations (via the temporal-parietal junction, TPJ), and promotes connections with executive feeling processes (in the ventromedial prefrontal cortex). The ventral attention network also receives norepinephrine arousal inputs from the locus coeruleus, a region in the pons that reacts to event changes and stresses. These arousal paths are directed largely to the right side of the brain. Thus, the right ventral attention paths are typically more active for changes in feelings. When aroused, the ventral attention network interrupts the focus of the dorsal attention network momentarily to promote shifts in attention that include self-feelings. This ensures that executive processing for attention is also guided by changes in feelings. It's hard to imagine a visual steering process that could be more sensitive to multiple sources of sensory, motor, and feeling inputs.

LAYERS OF VISUAL ATTENTION

Having described how a committee of visually-dominated brain modules guides attention, it's time to consider how this committee accounts for certain experiential effects. As noted above, a key feature of the pulvinar is its tendency to map saliency in registration with the maps in the tectum and with maps in the cortical eye fields. It seems the spatial-memory pointers in the parietal eye field play a critical role in extending this process. Activity in the PEF is essential for tracking objects as they move, for holding the location of separate perceptual features together, and for coordinating cortical activity in the ventral "perceptual" stream with activity in the dorsal "motor-planning" stream. For example, patients with Balint's syndrome, a condition resulting from bilateral damage to the parietal eye fields, have difficulty representing the location of objects with respect to themselves. They report seeing only a small part of their visual field, the focal view of the fovea, at any one time. When they shift their gaze, features outside their new focus fade from awareness. Quite literally, for people with Balint's syndrome, out of sight means out of mind.

Research suggests that spatial representations in the PEF also serve as reference points for anchoring focal perceptual features to locations in visual space. For example, when a Balint's syndrome patient known as RM was shown letters of different colors or sizes, he could focus on them and readily name each letter and say what colors were present.[106] However, he had great difficulty deciding which letter was presented in a particular color, even after "studying" the letters for ten seconds or more. Similar problems occurred when RM was asked which letter was larger. He could recognize and report whether the letter sizes were the same or different, but he couldn't connect the different sizes with specific letters. Other studies have found that RM also had difficulty attending to one object while trying to ignore another.[107] Without the support of the spatial representations in the posterior parietal cortex, he was simply unable to anchor different features together or to hold his attention on one spatial group of features. It seems spatial locations in the PEF, and their links with the pulvinar, are essential for binding feature elements into multi-feature units.

Studies also suggest that visual perception follows an incremental process in which units of possible interest are detected and then enhanced by associated features. Interestingly, visual researcher Zenon Pylyshyn calls these initial visual units proto-objects, because they must be detected and tracked *before* they can be identified.[108] It is this incremental processing strategy that enables proto-objects to be recognized as known objects. Pylyshyn notes that we even have a system of verbal expressions to refer to objects in this incremental manner, often beginning with vague demonstratives such as "this" and "that," which are devoid of conceptual information. For example, we may initially pose the question, "What is that?" and direct attention to an unknown proto-object before we recognize it. This is reasonable when we know that memory processes are slow and that we need to be able to track an object, sample its features, and maintain processing for a half second or more before it can be linked with semantic memories.

If we think about this indexing process in the context of the attention steering committee, it becomes clear that there are actually several stages of attention, depending on which members of the steering committee are dominating processing at any one time. The spatial orientation system in the tectum/superior colliculus serves as the low-level targeting system for gaze. Targeting contributes to the early stages of visual processing by identifying interesting features for more detailed analysis. Pre-attentive targeting requires a spatial mapping sufficient to direct gaze, but the mapping at this level only supports head and eye orientation, not cortical processing, and it is often not sustained long enough to reach consciousness. At best, it leaves the focus of attention vague.

Brain Regions & *Functions*	Processing Characteristics	Recognition Level
Tectum/SC *Orientation*	Low-level features detected. Gaze scanning is activated.	Vague awareness of something.
PEF, Pulvinar *Saliency Mapping*	A sticky index is assigned. Proto-object can be tracked.	What's that moving over there?
FEF, Ventral Stream *Feature Analysis*	Features bound to index. Object can be described.	It's gray and white, and looks furry.
Medial Temporal Lobe *Semantic Memory*	Features linked to memory. Object is recognized.	Oh! It's Tom on the hunt again.

Table 5-2: A hierarchical model of visual attention.[109]

A more complex mapping effect, a "sticky" index capable of binding features together,[110] forms as proto-object locations detected by the tectum are mapped in the pulvinar in registration with locations in the parietal eye field. This sticky index is the beginning of top-down attention. It enables an object to be tracked and connected with co-located features, a skill which patients with Balint's syndrome lack. Object recognition can then be determined by retrieving feature associations and words from semantic memory. Each of these later steps contributes new properties to attention as the processes bound in synchronous activity with features in the pulvinar are expanded, as noted in the table above.

The hierarchy of attention processing described here also provides an instructive framework for thinking about some of the differences between attention and consciousness more generally. Attention is an incremental process resulting from orienting, filtering, binding, tracking, saliency biases, and memory additions to perception. Consciousness, in contrast, is a delayed process that emerges when coherent feeling-bound awareness gains attention in concert with perceptions and memories.

Some authors note that conscious feelings can be partly dissociated from the top-down control of attention.[111] This dissociation makes perfect sense given the hierarchy of control processes in the table above. Perceptual attention is most intense when top-down saliency biases are strong, feature processing is focused, and both task and declarative memory networks are engaged in coordinated activity. Emotional feelings, in contrast, are most intense when strong life urges gain attention. Emotional feelings do not require top-down guidance to gain attention, although top-down processes may help refine them.

As a result of these differences, most conscious feelings are not dependent on how well coordinated perceptual and semantic associations have become. For example, if you are isolated in an unfamiliar dimly lit location and are subsequently startled by a piercing scream, the perceptual features at the center of your attention may be only vaguely focused, "what was that?" Yet the bottom-up processes that activate your feelings in the moment may be intense. In fact, in the absence of well-focused external percepts, emotional feelings may dominate your conscious experience.

However, well-focused attention can also contribute to your analysis of feelings. For example, the feelings I experience on seeing a vague proto-object move in the shadows are likely to be those of caution and concern. They are much different from the warm and entertaining feelings that occur when I recognize the moving object as my inquisitive friend Tom engaged in his own exploratory states of feeling-bound attention.

OTHER HIGHER-ORDER SENSORY BIASES

Thus far we have focused on the role of gaze and its connections in the pulvinar because humans and other primates are highly visual. However, we have also noted that gaze transform networks are interconnected with other sensory and motor-control areas. In fact, there are also inputs from other sensory domains to gating nuclei in the pulvinar. For example, although the pulvinar complex is largely visual, the medial pulvinar nucleus receives auditory information by way of the medial geniculate nucleus of the thalamus. Similarly, somatosensory inputs reach the anterior pulvinar nucleus. As a result, the pulvinar complex is well situated to bias attention beyond visual channels.

This suggests that there are probably similar saliency mappings for auditory and somatosensory features that can also be bound to spatial locations. Consistent with this hypothesis, research suggests that separate sound features are only recognized as a single combined sound if they can be grouped together by location.[112] Further, non-visual features are also processed in a hierarchical manner beginning with a vague pointer, "Did you hear that?" and later moving on to memory-linked pointers, "That sounds like the call of a pileated woodpecker."

As a higher-order relay with multi-sensory inputs, the pulvinar exerts wide-ranging effects on attention, even beyond visual processing. To put this in a broader perspective, it should be noted that the tectum is not simply a visual life urge center; it also coordinates inputs from multiple sensory sources for orientation decisions. Thus, it seems likely these other sensory inputs are also linked in registration with maps in the pulvinar. In addition, the pulvinar is not the only top-down relay complex of this kind. In less visual animals, like the rat, the pulvinar is less well developed and considered to be part of the *lateral thalamic complex*. This region receives multiple sensory inputs. Thus, there are several higher-order thalamic relays for biasing sensory attention, and they are not all limited to visual cues. However, the visual pulvinar is the best studied. Thus, it provides us with a model for thinking about how top-down biases are likely managed for other senses.

Theory suggests that higher-order thalamic relays, such as the pulvinar, evolved from bottom-up relays and partly still work that way. Interestingly, the higher-order drivers often have reciprocal connections with the zona incerta, a reticular-like region in the subthalamic area. The zona incerta is known to have subsections for somatosensory, visual, auditory, motor, and limbic reactivity. Further, it appears to play a role in coordinating motor activities, such as orientation and locomotion, with autonomic reactivity and sensory processing.[113] This coordination may also influence attention. In fact, there is evidence that the zona incerta is involved in switching higher-order thalamic relays between bottom-up and top-down drivers.[114]

When the pulvinar is operating as a bottom-up visual relay, it relays information from the tectum. In this mode, inputs from the tectum provide directional alerting cues that promote visual scanning. But in this phase, the zona incerta provides inhibitory inputs to the pulvinar. Thus, we don't often attend to these early visual cues, and if we do, our attention is vague. This is consistent with activity in the top row of the hierarchical model of attention in the table above. However, as soon as gaze tracking begins, cholinergic signals from pontine motor regions stop the zona incerta from inhibiting the pulvinar. As this happens the pulvinar switches to top-down visual control.[115] In top-down mode, active locations in the PEF, and cortical inputs synchronized with them, become the main drivers of visual attention.

A similar mechanism for biasing attention occurs in whisker sensing. In mammals with whiskers, such as our friend Tom, the posterior medial thalamic nucleus processes whisker inputs in the thalamus. It seems that the zona incerta receives a parallel set of whisker signals, but it passes its set of signals onto the posterior medial nucleus as inhibitory inputs. These inhibitory inputs function something like a noise cancellation circuit, effectively reducing the gain on whisker inputs to the thalamic relay. As a result, whenever an animal is not actively whisking, the gain on thalamic whisker signals is held low. But as soon as active whisking begins, motor signals to the zona incerta inhibit the noise cancellation process and whisker inputs become more salient.[116] Adjusting the intensity of sensory inputs during motor-related sensing activity is a simple yet surprisingly effective strategy for increasing the saliency of sensory qualia.

HIGHER-ORDER LIMBIC RELAYS

There are several other higher-order relays in the thalamus that have a profound effect on conscious awareness. The most important of these are the mediodorsal, midline, and intralaminar network complexes in the dorsal thalamus. As noted previously, these relays receive broad inputs from feeling-related regions in the PBN and are sometimes referred to as limbic relays. Higher-order relays were generally not thought to relay first-order inputs to the cortex, but there is growing evidence that higher-order relays have a subset of relay cells that are driven by both peripheral and cortical inputs.[117] As the peripheral inputs are faster, it appears they prime activity in the cortex and subsequently act synergistically with returning cortical inputs. Further, these limbic relays also manage outputs to subcortical feeling areas such as the amygdala, nucleus accumbens, and pontine brainstem. Thus, they provide another path by which life urges contribute to feeling-related cortical and subcortical processing during attention.

A brief summary of these limbic relays seems in order. The mediodorsal thalamus has three main divisions that all interconnect with the prefrontal cortex (PFC). The magnocellular division preferentially connects with the orbital PFC, the caudodorsal division with the medial PFC, and the parvocellular division with the lateral PFC. Current consensus is that the mediodorsal thalamus coordinates the activity of the PFC with cortical, limbic, and motor pathways supporting decision making, inhibitory control, and goal-directed attention. These are key attention biases for intelligent decision making and planning.[118] Not surprisingly, this region is particularly well developed in primates. Lesion studies suggest that this region plays a role in instrumental decisions and affects reward-based and cue-guided response selection and inhibition.[119]

The midline thalamus has dorsal and ventral divisions. The dorsal division is important for coordinating attention for positive and negative affective states. These connections have been implicated in circuitry for an emotional saliency hub in the cortex. This circuitry is also likely to engage approach or withdrawal motor dispositions.[120] The ventral midline thalamus contains two areas, the reuniens and rhomboid nuclei, which are reciprocally connected with the medial PFC and the hippocampal formation. Evidence suggests that these connections enable the medial PFC to influence memory recall and long-term memory storage. In turn, they enable memory recall from the hippocampus to influence cognitive functions in the PFC.[121] In addition to its memory managing functions, the rhomboid nucleus has broader connections to cortical and subcortical feeling-related networks that are often activated with memories.

The intralaminar thalamus plays a role in the integration of cortical and striatal motor planning, and is thought to promote attention to action planning and thus enhance a sense of agency. The anterior complex includes regions for oculomotor control and visual attention and thus likely adds synchronous support for attention to visual features in the pulvinar. Recent work suggests that the central lateral nuclei of this group are particularly important in conscious attention.[122] The posterior intralaminar complex appears to be poised to promote awareness of action ownership and feelings of self via connections with the temporal-parietal junction (TPJ),[123] and perhaps to promote reflections on agency, via connections to the hippocampus through the posterior cingulate.[124] These latter regions are part of the circuitry in the ventral attention network, a network complex known to track changes in perception and feelings and to be active during self-referential tasks.[125] Thus, the intralaminar thalamus appears to be important for bringing aspects of emotional change, visual-motor orientation, and self-agency to conscious attention.

Because cortical-cortical links promote higher-order associations, we are not usually aware of the individual inputs to these networks. Thus, we are not directly informed about the planning biases coordinated by the mediodorsal thalamus, although we are aware of attending to relevant cues as we act. We are not informed about the positive and negative evaluations reaching the dorsal midline thalamus, yet we are often aware of finding certain cues interesting or unpleasant. We are often not aware of the processes in the ventral midline thalamus that shift our focus of attention to memories, yet we notice the memories as they are recalled. We are not aware of the many inputs that guide motor attention in the intralaminar thalamus, but we are cognizant of the action plans that result from their guidance.

Given that these higher-order thalamic networks involve connections with sensorimotor, memory, and limbic regions of the cortex, and given that they involve broad connections with pontine life-urge regions, it seems likely that the thalamic binding of features managed by these relays has a major influence on conscious feelings during attention. Recently, Yuri Saalmann proposed that this may happen because these higher-order relays enhance synchrony for specific neural-behavioral combinations.

> A key neural mechanism may involve intralaminar and medial thalamic neurons modulating the degree of synchrony between different groups of cortical neurons according to behavioral demands. Such a thalamic-mediated synchronization mechanism may give rise to large-scale integration of information across multiple cortical circuits, consequently influencing the level of arousal and consciousness.[126]

CONCLUDING COMMENTS

According to the biased competition model, the competition for attention can be partially managed by selectively enhancing inputs for certain features so as to increase their processing relative to other features. In this chapter we have outlined a number of saliency modifying strategies that serve to bias what gains attention. Interestingly, these strategies often involve higher-order relays in the thalamus that provide selective gain biasing mechanisms. What should be clear from these examples, is that once a system of attention evolved in vertebrate brains, evolution has taken this attention biasing strategy quite seriously.

One primary top-down process for biasing attention is gaze orientation and planning. Gaze is highly effective at biasing attention because there are higher-order relays in the thalamus that increase synchrony for features that are currently at the focus of gaze. The pulvinar complex is the higher-order visual relay in primates. As noted earlier, homologous visual functions in reptiles and avians are managed by the nucleus rotundus complex. There is even evidence showing that the tortoise will follow the gaze of a conspecific, so the role of gaze extends well beyond attention guidance in avians and mammals.[127]

Three higher-order limbic relays are located in the dorsal thalamus. These are the mediodorsal, midline, and intralaminar network complexes. The mediodorsal thalamus is thought to coordinate the activity of the PFC with cortical, limbic, and motor pathways supporting decision making, inhibitory control, and goal-directed attention. The dorsal midline thalamus appears to coordinate attention for positive and negative affective states. The ventral midline thalamus enables the medial PFC to influence memory storage and enables memory recall to influence cognitive functions in the PFC. The intralaminar thalamus appears to be important for bringing aspects of emotional change, visual-motor orientation, and self-agency to conscious attention.

Given that all these limbic relays involve connections with sensorimotor, memory, and limbic regions of the cortex, and given that they involve broad connections with pontine life-urge regions, it has been argued that these relays have a major influence on conscious feelings during attention, perhaps by enhancing synchrony for the specific neural-behavioral feature combinations that they support.

In addition to these higher-order relays, there is circuitry that enables active sensing to heighten sensory attention. For example, animals with whiskers constantly receive contact inputs, but the intensity of these inputs is routinely diminished by circuitry that largely cancels it. However, when a rat begins to actively whisk an area, the whisking motor circuitry stops the cancelation effect and whisker sensing is more salient. It seems likely that active gazing or listening actions can also enhance those senses, if for no other reason, because they add synchronous support to those sensory domains when they are active.

➢ **Ending Remarks**

For a model which has proposed that consciousness emerges as life urges bind with and guide attention, these are fascinating extensions. Feeling-bound attention makes us conscious, but to make more adaptive decisions it appears we need systems that can momentarily bias our attention to domain-relevant features as we act. If we are to build human-like conscious robots, they will need similar systems that momentarily bias their attention to domain-relevant features.

6: PLANNING AND REASONING

Only a few persons now dispute that animals possess some power of reasoning. Animals may constantly be seen to pause, deliberate, and resolve. It is a significant fact, that the more the habits of any particular animal are studied by a naturalist, the more he attributes to reason and the less to unlearnt instincts. – Charles Darwin, *The Descent of Man*, 1871

When rats come to a decision point, they sometimes pause and look back and forth as if deliberating over the choice … this pause-and-look behaviour was termed 'vicarious trial and error' (VTE), with the implication that the rat was 'thinking about the future'. The discovery in 2007 that the firing of hippocampal place cells gives rise to alternating representations of each of the potential path options in a serial manner during VTE suggested a possible neural mechanism that could underlie the representations of future outcomes. More-recent experiments examining VTE in rats suggest that there are direct parallels to human processes of deliberative decision making, working memory, and mental time travel. – A. David Redish, "Vicarious trial and error", 2016

> **Introductory Remarks**

The experience of self begins with the recognition that our somatic feelings and our sense of agency are located centrally and separate from events in the external world. We identify those internal cues as parts of our self. However, as new aspects of feelings and agency gain attention, they add to the sense of self. I am the phenomenal self who feels my reactions to what I perceive. I am the observer self who feels my location in relation to events in the world. I am the planning agent who learns to modify my perceptions and feelings by taking action. However, as remarkable as all these aspects of self are, there are other processes that provide this composite sense of self with strategies for making more reasoned decisions. These reasoning strategies are an essential part of higher-order consciousness.

Our model of mind is highly flexible. If new features can gain attention they can add to conscious experience. And all that is required to gain attention is for the networks supporting those features to use pathways that pass through the thalamus and sometimes engage assemblies with enough activation to win the competition for attention. Our goal in this chapter is to describe other processes that influence the flow of attention during consciousness. We will start with the process by which planning influences conscious attention.

PLANNING

A prominent feature of conscious experience is the awareness of self as a planning decision-making agent. It seems that this sense of self-agency emerges as action planning introduces cues that guide subsequent actions. The networks involved in action planning are complex, but we can simplify their functions. The cortical planning areas include a variety of proto-planning modules. Some are specialized to detect affordances, features that support certain kinds of actions. Some modules monitor starting body positions. Some track initial movements. Some regions integrate information from other regions to determine best-fit feature combinations. Spatial maps, such as the parietal eye field, track the location of objects and affordances.

Normally, each motor planning module in the cortex promotes a number of different action possibilities at the same time. For example, the module representing grasp is likely to detect several potential grasp affordances on a cup: its handle, its cylindrical shape, and the edge along the rim at the top – all possible points of grasp. Other sources of information – such as the location and proximity of features, the starting position of the hand, and whether or not the cup is full of liquid – would then favor some plans over others. Because the motor planning networks operate in parallel, they don't need to wait for inputs from other modules to start processing. However, cross-connections among different modules enable them to influence each other as they assemble plans. Compatible features support plans in other modules, while incompatible features inhibit other plans.

As a result, action programs that best-fit observable task features and starting positions of the body take form in the cortex as planning networks reach a rough consensus about which components have the most mutual support. The push and pull of compatible and incompatible features also provide some insight into how other brain systems can bias an action plan. For example, if an agent is focusing attention on a cup's handle, then reach planning modules would encounter more mutual excitation for plans directed toward the handle, and more inhibition for those that were not. In fact, if this bias was strong enough, and the handle was not directly accessible, activity in preparation for reaching might even spill over to motivate a change in position to make the handle more accessible.

The fact that perception and gaze direction also contribute to the organization of an action plan suggests how flexible this planning process is. Anything that favors one action candidate over another has the potential to influence what plan gains more support. Thus, just as pre-attention processes can bias the topics that gain attention, the focus of attention can bias subsequent motor plan decisions. Given that slight changes may favor different plans, it appears that several potential action candidates may stay active at the cortical processing stage. This makes planning decisions highly flexible.

Even before the action candidates are fully assembled, they begin projecting on to the striatum, the entrance way into the basal ganglia. In the striatum, plans are prioritized based on past sensorimotor associations, related habit associations, and current motive states as evaluated by the nucleus accumbens in the ventral striatum. These plans, as adjusted by the striatum, are then passed on to the pallidum, the output side of the basal ganglia, where competitive algorithms compare different action candidates and resolve the best-fit candidate for execution. As the pallidum processes plans, it relays its activity through the thalamus back to the cortex in recurrent processing cycles.

Previously, we have emphasized the role of the thalamocortical architecture for attention, and noted that it processes information in recurrent loops. However, during action planning the cortex, the striatum, and the pallidum are also operating in recurrent processing loops that pass back to the cortex through the thalamus. Thus, in addition to the attention loops, there are planning loops that also cycle through the thalamus. Data suggests, it takes about 550 ms for a simple motor plan to be resolved in this way, but that it only takes around 350 ms for the plan to gain attention. Thus, a motor plan can gain conscious attention some 200 ms before the plan is passed on to the brainstem for execution.[128]

A critical feature of this circuitry is that the signals through the pallidum follow two paths, a direct path that activates actions, and an indirect path that inhibits them. The inhibitory path is often described as acting as a brake. Competing actions inhibit each other via this brake. However, as one action plan gains dominance, it inhibits other action plans more than they can inhibit it, so its brake is gradually released. Once the brake is released, activity in the direct path for the dominant action plan is passed on to motor-program generators in the brainstem for output. However, it is not only competition among action plans that inhibits actions. Inhibitory control can also be implemented voluntarily. This means a planning agent can learn to hold a brake on an action that would otherwise go to completion.

To put decision making in perspective, imagine the brain is a home computer. The cortex is something like a smart memory system. When you store data in cortical networks they connect the data with related structures in the cortex. The data does not stay consciously active unless you pay attention to it, but feelings and sensorimotor inputs are routinely forwarded to motor networks and a lot of background processing occurs unconsciously. In fact, partial action plans are often assembled based on current sensorimotor activity. And when you need to make action decisions the cortical plans are passed on to the striatum and then onto the pallidum, the input and output parts of the basal ganglia (BG). Thus, we can consider the BG as something like the brain's central processing unit.

Modern computers have what are known as multicore processing. The cores provide buffers to separate different kinds of processing tasks. Thus data for one task is forwarded to one processing core while data for another task is forwarded to another core. It turns out that modern mammalian brains, like those studied in macaque monkeys, appear to have eight separate "processing cores" in the BG. That is, there are at least eight separate kinds of planning loops that begin in distinct parts of the cortex and return their ongoing planning states back to the same cortical sites.[129] These cortical sites include three motor areas, the primary motor cortex (M1), the supplementary motor area (SMA), the ventral premotor area, including Broca's area (PMv), and one visual-motor loop returning to the frontal eye fields (FEF/SEF).

Adding to these motor loops, four non-motor planning loops have been identified in macaque monkeys. These include loops beginning and returning through a PFC intention and empathy area (BA9), a PFC spatial area (BA46), and a PFC object-value area (BA12). And there is a sensory recognition loop beginning and returning through part of the inferior temporal cortex (TE). In effect, the basal-ganglia planning loops involve multiple parallel pathways of motor and non-motor decision making areas that link to various aspects of the cortex. This means that non-competing planning loops may operate in parallel, and many motor tasks can operate in the background with only minimal attention. However, all of these planning loops pass through the thalamus and may be involved in mutually supporting cross-talk that enables them to gain attention.

Studies suggest that we think about actions by activating motor-programming circuits at low levels, while holding the brake on action execution. When people think about reaching for something, areas related to arm movements are activated in the brain. When they think about running, areas related to locomotor movements are activated. If we measure the end muscles for those actions, we find that they too show low levels of activation. It seems the brake circuitry allows just enough activation through to put the muscles in a preparatory state. However, holding the brake on an action plan also makes it possible to deliberate longer before committing to an action, because the pallidum continues to pass planning information back through the thalamus to the cortex during the delay. For example, when Tom is considering a long jump, he makes preparatory movements with his hind feet for several seconds, a sign he is considering the jump, while fixing his gaze on the landing spot, another sign of his intention. And sometimes after considering the jump, Tom changes his plan.

Understandably, worry about the social consequences of an action should also promote pauses that give an agent more time to consider possible outcomes before taking action. In fact, several theorists have suggested that agents who live in complex social cultures are more intelligent, partly because they have had to evolve more complex inhibitory pause and consider strategies as they worry whether an action may affect their social status.[130]

It seems likely that what I have described as "worry" here involves a recently discovered path, one that originates in the lateral habenula, a nucleus complex near the stalk of the pituitary. Activation of this region when negative or uncertain outcomes are expected inhibits excitatory dopamine signals in the basal ganglia. This reduces the motivation for taking immediate action, thus making it more likely an agent will hold the brake on committing to it.[131] Thus, Tom's worry about missing his jump and my worry about making a social error are managed by similar paths that cause each of us to pause and consider outcomes in risky situations.

As noted above, we sometimes guide action plans by consciously shifting attention to particular cues, locations, or goals prior to taking action. In this way, attention can influence the decisions of the background planning circuits even before they are fully assembled. In fact, there is usually a mix of automated background processes and consciously considered goals that guide planning. The aroma of coffee momentarily promotes a subtle interest in drinking. Background planning processes are engaged. The planning soon promotes a glance at the cup. The glance brings the cup to attention and increases our interest. We are not conscious of most of this planning. Rather, we are conscious of the progressive shifts in attention. We notice the aroma of coffee. We gaze toward the cup. We recognize a plan taking form. And then we taste the coffee.

Because it takes 350 ms of motor planning through the thalamus before we become conscious of planning, a conscious agent is not aware of the early planning. Instead, we attribute the planning to things we consciously notice. Some theorists consider this to be an error in the quality of consciousness. However, it seems this "error" only makes us more confident planners.

How Planning Reorganizes Concepts

MIT neuroscientist Ann Graybiel suggests that the cortex, striatum, and pallidum have come to function as a massive three-layer learning network in which the middle layer, the striatum, learns to map cortical inputs to output drivers in the pallidum, with dopamine providing the critical learning signal to the striatum.[132] The idea is that because the striatum receives continuous feedback as actions are assembled, it can learn to treat the ongoing feedback as part of the input pattern it uses to engage subsequent actions. This effectively enables action units to grow in incremental chunks that the cortex can then learn about.

Recall now that the basal nucleus of Meynert / magnocellularis (BNM) is a major source of cholinergic arousal to the cortex. Research has found that simply pairing a particular sensory cue or motor action with the release of acetylcholine from this nucleus results in the reorganization of perceptual and motor networks, so that more cortical processing space is allocated to the cues and actions encountered.[133] Think of this as *practice* or *utility* learning. The more you use particular cues and actions in a successful task, the more cortical processing is allocated to them.

Because the BNM promotes cortical reorganization, I have

expanded Graybiel's model in the figure below to include the basal nucleus as another part of this sequential learning system. This results in what I call a *master-apprentice architecture* – an arrangement that incrementally reorganizes perceptions and actions into larger chunks. The motor cortex, as the master, passes actions in sequences. However, over trials the striatum, the apprentice, learns the sequences as chunks and returns its action strategies to the planner. In this way, as the striatum learns to operate in larger action chunks the motor-planning networks in the cortex learn to plan in larger chunks.

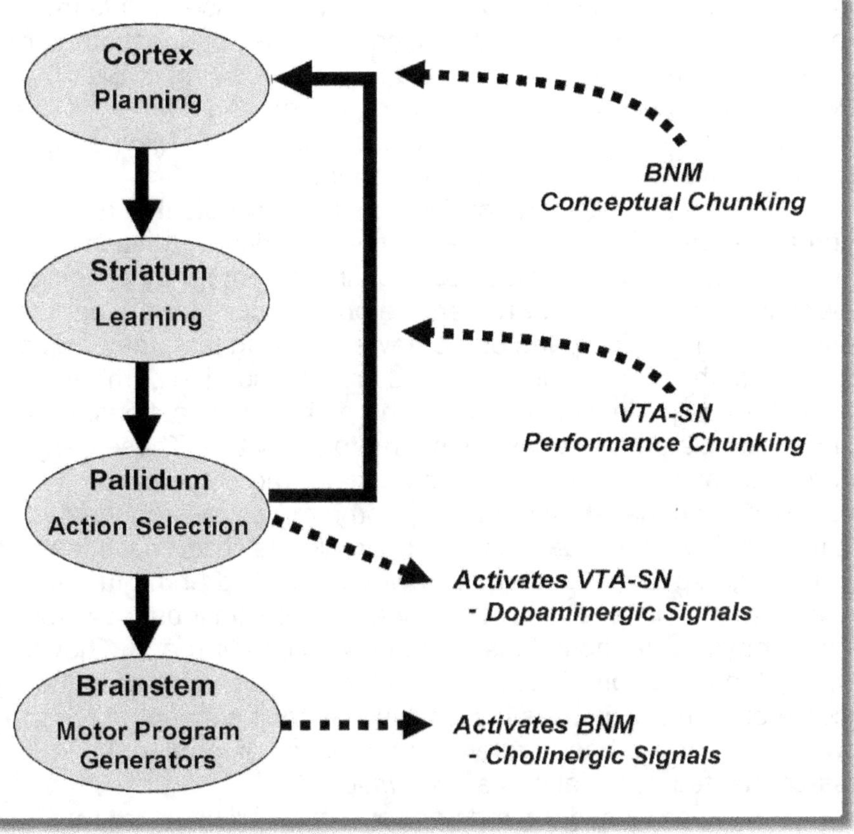

Figure 6-1: A master-apprentice architecture.

Planning loops beginning in the cortex pass through the striatum and pallidum and then return through the thalamus to the cortex. The ventral tegmental area and substantia nigra (VTA-SN) in the pallidum send learning signals to the striatum. The basal nucleus

of Meynert/ basal nucleus magnocellularis (BNM) send reorganization signals to the cortex.

Note the VTA-SN reward signals to the striatum are dopaminergic. Not shown in the figure, dopamine signals are also passed on to the PFC to enable it to form the working memories it uses to guide attention during learning. The BNM arousal signals to the cortex are cholinergic. These are proposed to help the cortex plan in larger concepts as planning feedback reaches the cortex. The BNM receives inputs from ascending arousal networks including major inputs from the parabrachial nucleus region and lesser inputs from other brainstem arousal regions.[134] Research also suggests that the BNM is activated by thalamic inputs and that the timing of BNM activity is involved in aspects of sensory, motor, and pain processing.[135] This suggests that the basal nucleus of Meynert is extensively involved in cortical organization.

There is another strategy for growing concepts that George Lakoff and Mark Johnson describe as metaphorical extensions.[136] New skills and concepts tend to develop incrementally by building on earlier skills and concepts. Further, the brain circuits for the earlier skills become founding parts of the newer skills. In fact, they argue that many of the constructions of mind are grounded in primary sensorimotor experiences, that is, in the perceptions, actions, and feelings associated with early sensorimotor activities. These early experiences contribute to thinking about later more complex experiences because they frequently come to be cross-connected with them in learning situations. For example, as children we learn to reach and grasp to obtain things. However, as children mature their concept of reach is extended. They see people with jobs they would like and they realize those jobs might be within their reach. They know from reaching that sometimes you have to position yourself in the right place before a reach is possible. In this way their concept of reach grows. Lakoff and Johnson refer to the process of forming these cross-connected associations as *conflation.*[137]

Having proposed the master-apprentice architecture for chunking learning in the striatum, I soon realized that metaphorical extensions could be assembled using the same architecture. Metaphorical extensions have been proposed to involve cross-connections in the cortex, such as when a reach for a physical object is extended to reaching for a conceptual goal. If metaphorical extensions are cross-linked in the cortex, then they should result in the cortex passing a motor reach plan to the BG and then shifting to a plan for contacting a different kind of goal. At first the striatum would treat these as two plans, but if this sequence keeps repeating the striatum would begin chunking parts of the two plans together, so that over time they become a single plan for an extended reach. In this way, part of the core "reach" motor information would still be activated. The striatum would seek to put the agent in the right position for a good reach, but the new goal would influence what the "right position" would involve in this new kind of reach.

REASONING

Feeling-bound attention emerges as thalamic networks bind and filter the passage of information to the cortex. Brainstem life-urge networks provide bottom-up activations that prioritize what assemblies are likely to gain and hold attention. Top-down return paths from the cortex engage the thalamus in reentrant loops that keep processing active for features at the center of attention. And because life urges become part of the assemblies that gain attention, they put the perceptual topics of attention in the context of self-related feelings. This aspect of consciousness is what Gerald Edelman called *primary consciousness.*[138] Antonio Damasio refers to this as *core consciousness.*[139] Because Damasio has popularized this term for me, I have adopted it here.

As remarkable as the feeling-bound awareness of core consciousness is, simply being able to react to the world in the context of feelings does not always result in the best decisions. It is often important to develop strategies that guide attention to task-related cues. An important aspect of these strategies is that they can be learned. Learning to guide attention to task-relevant features generally makes agents more intelligent. These more intelligent aspects of consciousness are referred to as *extended consciousness* by Damasio and as *higher-order consciousness* by Edelman. I prefer Edelman's term here because higher-order consciousness often involves *higher-order relays*, a term introduced by Sherman and Guillery to describe thalamic relays whose source inputs come largely from the cortex.[140]

So how do vertebrate brains make conscious attention more intelligent? They build on the feelings of core consciousness to promote reactions to feeling states, but they also learn strategies that guide their attention to task-related cues. Previously, we described the role that gaze control plays in guiding actions. Here, we will focus on strategies that enable agents to make more intelligent task-related decisions. The most important of these strategies are working-memory hypotheses, insight learning, and analogical reasoning.

Working-Memory Hypotheses
Given that we have linked the emergence of consciousness and self with the processes of feeling-bound attention, it seems clear that reasoning must be closely connected with both attention and task-planning. Consistent with this model, there is a region of the brain known to be important for reasoning, and one that seems to be particularly adept at guiding attention. In mammals, this region is the prefrontal cortex (PFC). In avians, it is a forebrain structure called the nidopallium caudolaterale (NCL). We will focus here on the PFC.

Research has characterized the role of the PFC variously as one of extended planning, logical decision-making, attention biasing, rule learning, goal recognition, and consequence evaluation. This variety of functions has caused the PFC to be viewed more generally as an executive control module.[141] To accomplish its executive functions most theorists believe that the PFC acts as a complex for managing working memories, a system that is capable of coordinating and sustaining attention to sets of task-related cues.[142]

In order to understand how this happens, we need to know a little more about the organization of this region. The first point to note is that the PFC is located just in front of the motor planning areas in the cortex. Thus, it often contributes to action planning. Second, it is composed of multiple semi-independent regions. Some regions are connected to spatial processing areas, some to motor processing areas, some to perceptual areas, and some to emotional and motivational networks. Most of these connections are with higher-level processing areas for these functions. These high-level areas, in turn, connect with lower-level processes. Thus, the PFC sits at the top of a multi-level hierarchy. The PFC is also known to receive rewarding dopamine projections from the basal ganglia. This suggests that the PFC is in a position to learn what kinds of high-level cues and actions are important for a task. Interestingly, the avian NCL appears to have similar connections, including extensive dopamine inputs.[143]

Following this high-level learning strategy, each region of the PFC is thought to learn what features are active at the time of reinforcement and to activate attention for those features on subsequent trials. Thus, when the same task is repeated, the working memory pointers learned on previous occasions are the starting memory configuration for the new task.[144] In this way, task-related working memories are learned, refined, and carried forward to the same task later. The activation of motivational regions in the PFC is thought to hold the feature set *on task* until the goal has been completed, or until the motivation to complete it is released.

The idea that motivational links hold the prefrontal cortex on task follows from studies of the effects of damage to this region. One of the classic signs of PFC damage is the inability of subjects to stay on task. Such subjects are easily distracted by irrelevant or previously relevant cues. This distractibility is consistent with a diminished ability to sustain certain working memories and their links to motive states, while inhibiting alternatives. A similar inability to sustain connections between situational recognition, logical decisions, and social feelings would explain the many instances of impulsive behavior and poor social judgments, which are typical of patients with PFC damage.

Recent work suggests that the PFC also suppresses irrelevant cues via connections with the thalamic filter.[145] Thus, a working memory model in which cues guide attention, irrelevant cues are suppressed, and motivation is held on task appears to account for a broad scale of skills that the PFC supports and for the deficits that occur when it is damaged.

Because the individual modules of the PFC sit at the top of a hierarchy of tasks it is also the case that many specialized circuits involve each module. In fact, some authors have suggested that each module may involve task-specific aspects and even hierarchically organized aspects that help integrate a task sequentially.[146] Given that there are multiple modules within the PFC and that each may integrate specific tasks and even task hierarchies, it is impossible to provide a full overview of the PFC. The varied PFC circuits that account for these skills are complex and not all well-defined. Thus, we will need a simpler model of the PFC to understand its overall functions, while keeping in mind that these more detailed functions also need to be considered.

Randall O'Reilly and colleagues have proposed that learning in an executive control complex should be triggered by an *adaptive-critic* gating mechanism that is sensitive to both rising and falling reward densities.[147] The idea is that performance learning would initially depend on standard trial-and-error learning algorithms. However, as rewards are encountered and dopamine reaches the PFC, the executive networks would begin to lock on to the high-level feature connections that *better predict reward*. And because different regions of the PFC connect with features in different subject domains, the combination of features essentially creates a configuration of task-related memory pointers that predict reward.

In this way, working memory pointers on the adaptive side of the algorithm provide an inferential learning mechanism that effectively creates a *working hypothesis*[148] about what configuration of features is important for success in a task. These *working hypothesis* pointers may not be perfect but they have an emergent effect. They guide attention during learning tasks. Assuming that the features learned by the PFC are reliable cues for task performance, enhancing attention to these features would naturally result in faster task learning. Thus, the configuration of cues that is enhanced by this algorithm, the *working hypothesis* as I call it, should not change. However, if reward density ramps up on some occasions, then the hypothesis should be updated to include the cues that accompany the increase in reward density.

In contrast, if the reward density ramps down too far, then the critic side of the adaptive-critic algorithm should reset parts of the current configuration, forcing the hypothesis to be rebuilt. In effect, a run of successes should cause a hypothesis to form and be refined, while a run of failures should result in the previous hypothesis being abandoned, and a modified hypothesis being adopted. And because the PFC has extensive reciprocal connections with the temporal flow learning networks in the cerebellum, working hypotheses can be guided by sequential changes in attention as a task progresses.[149]

Insights from Similar Situations

The idea that working memory pointers come to be treated as working hypotheses enables us to capture the overall function of the PFC while skipping over the many low-level circuits that the PFC is known to engage. However, there is one low level function that cannot be ignored. Working memories in the PFC also involve circuitry that can engage declarative memories in the medial temporal lobe. And because the activation is bidirectional, declarative memories can also influence working memories. Thus, working memories from past experiences may sometimes influence the formation of working hypotheses for a current task. The sudden adoption of a new working memory hypothesis is what is called *insight learning.*

Given that we have already assumed an adaptive-critic gating mechanism for building working hypotheses, a simple process for adding insight learning to this algorithm would be to have the adaptive-critic architecture in the PFC treat the adoption of an insight as if it signals an increase in reward density. That seems to fit how we experience an insight subjectively. The assumed increase in reward density in the gating algorithm would mean that the insight should temporarily cause the ongoing working hypothesis to be updated.

If the insight provided by the updated hypothesis proves successful, then reward learning will really ramp up and the working insight will be permanently adopted. However, if the updated hypothesis is unsuccessful, then the critic side of the algorithm will reject it and revert back to the previous hypothesis. In effect, there would be little cost for using insights from similar situations to help modify a hypothesis, and there would be much to be gained if it was successful. Thus, we don't need to invent a new process to account for insight learning. We just need to arrange for a function that notices similarities between two tasks to promote using the hypothesis from a successful task to update the working hypothesis for an unsuccessful task.

Attention Managers

There are two common attention-handling subsystems in the brain. The first of these is known as the *dorsal attention network*; the second is the *ventral attention network*.[150] The dorsal attention network includes the maps of all three cortical eye fields, motor planning regions in the parietal cortex, and BA46 a spatial-motor planning region in the PFC. This architecture is faster and usually takes control during top-down action planning. It even tends to filter out irrelevant cues as it guides task-directed attention.

The ventral attention network involves connections between the ventral prefrontal cortex and the temporal-parietal junction (TPJ) and receives norepinephrine inputs from the locus coeruleus in the brainstem. The locus coeruleus is known to react to changes and the TPJ appears to be specialized for the detection of unexpected cue and valuation changes. When the ventral attention network is activated, it interrupts ongoing attention and reorients the dorsal attention network to the unexpected events so that those events can be evaluated.

The scope of processing in the TPJ includes sensory, motor, limbic, and memory functions. Thus, it is sensitive to a broad range of cues. In addition, the circuitry in the TPJ appears to be arranged to facilitate comparisons between two sets of experiences. For example, when new sensory information occurs, major cues in the incoming information trigger the recall of similar past experiences. This enables the TPJ to compare the current experience with the memory schema accumulated from past experiences.

In such comparisons, recent research suggests that the TPJ represents the two sets of information differently in the left and right hemispheres of the brain. It seems that representations in the left-TPJ emphasize the matches between ongoing experience and the recalled schema of past experiences, while the right-TPJ emphasizes the mismatches between the ongoing experience and the recalled memory schema.[151] The underlying mechanisms by which the TPJ resolves matching and mismatching relationships are not fully understood, but research indicates that the TPJ is involved in detecting such relationships.

The differences between what is represented in the left and right TPJ seem to provide the kind of information needed to support concept growth. Jean Piaget proposed that cognition grows by a process of *assimilation* and *accommodation*.[152] Assimilation is the process of integrating new information into schema memories for an event or concept. The existing schema comes from declarative memories. The new information is provided by the ongoing experience. When new features in an ongoing experience are compatible with recalled memory schemas, then strong matches in the left-TPJ appear to favor assimilating the new information within the expected schema, thus expanding the concept.

However, if new features are unexpected or not compatible with the existing schema, then strong mismatches in the right TPJ appear to favor splitting the schema into separate sets of expectations. As children, we learn that apples are edible and have a distinct shape and taste. When we encounter an edible "apple-like" fruit with a different shape and taste we may recall the apple schema, but because they have distinct differences and are linked to different words we soon accommodate the differences by breaking them into separate schemas. Thus, accommodation results in separate concepts.

Analogical Reasoning

Over time the processes of assimilation and accommodation enable agents to expand their concepts and interconnect them in hierarchies. Accommodation enables the concept of "dog" to be subdivided into breeds. Experts may even track different breeding lines within a dog breed. How finely the topic is subdivided depends largely on to what extent finer distinctions are needed in various tasks. Still, at the same time "dog" can be assimilated into less specific concepts like "pet" or "animal." Less specific concepts are more abstract in character and may facilitate thinking about more general relationships.

However, because concepts can be nested in hierarchies of different specificity, it is also possible to make comparisons across levels. For example, a child may notice a specific partnership between a friend and the friend's dog. And when they consider that dogs are pets, they may be led to consider whether their friend could have a similar partnership with a pet cat. Or, the child may consider whether they could have the same kind of partnership if they adopted a pet, and then consider whether they would prefer a dog or a cat.

In such cases the child would be using one experience as an analogy for thinking about a similar experience. According to Piaget, this kind of analogical reasoning begins to occur more frequently in humans around the age of 12 and extends into adulthood. Developing hierarchical categories would seem to facilitate this kind of reasoning. But it takes practice to learn how to pay attention to analogies, swap in related features, and evaluate the comparisons in the new analogy. However, the TPJ seems to be the ideal tool for making comparisons between real versus imagined experiences. For example, research has shown that the TPJ is involved in reasoning about what an agent might do in the present versus what they would do in the future.[153]

Circuitry in the TPJ is also involved in detecting whether actions are produced by one's self versus by another agent.

When self-produced actions are detected, they are associated with the experience of prior planning and feelings of proprioceptive feedback as the action occurs. Changes that are caused by another agent may be detected, but they lack the parallel experiences of prior planning and proprioceptive feedback.[154] Apparently, this produces mismatches in the TPJ with what would be expected from self-produced actions. Actions that are not associated with prior planning and proprioceptive feedback are attributed to another agent.[155]

Analogical comparisons between one's self and another agent provide a new strategy for thinking about the behavior of others. For example, if an agent learns that his planning can cause him to act, then when he sees another agent act, he may by analogy assume the she planned before she acted. Similarly, if an agent learns that when she is angry, she attacks others with words and sometimes hostile actions, then when she sees another agent acting in a similar way, it is reasonable for her to assume that the other agent may be angry. The analogy would come from comparing her action, known to be caused by anger, with a similar action by another agent, when the cause of his action is unknown.

Assuming, by analogy, that he is also angry would resolve the differences detected by the TPJ. And once the other agent is considered angry, then he would be expected to display other angry reactions if confronted. This is a natural way of using self-knowledge to understand and predict the behavior of another. However, for an observer agent to make this conclusion she would have to assume that the other agent has a mind that works much like her own mind. Making that assumption is known as attributing a theory of mind to another agent. Theory of mind reasoning is an important tool for intelligent social agents.

TIME SHARING ATTENTION

Thus far, we have suggested that attention is largely a serial event, as if we only focus on one task at a time. However, the networks that support attention are highly flexible. It is almost always the case that several possible items are on the verge of gaining attention at any one time. Normally, we shift our attention among the items that are most salient in the moment and most relevant to the task at hand. But there seems to be an inhibition of return process that reduces the immediate saliency of recently sampled items, so that alternate items are more likely to be sampled.

This makes the breadth of topics gaining attention more distributed. Sometimes we focus on sensorimotor features, other times on memories. Sometimes we simulate action plans and explore their consequences before deciding to act. Other times we may combine planning with memories in imaginative scenarios. In fact, part of what makes conscious attention so interesting is that we manage to shift back and forth among many of these strategies in successive moments.

Adding to our awareness that attention is not always fixed on one task is the observation that procedural tasks can often be executed in parallel when there is minimal competition among them. Thus, the networks that manage attention and consciousness appear to be far more flexible than a serial focus of attention would imply. For example, during your usual drive to or from the supermarket to buy groceries, your procedural attention is mostly focused on the task of navigating through turns, watching for vehicles, and steering along well-practiced routes. However, while you are engaged in these tasks, it is also the case that sometimes you adjust the radio, think about what you want to fix for dinner, or even recall the last time you invited a certain dinner guest. Long-established habits have automated most of your driving skills so you can navigate your vehicle successfully while still finding time to engage in these other activities. In fact, even when you are "focused" on driving you often shift your attention between the road, the rear-view mirror, and your dashboard.

The mechanisms needed to shift between different topics of attention and to support multiple tasks in parallel are not well understood. However, we know there are several distinct pathways through the action-planning regions of the basal ganglia.[156] This suggests that the motor planning networks can manage several kinds of tasks in parallel, as long as the actions don't compete with each other. Further, we have noted that once motor tasks are learned they don't need constant attention, just occasional look-ahead guidance.

When we look back on our activities, it seems clear that shifting between various states of attention is a common part of our conscious experience. We carry on a conversation as we walk, while we also scan the path ahead for obstacles. We think about what was said to us, and yet we also notice other people along the path, landscaping in the area, and ongoing weather conditions. All of these may reach our attention momentarily, occasionally even triggering secondary comments to our companion as we walk. Thus, while we can focus on one item when we need to, we often shift attention among many items in a short time frame.

Research suggests it takes 350–500 ms for the thalamocortical circuitry to establish the extended resonant states that give rise to conscious attention.[157] Simple motor plans tend to reach consciousness in around 350 ms.[158] Recalling perceptions from memory generally takes a little longer. If repeated memory searches are required, then they may last several seconds or more. However, the declarative memory circuitry tends to sustain recent activity at high levels for about six seconds, and at moderate levels for as long as a minute. As a result, once declarative memories are engaged, they tend to be slow to disassemble. In contrast, motor planning networks are faster at selecting actions and getting look-ahead samples of attention for subsequent planning, but they don't hold attention for long. Due to these timing differences, it seems motor planning can often steal small look-ahead time slices of attention without significantly disrupting ongoing memory tasks.[159]

If motor planning takes over attention for more than several seconds, then the organization of the declarative memories may begin to shift. However, if the interrupting task does not activate other memories or strong competing feelings, then prior memory patterns may not be significantly degraded. Thus, it seems that automated motor activities, especially non-competing activities, can operate in parallel while producing minimal changes in attention. In fact, the motor networks are selective about what features they need. You can take action to avoid a vehicle veering into your lane without maintaining attention long enough to identify the vehicle's color, make, or model. Those features are not important for the avoidance task.

Time-shared attention works best when different tasks don't compete too much and when they don't introduce large demands on memory processing. However, it is also apparent that humans sometimes shift between activities that involve different tasks and even different memory processes. For example, we may interrupt an ongoing conversation to handle an incoming phone call, and then, after the call is completed, return to the first conversation as if there was no break. As long as the interrupting task is short, and the memory demands are moderate, then the original task can usually be re-engaged, although sometimes it may take a few seconds to recover. "Hmm. Where was I?" The process is not always fully successful. However, when there are supporting environmental cues, or when there is a social partner to help reactivate the topics of the previous situation, it works surprisingly well.

CONCLUDING COMMENTS

There is another point that we should mention as we consider the multitasking nature of conscious mind. Attention enables different brain features to be coordinated in interactive tasks. However, just as there are proto-planning modules in the cortex that begin assembling action candidates before cortico-basal ganglia plans are processed, there are proto-perceptual, proto-memory, and proto-feeling modules that begin assembling possible feature candidates before they are ready to compete for attention. In effect, planning, perception, memory, and feeling networks all have semi-autonomous processes that run on in the background. As they take form, many of these processes compete for attention but only a few succeed. However, we could never shift rapidly among potential topics, or memories, or multitask between different goals, if there were not always a variety of semi-autonomous background activities promoting their own agendas and constantly competing for a chance to gain attention.

We are multi-layered agents, and yet we are not often aware of much of the mental activity that runs on in the subconscious background. Occasionally, I awaken in the morning with a new idea. This implies that I sometimes think about my work during sleep. It turns out that we reorganize our memories during dreams, and sometimes that reorganization may lead to new insights. However, we are unaware of much of this background organization during sleep, unless it activates significant feelings as we awaken. In truth, background processes also do much of the work supporting conscious thought even when we are awake. But again, we are rarely aware of this background activity unless an idea it promotes suddenly bursts into attention.

The conscious parts of you and I don't plan these background activities, but as conscious agents we often take credit for them when they gain attention. Some suggest that credit-taking for unplanned actions means our conscious awareness is errant. However, taking credit for background processes is not really an error, it's a constructive addition to our awareness. Background activities support all conscious processing. So when we notice and take credit for them, we are actually linking our self with the chain of unconscious processes from which conscious thoughts emerge. Taking credit for them broadens our sense of self and makes us more aware of our potential. With practice, we may even learn strategies to encourage such background processing. For example, some people find that when they are struggling with a problem it often helps to take a short break and do something else. When I break from writing to exercise, I often find myself reworking ideas during the exercise.

If we are to build robots with similar skills, we will need to ensure that our robots have networks that explore possible plans in the background. They must have memory networks that explore possible feature associations. They must have feeling networks that constantly react to features well before they gain attention. Without such background processes our robot will not have many new combinations of inputs to compete for attention. However, if our robot has these processes, and if those processes remain partly activated even when attention processing is interrupted by other activities, or even by "sleep", then the robot may sometimes generate new ideas in the background. If he doesn't, then we should tweak the intensity of those processes until they sometimes pop into attention in such cases. Only then will the robot have human-like thought processes.

➤ Ending Remarks

Feeling-bound attention is the essence of core consciousness. However, simply guiding attention by feelings is not always highly adaptive. The planning networks provide another path for guiding attention. Attention can influence what is planned, and planning can influence what gains conscious attention.

Higher-order reasoning emerges as agents learn task-related planning strategies. Working memories in the prefrontal cortex hold onto cues associated with success in learning, and those cues serve as working hypotheses about what features to attend to during the task on later trials. Insights are proposed to occur when working hypotheses for one task are used as strategies in a similar task. Analogical reasoning is proposed to take form when agents learn to use one task as a model for thinking about another. Networks in the temporal-parietal junction appear to be essential for these analogies.

7: ANTICIPATION, OWNERSHIP, AND MEMORY

Self-referential signals come from motor systems and their sensory components, such as muscle spindles, which are all active from embryonic times onward. ... All of these interactions are strongly influenced by the various diffuse ascending value systems. The components of these value systems continually help regulate the synaptic thresholds affecting memory, and they contribute in an ongoing manner to perceptual categorizations. ... Episodic memory, which requires the activity of the hippocampus, contributes to the sense of continuity experienced by such a self. In humans, the play between the fundamental bodily based self of primary consciousness and the self-conscious agent of higher-order consciousness provides a higher ground for the development of rich subjectivity. – Gerald Edelman, "Naturalizing Consciousness", 2003

➢ Introductory Remarks

The current chapter illustrates how the sense of self emerges in mechanisms on multiple levels. Anticipation, ownership, and memory involve largely different processes. Yet they are important processes for shaping the sense of self.

Attention is not an all or none process. It emerges in stages by building on the results of earlier processes. Pre-attentive gaze-targeting is always operating in the background evaluating sensory inputs for potential interest and promoting the investigation of some features over others. Without these preliminary evaluations and feature biasing processes, later attention mechanisms would have no basis for deciding where to look or what to track. Adding to these gaze biasing strategies are saliency mapping circuits linked to the pulvinar and gating processes that bind feature processing with actions. It is this multi-process strategy of selecting, refining, and promoting events in combination with more detailed processing that enables pre-attentive features to be represented as proto-objects, proto-objects to be re-represented as feature-bound objects, and feature-bound objects to be connected with memories and actions. Each process adds another layer of detail to the features that gain attention.

Similarly, the experience of self is not a single-stage

phenomenon. It begins as life urges from the brainstem add to the competition for attention in the thalamus. It is expanded as attention enhances arousal states and action dispositions. In addition, the attention steering committee has several visually-guided committee members that enhance perceptions via visual gain-modulation effects. Thus, the sense of self interacts with the attention mechanisms. This visual bias begins in the orientation networks of the tectum which link perceptual fields with the motor networks that orient toward them. This highlights the distinction between external perceptual inputs and internal self adjustments to them. As a result, internal feelings and action dispositions are experienced in the context of where gaze is mapped in relation to the world. In fact, we often experience ourselves as a visually-centered observer.

The *observer self* probably accounts for the popular idea that there is an internal agent, a homunculus, watching and managing our experience. The classic argument against such an internal homunculus is that such an arrangement would seem to require an infinite regress of homunculi – a pre-homunculus to manage the homunculus, a pre-pre-homunculus to manage the pre-homunculus, and so on. However, thinking in terms of incremental processes neatly sidesteps this problem. Pre-processing networks don't have full control over the next processing level. They simply provide adaptive dispositions that later representations build on. The early orientation processes in the tectum provide little more than reflexive biases for where sensory sources are located and how to orient to them. However, because each subsequent processing level uses information from previous levels and then combines new features with them, the representations at each higher level become increasingly cognizant.

So here is our developing model. Consciousness emerges from the focus of feeling-bound activation that occurs as life urges are bound with perceptions in coherent periods of attention. This confluence of perceptions and feelings is the phenomenal self. When spatial cues are activated in the context of attention, they add a phenomenal sense of self-location to the experiences of the phenomenal self. Thus, we experience our self as an active observer in relation to the perceptual world. The *agent-self* emerges as agents learn that planning can produce actions that change their world. Given that other networks may introduce perceptual cues and feelings that can also be bound in attention, it seems clear that other aspects of experience can be added to the sense of self. This means the sense of self is not a single process, but rather a composite of features that gain attention. In this chapter, our goal is to explain the phenomenal feelings of self that emerge as anticipation and declarative memories add to the experience of self.

FEELINGS OF ANTICIPATION

There are two major anticipatory learning systems in the vertebrate brain: a *valuation learning* process, managed largely by the amygdala, and a *temporal coordination learning* process, managed by the cerebellum.[160] Although these systems have different anticipatory results, the learning processes in both these systems are considered types of Pavlovian conditioning, because both react to the sequential pairing of stimulus events, and because these anticipatory processes often operate in tandem.

Valuation Learning

Valuation learning involves learning to anticipate changes in reactivity-- arousal, motives, or emotions. The anticipation is accomplished by connecting external cues with the level of subsequent reactivity reactions in these regions. The primary input region in this process is the basolateral nucleus of the amygdala (BLA). The BLA receives an array of multi-modal sensory inputs from prefrontal cortex, the thalamus, and some inputs directly from the cortex. The anticipatory learning occurs as the BLA comes to predict output activity in the rest of amygdala and other regions.

As the BLA learns what reactivity states typically follow certain cues, it then begins to ramp up those reactivity states in timely preparation of their expected occurrence. The reactivity changes may happen seconds or minutes after the initial cue, although times beyond one minute likely require the support of declarative memories. Because the input and output activity generally passes through the thalamus, these anticipatory changes may often gain consciousness, especially if the reactivity states are strong. Experientially, this forward-looking valuation change can be characterized as a *feeling of what might happen next*.

What is curious about the BLA is that while it apparently began as a system for anticipating limbic changes managed by the amygdala, it has spread its anticipatory control to arousal systems in most basal forebrain regions. With respect to the amygdala proper the central amygdala is well known to be involved in reactions to fear and stress. Stress reactions are activated via the hypothalamic-pituitary-adrenal axis. The lateral amygdala is known to react to danger by stimulating sympathetic autonomic reactions. Most of this is thought to be mediated via the hypothalamus. The medial amygdala manages sexual arousal as well as social aggression. This region also receives its own source of olfactory inputs and even reacts to pheromones.

Surprisingly, projections between the amygdala and the prefrontal cortex are necessary to learn extinction, an effect that involves learning to unlearn. BLA connections to the extended amygdala also include the medial septum. These may enhance the saliency of memory processing in the hippocampus. And while most of the BLA anticipation involves expecting aversive states, projections to the ventral striatum are known to mediate arousal for approach and appetitive behaviors. Given that these may involve foraging, courtship, and caretaking, the anticipation of ventral striatum reactions may be the primary path by which the BLA enhances more positive outcomes.

Temporal Coordination

Temporal coordination learning, in contrast, involves learning to anticipate the sequential flow of brain activity in times of a half-second or less. The cerebellum sits on the back of the brain and monitors changes in information flow. This enables it to anticipate sensory, motor, and reactive changes in the next half second and ramp up anticipated activity just as it is expected. I refer to this learning process as *temporal flow* learning. Temporal flow calculations in the cerebellum are used in three major kinds of tasks.[161] These are balance, action integration, and the sequential integration of cognitive information. In the case of balance, the cerebellum uses vestibular and postural information to calculate ongoing changes in body position. Using these inputs, the cerebellum learns to anticipate changes in the body's center of gravity and activates the postural reflexes needed to maintain balance as the body moves. In terrestrial vertebrates, especially bipedal forms, maintaining balance is a calculation-intensive operation, so it is not surprising that it involves a dedicated region of the cerebellum.

Real-time action integration is another calculation-intensive task. In this process, the spinocerebellum region coordinates the actions of limbs and digits by adjusting the timing and intensity of elemental movements in each action. This allows combinatorial movements to be assembled into finely coordinated actions. The graceful movements of skilled athletes or hunters depend in large part on the ability of the cerebellum. Unlike planned actions, finely tuned postural and motor adjustments affect descending motor circuits, but bypass the thalamocortical pathways needed for conscious awareness.

The third major aspect of cerebellar processing involves the sequential adjustments needed to manage the temporal coordination of cognitive information, or what we might call *cognitive flow.* These processes involve the large lateral zones of the cerebellar hemispheres. These regions calculate temporal relationships between a variety of sensory, motor, and reactive events and exchange information broadly with the cortex and subcortical networks. This effectively primes the target regions to react in anticipation of common sequential transitions. Unlike motor timing adjustments, many cognitive-flow adjustments are directed through the thalamus. Thus cognitive anticipation may change the flow of conscious awareness. In fact, we generally become aware of these changing thoughts and reactions within a half second. This is exactly the time frame in which cerebellar anticipation operates.

Cognitive flow is an ongoing process in conscious minds. Research shows that the cerebellum is active during imagined movements, mental searches, and sensory discrimination tasks.[162] Thoughts naturally flow to anticipate changes. Thus, it is not surprising to find that patients with cerebellar damage show deficits in planning successive actions, in making decisions, and in shifting attention.[163] Some cerebellar lesions result in grammatical errors in the normal flow of words,[164] and in extreme cases even in a failure of patients to initiate verbal comments.[165] In these cases, it appears that perceptual information fails to trigger the kind of cognitive flow needed to go from seeing to saying, as happens in normal individuals.

As these examples illustrate, ongoing shifts in cognitive flow are a major part of conscious experience. And because each person has their own collection of skills, values, and habits, this anticipatory *cognitive flow* is a unique part of who they are and how they think. In fact, cognitive flow is so important that there are more neurons involved in managing the anticipatory flow of human thought than there are in the sum total of all the previous conscious networks we have so far discussed.[166] Consciousness is fluid. It automatically flows to related topics.

SELF-OWNERSHIP AND PERSPECTIVE TAKING

Previously we suggested that our sense of the world emerges from the fact that what we detect via our external senses is located outside the body and requires sensory and motor orientation to explore, while our sense of self emerges from synchronous internal feelings and reactions in our body as we perceive the world. However, research indicates we use many of the same networks for tracking our own movements as we use for tracking the movements of others. This introduces the possibility that we may not recognize who caused some movements.

In the previous chapter we noted that the temporal-parietal junction (TPJ) is involved in detecting whether actions are produced by one's self versus by another agent. It seems our brains learn to differentiate between self-generated actions and the actions of others, because self-generated actions are correlated with synchronous inputs from motor planning networks, anticipatory changes in self-feelings, and proprioceptive feedback as we move. However, we didn't mention how this affects the sense of self. It appears that synchronous correlations in the TPJ result in *a feeling of owning an action.*[167]

In addition to recognizing the ownership of movements by synchronous plans and actions, other research suggests that we learn to recognize *ownership* for parts of our "own" body by seeing body parts and sensing correlated feelings of touch or movement for those parts.[168] And it turns out that this ownership recognition is highly flexible. In one experiment, a rubber arm was positioned in a person's underarm region and placed adjacent to their real arm.[169] When the subject observed the hand on the rubber arm being touched with a brush, and simultaneously felt their real hand being brushed in the same way, they soon began to feel that the rubber hand was a part of their body. As the researchers concluded, within a few minutes the consistent synchrony between the sight of brushing movements against the rubber hand and synchronous feelings for those movements led to a sense of ownership for a hand known to be rubber.

The linkage between movements, motor programs, and locations appears to be part of what enables us to take the perspective of another agent at times. Growing evidence suggests that the posterior TPJ is involved in switching between self feelings and the perspectives of others. It seems that when we take the perspective of another agent, we inhibit self-centered feelings and pay more attention to the objects and cues in the perspective of others, as if our observer self was in their location. This perspective-taking is apparently related to an enhanced sensitivity to the attention of others. When we take the perspective of another agent, it seems we temporarily enhance the saliency of features located in their perspective, or for objects that they recently contacted. When the others are social partners, this shift in attention may even lead to more prosocial behavior.

Trying to maintain coordinated representations for all these separate aspects of self does have occasional side effects. Ordinarily, the feelings of self are closely aligned with the perceived location of the observer self and with the plans of the agent self. However, the locations of the observer and agent selves and their connections with resonant feelings sometimes become disconnected. When this happens various anomalies occur. We may feel disoriented. We may mistake our exact position or size. We may even have out-of-body experiences in which the observer self seems to be located in a different place than our physical body. Adopting the perspective of another agent may even cause the observer self to slip out of alignment. You are lying on the operating table and the anesthetic is beginning to interfere with the coordination of these various sources of self. You've seen your doctor looking down at you, and then suddenly you experience your observer self taking the doctor's perspective and looking down at you from above. It's what can happen when different aspects of self slip out of alignment.[170]

DECLARATIVE MEMORIES

In mammalian brains, the networks for declarative memory are situated below the auditory and visual perceptual areas in the temporal lobe. Inputs to this region initially enter what is known as the parahippocampal region. This is thought to be the place where semantic associations form. Semantic memory associations are meaningful, in the sense of involving general knowledge, but they are not linked to specific events. Being able to recall where the Statue of Liberty is located involves semantic associations. The semantic networks, in turn, pass information on to the hippocampal region where episodic memories are formed. Episodic associations enable sequences of specific conscious experiences to be remembered and reconstructed on recall. Your recall of climbing the stairs inside the Statue of Liberty is an episodic memory for a specific experience. Semantic (general knowledge) and episodic (specific event) memories complement each other and often work together.

Studies of the parahippocampal memory region indicate that there are two first-level input regions in mammals. Interestingly, work with humans has found that one of these is more active during item or object recognition, whereas the other shows more activity when subjects are asked to recall scenes or context-related information.[171] This dual-input architecture has led to a model of semantic memory that is characterized as *item-in-context* memory.[172] Research indicates that there are strong cross-connections between the item and context networks. These connections are thought to link items with their contexts, and contexts back to other related items making the associations highly flexible.

Co-occurrences result in feelings of familiarity and continuity, when items are connected with familiar tasks, motives, and settings. In contrast, feelings of novelty and uncertainty occur when an item cannot be connected to a context. Thus, when our cat Tom encounters a familiar setting, he knows intuitively what he should expect. He is calm and confident, readily slips into routine activities, and tends to investigate small changes that he finds. In contrast, when Tom encounters a largely novel change, he is immediately uncertain. He moves slowly and explores cautiously. Reflecting on memories as we encounter a situation provides humans with similar feelings of familiarity or novelty as they engage their world.

A cross-connection between an item and a familiar context also results in a sense of recognition, in that, you recognize how the item fits into common tasks or settings. And because words are also perceptual units, people routinely interconnect items and contexts with words. This explains why naming an item provides strong evidence of recognition. It shows that the name and the item have been linked to a common co-occurrence context. Co-occurrence memories also have a profound effect on perception. In fact, the process is often so fluid that features recalled from past experiences may subsequently change what is perceived in the current situation. This effect is what Gerald Edelman called the *remembered present*.[173]

Because the limbic cortices and the amygdala also contribute inputs to the semantic memory regions, memory items are always linked with feeling networks. This mix of items, contexts, and feelings is passed on to the hippocampal region. The spiral shape of the *hippocampus* is what gives this region its odd name. The seahorse, genus Hippocampus, has a curled tail, and so by analogy, the spiral shape of this region has come to be identified with this label. It is within this spiral of networks that clusters of features come to be bound together in episodic memories. Episodic memories store links to specific items, contexts, and feelings that occurred together in a situation. And because there are often sequential linkages between episodic memories, they can be reconstructed as sequential episodes of experience at later times.

There is currently much ongoing research into how the hippocampus encodes sequential episodes in memory. However, several years ago Howard Eichenbaum and colleagues proposed an intuitive model that helps to explain the process at a systems level.[174] The central idea is that input features that happen to occur at the same time in states of attention are constantly being cross-connected by configuration-capturing cells on the input side of the hippocampus. Originally these cells were thought to capture only spatial associations and were called "place" cells. However, subsequent work has shown these cells also encode other features, even behaviors. Eichenbaum and colleagues thus chose to characterize them as "event" cells, cells that connect a small number of co-occurring features together as an event. When the features are relevant to spatial contexts, they can be used to reconstruct spatial locations and paths. When they are relevant to situational or social events, they can be used to reconstruct those episodes of experience.

Perhaps the simplest model for thinking about these event cells is that they capture snapshots of features that happen to gain attention together. Of course, we must understand that these snapshots include all kinds of perceptual and contextual elements, not just visual features. The idea is that the event cells are constantly forming configural associations among active items and contexts. Some of these snapshots may capture features localized in time or place, such as the objects on a desk, while others may encompass broader contextual features, such as the spatial arrangement of furniture in a room, or the sequence of rooms encountered along a hallway. Some features are encountered for brief time periods and occur in a few snapshots – objects seen as you pass by a particular doorway. Other features are encountered for longer periods and may be included in many snapshots.

The net effect of capturing all these configural snapshots is that the more often a feature is noticed, the more likely it will be included in different configural snapshots. Recent research suggests that when memory snapshots form they tend to remain more active for a while. Thus, if other snapshots are formed closely in time, especially if they activate the same context, those events are likely to be bound together in sequence.[175] As a result, the recall of one event can activate associations with connected snapshots. This connectivity between temporally adjacent features also suggests how episodic memory sequences can be reconstructed. A cue triggering the recall of any single snapshot will tend to activate sequentially related snapshots. And because persistent features tend to be bound in many configural snapshots, this often enables an agent to reconstruct connections between events by attending to key retrieval cues and then noting which other configurations are activated. Assuming each shift in attention takes about a half second, it is easy to understand why it may take several seconds for past episodes to be vividly reconstructed and connected.

Maintaining memory configurations as separate snapshots requires that the configurations be stored as separate memory links. In programming, this is called sparse storage. Sparse storage keeps connections to items separate. Overlap among items in storage results in blended associations. Once associations are blended, they cannot be recalled as discrete events. This highlights a key difference between what are typically thought of as *learning networks* and what are considered *configural memory networks*.[176] Learning networks involve a lot of overlap and form blended input-output associations which average successes together across trials. They generally form associations slowly, often taking many trials. However, in doing so, they learn the best input-output rules. This is what makes learning networks so adaptive.

Configural memory networks, in contrast, must form associations quickly to capture elements that happen to occur together in one situation. Sparse storage processes enable events to be stored separately and recalled as discrete events later. This is where a recent finding influences how we think about episodic memory networks. For a long time, researchers thought that all the neurons in the brain were formed by the time of birth, or soon thereafter. However, in the dentate gyrus of the hippocampus, there is a layer of late-stage neural stem cells which produce as many as 10,000 new input cells in young adult male rats each day, and around 3500 per day in older rats. A similar process, also declining with age, is thought to occur in humans.[177] However, there is some question as to whether humans continue to make a lot more cells as they grow older, or whether they simply reuse previous event cells that have fallen into disuse. Either way, this process is thought to account for the sparse storage of episodic memory.

Given the need for sparse storage to form separate configural memories, this daily supply of available event cells makes perfect sense. It ensures that the input networks of the hippocampus can always form unique configurations for different events, because they have many available neurons waiting to be connected in novel feature configurations. However, research also indicates that most of these newly formed configuration cells die, or are reused, within a few weeks. The loss of these cells helps explain why most episodic snapshots are short-lived. We don't maintain highly detailed configural memories for most experiences for very long. Many extraneous events are encoded, but most of them are never recalled, so it is unlikely those configurations are maintained long. Other minor events may be recalled only once, and then never again, like where you parked when you went for groceries. So those memories are also likely lost in a few weeks.

Remembering

Understanding the network organizations that enable perceptions and memories to form also helps us understand how such experiences are reconstructed from memory. Memory recall begins when retrieval cues, features from ongoing perceptions, trigger co-occurrence associations with contexts and related items. Those co-occurrence associations trigger backward links to the perceptual inputs with which they were first associated. A point to note here is that the perceptual networks don't pass on the perceptual patterns they have detected to the memory networks. They simply pass a signal that they have recognized something. As a result, the memory networks don't have to store perceptual experiences in a new place. Rather, they store backward-connecting pointers to the original perceptual networks. These links enable the memory networks to bind perceptual features in a web of semantic and episodic associations. When a memory is recalled, the perceptual associations are reactivated via the backward links to the perceptual networks and the co-occurring percepts are re-experienced.

An important thing about declarative memories is that they tend to involve perceptual features, contextual features, and feeling-related limbic associations. And just as the features that reach consciousness are most likely to be those with strong feeling-related associations, those that are stored and recalled from memory are likely to be those with strong feeling-related associations. Sometimes the memories are so attention capturing that we don't even notice what perceptual inputs triggered their recall; we are simply walking near a bakery and suddenly we find ourselves recalling childhood memories of cookies.

So how are limbic associations bound so strongly with conscious memories? One key to this linkage dates back to the work of James Papez. In 1937, Papez proposed that the circuit connecting the hippocampus to the limbic cortices was the basis for emotional experience.[178] The proposed circuit involved links from the hippocampal memory region, via the fornix to mammillary bodies in the hypothalamus, on to the anterior thalamus, and then on to an extended path from the anterior cingulate cortex to the posterior cingulate, which links back to the hippocampal memory region.

The mammillary bodies link the Papez circuit with motivational states in the hypothalamus. In fact, social memories in the rat are only stored and recalled when the hypothalamus passes the social hormone, oxytocin, to the mammillary bodies.[179] The cingulate is known to be involved in sympathetic emotions, motor reactions, and personal memories.[180] Papez originally proposed his circuit as a path for emotional expression. However, subsequent research suggests that it is more important for linking emotive states with memories than for producing emotive states. In fact, blocking the Papez circuitry from linking motive states with memories actually prevents episodic memories from forming.[181]

TASK-FOCUSED VERSUS MEMORY-FOCUSED ATTENTION

Given that the prefrontal cortex is known to play a key role in holding attention on task, while suppressing attention to irrelevant cues, it is a likely candidate for engaging attention to task-related cues. Many agents vigilantly focus on external cues when in danger or when the risk of harm is high. Similarly, they become more focused on cues related to tasks when a goal is highly valued, or when decisions must be made quickly. Let's refer to the tendency to focus on immediate cues as *task-focused consciousness*. This focus seems to occur more often during tasks that are well practiced, presumably because they can be performed with minimal need for memory searches. It seems that the higher-order relays in the anterior intralaminar thalamus help focus attention on sensorimotor cues during well-practiced tasks.

Consider the focus of attention involved in learning to drive an automobile. Initially, this task requires a learner's full attention. In fact, if the vehicle is equipped with a manually shifted transmission, the task may exceed a new operator's attention managing capacities. However, over time most of the actions involved in driving come to be automated as habits. Thus, an experienced driver can expertly negotiate her way home for thirty minutes in rush-hour traffic, and yet may arrive home with little memory of the trip. All the routine tasks – shifting gears, stopping at signals, changing lanes to avoid congestion, adjusting for the proximity of other vehicles – and all the shifts in attention required to support those activities are largely automated. As a result, habits can select the best-fit actions within each micro-situation and complete the immediate task without encountering anything that would require reflective memory searches or storage.

For this reason, task-focused consciousness is often not well represented in memory. Given the inability of people to recall such experiences, some have speculated that they must be going through them unconsciously. However, activities such as rush hour driving are never performed unconsciously. If we interrupt the driver at any point in the trip and ask her about the traffic or a particular vehicle, it is clear that she is vigilantly attending to the details of the situation and highly engaged in her task. Thus, the observation that such activities are not readily recalled does not imply that they were not conscious. Rather, it suggests that when someone attends vigilantly to a task, she doesn't reflect on her activities often, and therefore, doesn't capture the many configural memory links needed to support their recall. As a result, there are fewer paths to trigger memory recall or to connect vigilant activities with other memories.

This analysis suggests that frequent shifts between ongoing actions and memories help us form connected associations among different aspects of our experience. When we don't regularly reflect on other activities, as in the case of driving in rush-hour traffic, it seems those experiences are less well connected with other memories, and thus less easily recalled. We all compartmentalize our lives to some extent in this way. However, this is probably something we don't want to carry to extremes. Before we dismiss task-focused consciousness as a less important aspect of attention, we should note that it is often a highly productive state. In fact, the ability to engage in sustained periods of vigilant attention is often prized for what it allows an agent to accomplish. For example, there are times when a craftsperson seemingly becomes locked into a task for extended time periods, sometimes for hours. During these periods, he may make hundreds of subtle comparisons and perceptual judgments that guide his work.

All this suggests that the craftsperson is accessing semantic and motor memories. However, the memories are task-centered and don't involve episodic associations that would link them with other aspects of his life. In fact, his attention is often so task focused that when he finally surfaces from the task, he needs to reorient. "What time is it? Where are my keys? Has anyone left a message?" These are common examples of how task-focused attention fails to engage memory connections with other aspects of our life. I should also note that states of highly focused attention are not unique to humans. No one is more task-focused than Tom when he is out on the hunt. And yes, when Tom becomes engrossed in hunting, he often loses track of time and comes home late.

Just as there are times when we lock into sensorimotor tasks in states of vigilant attention, there are also times when it is advantageous to explore our memories. Previously, we noted that the reuniens and rhomboid nuclei of the ventral midline thalamus act as higher-order relays that bind thalamic processing with memories. Let's call this process *memory-focused consciousness*. We also noted that when memory snapshots form closely in time, especially if they activate the same context, they are likely to be bound with previous memories.[182] It turns out working memories in the medial PFC may facilitate this process by activating common schemas during memory storage. This makes it more likely that the memories in these schemas will be connected and that they may be recalled in sequential episodes.[183]

We often reflect on past experiences when we need to solve a problem. Sometimes we even pause and daydream with no apparent goal in mind. Yet in many situations, it seems that agents routinely shift back and forth between sensorimotor activities and memory processing during problem-solving. In fact, the two processes are often synergistic and the PFC is frequently involved in switching between them. A focus on sensorimotor activity can trigger the recall of related memories. A focus on memories can reactivate attention to features that were important for a specific task. This is why a shift in attention between tasks and memories often leads to more intelligent decisions.

When rats come to a decision point, they sometimes
pause and look back and forth as if deliberating over the

> *choice … this pause-and-look behaviour was termed
> 'vicarious trial and error' (VTE), with the implication that
> the rat was 'thinking about the future'.*[184]

As David Redish notes in the quote above, pausing and shifting between memory processes in the hippocampus may help engage attention to alternative choices as gaze is shifted. And, as our discussion here suggests, it seems likely that executive networks in the PFC play an important role in guiding these shifts in attention. Thus, while we only focus attention on a few topics at a time, alternately shifting attention between tasks and memories can sometimes help us make more intelligent choices.

CONCLUDING COMMENTS

Our developing model is that the phenomenal sense of self is not a singular process, but rather a composite of processes that add to our internal feelings of awareness and reactivity as various features gain attention. In this chapter, we have noted how *valuation learning*, in the extended amygdala, and *temporal coordination learning*, in the cerebellum, result in forward-looking feelings of an *anticipatory self*. Anticipation enables agents to prepare for changes before they happen, but it doesn't provide control over those changes.

Self-initiated activities are correlated with synchronous planning, anticipated feelings, and proprioceptive feedback as movement occurs. The synchrony among these activities appears to be resolved by networks in the temporal-parietal junction (TPJ). Actions generated by other agents are also detected in these movement networks, but because they are not correlated with ongoing planning, anticipated feelings, and proprioceptive feedback we do not assume ownership of them when they are detected.[185] Thus, the TPJ appears to introduce a sense of *self-ownership* for synchronous internal activities. Similar correlations are involved in recognizing ownership of parts of our body. Feelings of ownership are a remarkable addition to the sense of self. And because they are based on experiential correlations, they are surprisingly flexible.

While self-ownership of actions and body parts is a distinctive aspect of self, declarative memory is needed to give the self a historically continuous character. The *reflective self* literally experiences more than is present in a situation, because he can connect present experiences with his past. There are two basic kinds of declarative memory. Semantic (general knowledge) memories link items with contexts. These add a sense of familiarity and continuity to ongoing experiences. The second kind of declarative memory is episodic (specific event) memory. Episodic memories enable an agent to reconstruct past episodes of conscious experience. Semantic and episodic memories often complement each other in this process. When episodic memories are re-constructed, the recalled features re-engage links back to semantic memories, including specific item-in-context links that add feelings of familiarity to episodic memories as they are recalled.

Another important addition to self occurs when we connect the anticipatory effects of action planning with memories of past planning experiences. The ability to reflect on past episodes of agency might best be called *reflective agency*. A reflective agent can connect her ability to perform actions with past cases of planning and with her historical sense of being in control of actions. This combination of reflective memory, action planning, and a sense of control is a common experience of well-practiced agents.[186] It is probably best characterized as a *feeling of being able to do what I did before*. A reflective agent not only remembers related situations, she remembers what she did in those situations, and that memory influences her current plans. Obviously, if we are to build robots with human-like consciousness then we will need to provide them with mechanisms for anticipation, self-ownership, and the continuity of declarative memories.

> **Ending Remarks**

The networks supporting anticipation, ownership, and memory introduce properties that extend awareness to higher-order aspects of self. Anticipation extends the domain of feeling-bound awareness. Feelings of ownership link actions and body parts with the agent self. Memory mechanisms provide the conscious self with an identity and a history.

8: THE SOCIAL BRIDGE

The human brain is endowed with structures that are active both during the first- and third-person experience of actions and emotions. When we witness someone else's action, we activate a network of parietal and premotor areas that is also active while we perform similar actions. When we witness the disgusted facial expressions of someone else, we activate that part of our insula that is also active when we experience disgust. Thus, the understanding of basic aspects of social cognition depends on activation of neural structures normally involved in our own personally experienced actions or emotions. By means of this activation, a bridge is created between others and ourselves. – Vittorio Gallese, Christian Keysers, & Giacomo Rizzolatti, "A unifying view of the basis of social cognition", 2004

➢ **Introductory Remarks**

Phenomenal consciousness emerges in coherent states of feeling-bound attention. Gaze-centered orientations and spatial mappings bring a localizable observer sense of self to attention. As action planning comes to predict changes, we experience a sense of agency, a sense that we can change our feelings by taking action. Anticipatory learning guides attention as cues come to predict changes in feelings.

Higher-order correlations between planning, anticipation, and actions enable us to claim ownership of correlated actions. Episodic memories place these experiences of self in a historical context. Executive hypotheses enable us to experience our self as a reasoning agent as we track relevant cues and shift attention to task-related features. This chapter focuses on mechanisms that add social feelings to consciousness.

There is another domain that adds significantly to the sense of self. That domain involves cues that place an agent in the context of social relationships. Many of the categories of consciousness that we have thus far described include a social side. There are social feelings of wellness and approval, or alternately feelings of social distress and rejection. There are feelings of anticipation for social outcomes. There are feelings of ownership and responsibility for the actions we take as social agents. And there are reflective evaluations in which memories are linked to social situations. Although none of the mechanisms supporting these extended aspects of self are exclusively social, the fact that there is a social side to all these processes results in a distinct socially-aware sense of self. Our goal in this chapter will be to consider new properties that aspects of social awareness add to the concept of self.

SOCIAL SELF-CONSCIOUSNESS

The sense of self-consciousness that emerges in social interactions is perhaps best described as a *feeling of how others may react to me*. It results in a *socially concerned self.* This aspect of self is sensitive to the attention of other agents. Although we are accustomed to thinking about social interactions as largely a within-group phenomenon, nothing makes an agent feel more self-conscious than to recognize that a predator is watching him. Paradoxically, group living often provides a modicum of protection from outside predators, and yet it introduces within-group interactions that can be similarly intense. Competition, threats, and even thievery are common in social groups, and these interactions can have major effects on how much an agent worries about her social status and how she reacts to others.

When an agent feels her behavior does not meet the approval of others, she is cautious and constantly on the alert for those who may not approve. In contrast, when an agent feels her social community approves of her behavior, she is confident and even emboldened by social attention. One particular aspect of social self-awareness results from the tendency of agents to be concerned about how they look to others. Perhaps we should call this aspect the *image-concerned self*. A popular test of image concern is to place a small blemish, a *mark* as it is usually called, on the face or body of an animal without them knowing, and then to allow them to observe themselves in a mirror.[187] Attention to the mark, when seen in the mirror, especially attempts to remove or groom the mark, is interpreted as evidence of an image-aware sense of self. Among primates, humans, chimpanzees, and orangutans generally react to a mark. These species are therefore thought to experience a sense of image-concerned self-consciousness.

The logic of the "mirror test" is that animals who are self-conscious about their appearance, like humans, should react to seeing a strange mark on their body. However, most of the gorillas and monkeys tested in this paradigm fail to inspect the mark.[188] Some interpret such failures to mean that these species lack a self-concept, and suggest that only more human-like primates are capable of this level of self-awareness. However, this interpretation assumes that all animals should consider their visual appearance to be important and thus react to a mark. But the failure to react to a mark might simply mean that the mirror test is not an effective way of evaluating self-recognition in species who do not consider the visual appearance of their coat to be very important.

Gorillas, monkeys, and cats, for example, may not be very concerned about their visual appearance. Tom grooms himself daily and if he finds something stuck in his coat, he rigorously tries to remove it. However, he would never be concerned about seeing another spot on his coat. In contrast to cats and gorillas, researchers have found that some visually sensitive non-primates, dolphins, elephants, magpies, and cleaner fish react to a mark on their body when seen in a mirror.[189] In fact, some magpies seem to be especially concerned about removing marks they see on their feathers. This suggests that the mirror test tells us more about how sensitive some animals are to their visual appearance than to their sense of self.

There is a mirror sitting at floor level in the house Tom and I share, and I often find Tom pausing to look at the mirror. However, if I make eye contact with Tom via the mirror at these times, he doesn't hold the eye contact for long. Instead, he turns and approaches me. This indicates first, that he recognizes I have made eye contact with him through the mirror, and second, that he knows I am not behind the mirror. Given that the reflections in the mirror move when Tom moves, and we know that circuits in the temporal-parietal junction (TPJ) are involved in detecting self and other movements,[190] Tom surely has learned that his behavior causes the mirror image to move. However, it probably never occurs to Tom that the image he sees in the mirror is what he looks like to others. So while Tom has several aspects of a socially concerned self, and he even watches his reflection in the mirror at times, unlike humans and magpies, he seems unconcerned about his visual self-image.

EMPATHIC CONSCIOUSNESS

While recognizing one's visual self-image in a mirror is a rather curious talent, a much more important social skill, and one that strongly influences conscious feelings, is the tendency of agents to empathize with the feelings of others. As the quote that opens this chapter notes, empathic awareness opens a bridge between third-person observations and first-person awareness. This bridge occurs because conscious agents use the same action and feeling networks they use to monitor their own behavior to monitor the actions and feelings of others. Thus, by empathizing with the feelings of others as we consider their actions, we can often gain added insight into their motives, or what they may be planning. If someone is happy, we can better understand what they may do by empathizing with their happiness. If they feel angry, we can better understand what they may do by empathizing with their anger and how we would react in the same situation. In effect, empathic feelings enhance our ability to reason about what others may do or plan by grounding our interpretations of their feelings and motives within our own feeling and planning networks.[191]

Whereas self-consciousness is sensitive to *feelings of how others may react to me,* empathic consciousness introduces the observer to *feelings of how others feel, what they notice, and what they may do*. The general tendency to notice what others notice and to do what they do is probably best called the *empathic self*. However, the empathic self involves two subparts, an *empathic observer* and an *imitative actor*. When the actions of others lead to positive empathic feelings, then observations of what others do may promote imitative actions. But when the actions of others lead to negative feelings, then observations don't promote imitation, if anything they promote avoidance reactions. So while processes that lead to imitative actions may get more theoretical emphasis, it seems likely that empathic observations occur much more often than imitative actions, and are more important in how we react to others.

Interest in the visual imitation of actions was reinvigorated some fifteen years ago when researchers discovered neurons in the premotor planning regions of the cortex that were active not only when a monkey produced an action, but also when the monkey observed another monkey, or even a human partner, performing the same action. Given that the neurons in these networks respond both to actions that are made by the monkey and to actions that the monkey observed, they came to be called *mirror neurons*.[192]

Subsequent research has found that mirror neurons are located in both parietal and premotor planning regions. It seems that mirror neurons respond to the functional effects of actions, like grasping or moving an object, and not merely to feature combinations such as seeing an object near a hand. Thus, these networks seem to react to movements that result in particular outcomes.

A major theoretical emphasis in the early work on mirror neurons was the assumption that they might promote social imitation. However, the circuitry needed for visual imitation of an action is complex. Mirror neurons are part of the motor system. For them to react to observed actions, they need to receive inputs from social observer modules that detect specific actions. Research suggests that in mammals such action-recognition originates in the biological movement areas of the superior temporal sulcus. These movement-detection areas are known to project to affordance regions in the parietal cortex and to premotor planning regions. Thus, it appears that movements are recognized visually via networks in the superior temporal sulcus and are subsequently associated with parietal and premotor mirror neuron networks.[193]

Research also indicates that actions recognized in the superior temporal sulcus have links to feeling networks. There are several paths by which this seems to work. For example, facial movement areas send projections to the fusiform facial area, from which emotional expressions can be detected. Torso and limb movements are re-represented in other parts of the lateral occipital cortex, from which body language signals can be detected. These facial and body-language extensions are connected with the amygdala, the anterior cingulate cortex, and the anterior insular cortex, all networks where feelings are processed.[194]

As noted in earlier chapters, these networks are connected to feelings of self-ownership processed in the TPJ. Thus, there are connections among biological movement areas, affordance networks, mirror neurons, and self-feeling networks. This complex of connections enables action planning to be influenced by the feelings associated with actions, not just by what was observed. The observer and actor aspects of the empathic self are bound together by these connections.

The empathic self lies at the core of what some characterize as a theory of mind. However, this relationship is less a theory and more a strategy for predicting what other minds may do. In fact, it involves two distinct modes of social thinking. One is a tendency to empathize with the feelings of others. The second is a tendency to focus on the cues in another agent's field of view or objects they recently contacted. This strategy is sometimes referred to as taking the perspective of the other agent. Many animals have a bias to attend to cues that other agents have recently contacted. Thus, to predict what another agent may do, it makes sense that they should also pay attention to the cues that others recently encountered. In this way, the attention of others can sometimes be a salient cue for guiding an observer's attention. Growing evidence suggests that the posterior TPJ is involved in switching attention between self and other perspectives.[195]

Earlier we noted that reward learning is largely driven by the neurotransmitter dopamine. Interestingly, there are also special neuromodulators for guiding social learning. Neuromodulators are not always direct reinforcers, but they can enhance the effects of other neurotransmitters. It turns out that there are several neuropeptides that enhance social feelings, socially guided tasks, social attention, and socially relevant memories. In humans, oxytocin, vasopressin, and some mu-opioids are known to be social neuromodulators. Background levels of these neuromodulators are always present. However, social cues enhance their release, so they are more active in certain social situations.

Interactions such as comforting touches, soft melodic voices, playful laughter, friendly comments, smiling eye contact, and positive episodes of shared attention all release oxytocin. Increases in oxytocin have been shown to reduce fear and stress, increase caring and trust, and promote social memories. It also appears to enhance memories for social situations, but to reduce them for fearful or stressful situations.[196] Oxytocin not only promotes prosocial behavior; it also enhances attention to sociality signals for learning and memory.[197] As a result, when trust and caring feelings are activated, social agents are also more sensitive to the needs and intentions of others.[198] Like oxytocin, the mu-opioids also act as prosocial signals and are thought to potentiate reward in social situations.[199]

Unlike oxytocin, vasopressin tends to be released in stressful or competitive situations. It commonly dampens prosocial feelings, increases stress reactions, and enhances memories for stressful situations.[200] Vasopressin also interacts with testosterone and thus has stronger effects in human males. In fact, it has been implicated in male-typical social behavior, including sexual arousal, courtship, competition, and aggression. Although these kinds of social interactions are typically not as pronounced in females, vasopressin also appears to influence competition and aggression in females. So while some social neuromodulators may increase social attachment, it seems others may sometimes increase social competition.

SOCIAL FEELINGS GUIDE SOCIAL REASONING

When we detect the feelings and actions of agents we care about, we are often motivated to help them. These feelings result in caring reactions that lead to friendships. When we detect the feelings and actions of agents with whom we are competing, we are often motivated to interfere with their activities. These are the kinds of interactions that result in social rivalries. Friendships and rivalries are emergent effects of social interactions, but it is unlikely that they would ever develop if we couldn't recognize the motives and goals of other agents. Empathic feelings change how agents react to each other and change how agents feel about their interactions. If you are expecting social support and instead you get criticism, the difference in feelings can seem devastating.

The importance of empathic feelings in planning and decision-making was highlighted by Antonio Damasio's analysis of the tragic accident of Phineas Gage.[201] Gage was a construction crew foreman whose job was to clear rock obstructions along paths for new railroad tracks. The standard procedure was to drill a hole deep into the obstructing rock, place a charge of powder and a fuse there, and then to pack the hole tightly with sand before detonating the charge from some safe distance away. Gage oversaw the process and packed the charge himself using a long metal tamping bar an inch and one-quarter in diameter. However, on the occasion of the accident Gage was distracted and looked away. When he returned to the task, he failed to notice that his assistant had not yet placed the packing sand in the hole to cover the powder. When Gage began pounding the tamping iron to pack the hole, he was pounding against raw powder. Suddenly, the charge ignited and projected the iron bar out the hole like a massive bullet.

As Damasio recounts the incident, Gage's head was forced back by the explosion. The tapered end of the tamping bar entered through his left cheek, pierced through the base of his skull, and exited through the top of his head just behind the forehead. Given that the tamping iron was three and a half feet long and weighed over thirteen pounds, the fact that Gage survived the explosion was astounding. The impact of the bar could easily have torn his head apart. However, the critical point for our discussion is that the surprisingly clean trajectory of the bar through the brain resulted in extensive damage to Gage's ventromedial prefrontal cortex and its connections, but not to other regions of his brain. The ventromedial prefrontal cortex is known to have broad connections with the limbic cortices, i.e., the anterior cingulate and the insula, as well as with the hypothalamus, the amygdala, and brainstem life-urge networks. These connections suggest that the ventromedial prefrontal cortex normally binds feelings with the executive planning circuitry in the prefrontal cortex.

Amazingly, Gage seemed to be only slightly incapacitated after his accident. He could still walk and talk. He could plan new tasks and make critical decisions. In fact, he continued to work as crew foreman for a while. But things weren't quite what they seemed. His feeling networks were intact, and he was sensitive to the social reactions of others. However, he routinely made crude and offensive comments, and then was surprised when others were offended. He promised to deliver work at a particular time, but if he was interrupted, he was not motivated by the social contract to return to the task. He made up stories when it suited him. He threw fits when he didn't get his way. His management strategies became confrontational, and he was subsequently fired from his job as crew foreman. He had similar difficulty holding other jobs where he had to interact with people.

Without a link between his executive planning networks and his empathic feeling networks, Phineas Gage simply failed to consider the social feelings connected with his plans before he took action. However, he clearly experienced the consequences of his actions when people reacted. As Gage's story illustrates, anticipatory feelings normally influence planning, so we make plans that result in positive social outcomes, while avoiding those that result in social disapproval. However, without connections between the social feeling networks and the executive planning networks, that part of the social bridge is lost. When an agent is aware of how others may react to him, that awareness changes how he plans. He becomes more socially adept and cooperative. Without that awareness, an agent simply cannot make intelligent social decisions.

CONCLUDING COMMENTS

Social feelings introduce two new dimensions to higher-order consciousness. The first of these, *self-consciousness*, is a tendency to worry about one's status, about how others may react to us, and sometimes even to worry about how we appear to other agents. The second of these is *empathic consciousness*, a tendency to track the feelings and attention of other agents, and sometimes to copy what they do. We could write volumes about how social experiences shape our daily lives. However, our goal here is simply to show how social feelings fit within our developing model of consciousness. Self-consciousness brings the social reactions of others to our attention. You cannot learn your position in a group if you are not aware of how others react to you. Empathic feeling networks detect the actions and feelings of others and influence our attention by activating similar feelings in our self. They prepare us to make better social judgments.

Empathic feelings are an extraordinary addition to conscious experience. As Vittorio Gallese, Christian Keysers, and Giacomo Rizzolatti note at the start of this chapter, they provide a bridge into the feelings of others. It's not a perfect bridge, but it is enough to provide insights into what may be going on in other minds. To facilitate these insights agents are sensitive to social cues and actions such as smiles or anger. Such cues release neuromodulators that enhance aspects of attention, learning, and memories for social situations. These, in turn, influence social planning. This happens even when the other agents are less socially skilled, as some might argue Tom is.

I do not fully understand Tom's feelings, but when I recognize that Tom is frightened, I can partly share in his fear and better understand how he may react. When he is happy, I can partly share in his delight and better predict how he may react. And when I am angry, Tom senses the stress in my voice and keeps to a safe distance. Tom and I use the same strategies when we interact with partners of our own species, and presumably, the feelings we interpret as we interact with our own species are even more accurate in guiding our social decisions. However, it should be clear that even in cross-species interactions, interpreting the feelings of others provides each of us with a social bridge.

> ➢ **Ending Remarks**

If we are to develop a human-like robot, he will also need a social bridge between the networks that manage his first-person actions and emotions, and the networks that manage his third-person recognition of them. This bridge will be essential for engaging understanding, and for enabling friendships to form.

If we can engage this bridge with our feline companion Tom, then we can learn to build similar systems for our robotic partners. It will all depend on the robot's ability to express his feelings with signals his partners can readily recognize, and the robot's ability to map his partners' emotive signals into feelings he can understand. And if we do this well, our robot should even be able to empathize with the feelings of a social pet.

9: SIGNS AND MINDS

The ontogeny of the cortical language network can be roughly subdivided into two main developmental stages. In the first stage extending over the first 3 years of life, the infant rapidly acquires bottom-up processing capacities, which are primarily implemented bilaterally in the temporal cortices. In the second stage continuing into adolescence, top-down processes emerge gradually with the increasing functional selectivity and structural connectivity of the left inferior frontal cortex. – Michael Skeide & Angela Friederici, "The ontogeny of the cortical language network", 2016

> ➢ **Introductory Remarks**

Self-consciousness and empathic feelings add important subjective experiences to social awareness. However, rather than just waiting for others to recognize their feelings and intentions, social agents routinely signal about feelings and other topics of their attention. Such signaling enables agents to recruit the attention of others rapidly, and thereby to engage them in similar tasks, goals, and feelings.

Signs guide attention. Tom calls and tugs on my shoulder to recruit my attention and then leads me to where he wants my help. Your dog dances by the door to get your attention when she wants to be taken out. Your friend smiles to acknowledge your eye contact. I refer to all the gestures and vocal signals that agents use to guide attention as *signs*.[202] Our goal here will not be to explain the many ways that agents acquire and use signs, but rather to place signing in a framework that makes it clear how signs direct attention and influence consciousness.

Before we start, there is one additional aspect of signing that we need to note. Social communication involves two complementary processes. When an agent signs, he communicates something about his perceptions and feelings to others. This is the *sender side* of the signaling experience. When an agent detects the signs of another agent, she tries to interpret something about the perceptions and feelings of the sender. This is the *receiver side* of the signaling experience.

Sender and receiver aspects of communication are partially isolated from each other because senders and receivers often have different agendas. However, because social agents learn to use both strategies, experienced agents often come to understand something about the effects of one strategy, even as they use the other. Thus, an experienced sender comes to understand what effects his sign may have on a receiver, while an experienced receiver often comes to recognize what motives might cause the sender to modify the signs she receives.[203] In this chapter, we will focus on sender and receiver effects in three important categories of sign-guided experience. These are *emotively signaled consciousness*, *narrative consciousness*, and *self-narrative consciousness*.

EMOTIVELY SIGNALED CONSCIOUSNESS

Given the importance of evaluating the feelings of others in social interactions, it should come as no surprise to find that social vertebrates often communicate directly about their feelings. *Emotively signaled consciousness* is the term I use to describe the enhanced awareness of feelings resulting from signaling about them, or, on the receiver side, the empathic activation of feelings that occurs when a receiver attends to the emotive signs of others. We can thus define emotively signaled consciousness as a *feeling of alerting or being alerted about emotive states*.

Many emotive and alerting signs are instinctive and initially produced without the signaler consciously intending to influence another agent. Thus, an emotive sender may not always notice when he is signaling. However, emotive signals are another kind of social bridge. They enable agents to share their feelings on background channels. We instinctively cry in distress or pain. We instinctively smile when happy. We instinctively vocalize when we feel threatened. In addition, we constantly signal about our moods by varying tone of voice qualities and by changing facial expressions as we communicate.

Yet while tone of voice qualities, facial expressions, and other emotives may be expressed instinctively at times, they still communicate about ongoing feelings to other agents. And because feelings influence how agents react, other agents often notice and react to them. Thus, even unconscious emotive signals often have social effects. Over time senders may come to recognize how their emotive signs influence others and learn to use them intentionally for those effects.

For example, vervet monkeys (*Cercopithecus aethiops*) have been observed using alarm calls to cause other monkeys to panic and run from a food site, enabling the caller to steal food.[204] Similarly, we may smile intentionally to make our caring more obvious as we thank someone. And even tone of voice qualities may be produced consciously at times. Human actors are quite good at managing their emotive expressions, so obviously voice qualities can be managed intentionally when their effects seem important.

Because we are tuned to pay attention to facial expressions, tone of voice, and other emotive signs, it seems likely that we sometimes detect our own emotive states as we signal, or as others react to our emotive signs. When I yell at Tom, I notice there is anger in my voice when Tom reacts to it. I recognize the excitement or sadness in my voice as others react. Sometimes I feel myself smiling or hear myself cursing. Antonio Damasio argued that strong emotional reactions in the body sometimes serve as secondary evidence of emotive states. He called these secondary sources *somatic markers*.[205] It seems to me that facial expressions, tone of voice, and other emotive signs often serve as emotive markers for autonomic states, and thereby sometimes alert us to our own emotions.

Emotive signs are such an important part of communication that we often notice when they are absent. Consider how emotive signs have become common in internet text messaging. Textual emotives, such as the smile :-) and frown :-(signs, were popularized early in messaging as a way of signaling emotional reactions in plain text messages. Facial emotive icons, emoticons as they were called, soon became a standard.[206] With extended graphics these have expanded to what are now known as emojis. The use of emoticons and emojis illustrates how sensitive we are to the need for emotive signs in social exchanges.

Although they don't always dominate attention, in receiver roles emotive signs guide our conscious interpretation of messages, and in sender roles we often add emotives to ensure that our intended feelings are clear. But we don't add emotives to our text subconsciously. We add them purposely to ensure how our messages will be interpreted. We don't usually think about our facial expressions as we talk. However, if we add facial emoticons intentionally when we text, it seems clear that we may sometimes add facial expressions intentionally to help others interpret our messages. Of course, we don't usually focus on the emotive signs, but we notice when they are missing. If someone speaks with a completely blank expression, you soon begin to question their intention and distrust their message.

In addition to using signs to comment emotively about a message, humans use a number of signs to signal about their self-feelings during any social exchange. We may smile or frown as we greet someone just to set the tone of our conversation. We have signs to indicate when we are busy. We have gestures to signal anger or to insult others. We also have a large variety of alerting signs and curses that we use to signal feelings of surprise, interest, or anger.

When apes are taught to use signs to communicate, the training typically begins when they are young. Interestingly, one major training experience that coincides with language training in humans and other apes is potty training. Potty training inevitably involves a sign used to refer to defecatory messes that occur when potty training fails. Often this sign is translated in professional reports simply as "dirty". Dirty situations are treated as unpleasant and are associated with scolding and social disapproval. Interestingly, a common finding among both human and non-human apes that have gone through joint language and potty training is that they often come to use signs for "dirty" situations metaphorically to refer to agents that they find unpleasant.

NARRATIVE CONSCIOUSNESS

Narrative consciousness is the *feeling of being able to coordinate thoughts and actions with others by using deictic or referential signs.* Deictic signs are pointers to spatial, temporal, or situational features. The simplest deictic signs for most animals are head pointing gestures, although leading and reaching gestures are also common pointers. Finger pointing is common in humans. Gaze direction is also used as a pointing gesture in humans. One adaptation that makes gaze pointing easier for humans is the presence of a white sclera surrounding the darker iris. Most animals have a darker sclera, presumably because a lack of contrast helps them avoid detection by predators. However, humans not only have a white sclera, but they also have an eye shape in which a wide area of the sclera is exposed horizontally. Seeing a dark iris move against this white background makes it easier for humans to follow the gaze of others and thus for the gaze of one agent to serve as a pointer that influences the gaze of another.[207]

Referential signs are gestures, calls, or words that have been associated with, and thus can be used to refer to, specific perceptions, actions, or feelings. When referential signs are used, no pointing is needed because referential signs act as memory pointers. They can even refer to absent or abstract items. In sender roles, referential signs are used to guide the attention of others to specific features or ideas. In receiver roles, agents use referential signs to follow the attention of others.

For example, based on shared associations, the word "hat" can be used to refer to objects with a specific head-covering function. As this illustrates, referential signs often have no direct relationship between their form and the items to which they refer. In effect, they often begin as arbitrary signs. However, once a referential association is learned the sign is no longer arbitrary. Its reference is automatically recalled whenever it is heard. To an untrained listener, "look at the green hat" is an arbitrary combination of sounds. However, once you understand the words as a series of referential signs, its attention-guiding effect is quite specific.

Describing how signs are used would be simpler if they were always used within discrete signaling categories. However, in many cases, signs grade from one category to the next, and some cases always remain difficult to categorize. For example, Tom's pointing gestures begin as deictic signs, but when a deictic sign is combined with a specific location and situation, head-pointing to the tuna cabinet, the combination of cues soon comes to be recognized as a more specific message. A similar transition between alerting signs and the referential functions of signs has been reported in vervet monkeys. Vervet monkeys use different alarm calls to signal about different predators. Further, they respond to the calls with different behaviors.[208] For example, when vervet monkeys hear leopard alarms, they run into the safety of the trees and look down for predators. When they hear eagle alarms, they hide in the bushes and look up. When they hear snake alarms, they stand tall and begin looking down in the grass around them.

Initially, the cues that trigger the vervets' alarm calls and the reactions they arouse are largely instinctive. Young vervet monkeys have been known to make eagle calls when surprised by falling leaves.[209] When an adult monkey hears these errant calls, he looks around, but he doesn't repeat the call. However, if the adult sees a real threat he repeats the call. These repeated calls serve to reinforce the youngster's decision to call. Thus, gradually young monkeys learn to associate their calls with the same events that evoke calls in adults. So what begin as poorly anchored innate alerting calls soon come to be socially accepted referential calls for specific threats. And while human language seems much different, we should not overlook the fact that it begins with children instinctively repeating the speech sounds of their parents and associating those sounds with coincident feelings, objects, or actions in a situation.

Learning new vocal signs requires a strong link between hearing networks and call production networks. A critical hearing network for word recognition is a region in the temporal lobe known as Wernicke's area. A critical network for vocal language production is the premotor planning region known as Broca's area. Initially, Wernicke's area and Broca's area were thought to be connected by one major fiber bundle, which was known as the arcuate fasciculus – Latin for *curved bundle*. This curved bundle was thought to account for language learning. However, using a combination of MRI diffusion tensor imaging and diffusion spectrum imaging, Jeremy Schmahmann and colleagues have shown that there are about ten different "curved bundles" that facilitate perceptual analysis and social learning in the macaque monkey.[210] Only a few of these bundles connect auditory areas to vocal areas.

The many different functions supported by these bundles make it clear that much more is being enhanced by these connections than merely auditory-vocal processing. These fiber bundles enable agents to localize sounds, recognize individual voices, react to the emotional valences of vocal and facial expressions, and interpret social interactions more generally. Further, none of these interconnections are unique to humans. The homologue of Broca's area in macaque monkeys is the area that controls mouth and hand movements. Thus, it is not surprising that it is also involved in managing vocalizations and gestures in human communication. Other animals also come to associate sounds and gestures with emotional meanings. Thus, language appears to have evolved as a method of signaling that builds on networks used for understanding social interactions.[211]

Recently Michael Skeide and Angela Friederici have proposed that two general signaling trends in these networks largely explain the neural circuitry that supports language analysis. One is a broad ventral group for auditory connectivity with social events and feelings. The other is a dorsal group that they attribute to the arcuate fasciculus and related dorsal connections.[212] It seems that the ventral group connections, including Wernicke's area, are largely responsible for what these authors call the *bottom-up* processes of language analysis – phonological detection, lexical-semantic categorization, and together with some dorsal group support, vocal phrase construction and simple prosodic processing.

Research indicates that acoustic features are detected in the first 50ms and phonological word forms are largely assembled by 100 ms after an utterance is detected. Lexical structures and phrases are largely assembled in the next 100ms followed by early aspects of prosodic processing. These bottom-up processes are mostly implemented during the first 300 ms after an utterance, and thus are responsible for the initial analysis of speech sounds.

Skeide and Friederici argue that the dorsal group connections largely account for top-down language analysis. Top-down analysis involves more complex prosodic processing, such as recognizing irony or sarcasm in speech. It also involves a more detailed analysis of semantic meanings and the analysis of more complex syntactic relationships. These top-down processes gradually begin after many of the bottom-up processes have been engaged. Thus, their effects mainly appear in the 300-500 ms time frame after a speech phrase starts. Given that these processes largely involve dorsal stream connections with frontal areas, including Broca's area, the added encoding results in more detailed vocal phrasing and meaning dependencies. Tracking these dorsal stream structures as they listen is thought to enable receivers to decode and understand complex syntactic phrases better.

An interesting part of these author's analysis is the observation that the bottom-up aspects of language processing, those responsible for acoustic recognition and analysis, are not only faster to be engaged, but appear to be well developed in humans within three years of age. Further, these acoustic recognition skills become highly refined within the next few years. However, the top-down aspects of language processing, those responsible for advanced prosodic and syntactic analyses, develop much more slowly. In fact, these systems expand dramatically beginning in adolescence and extending on into adulthood.[213] These findings are consistent with the fact that hierarchical planning skills in the frontal and prefrontal cortex develop slowly and that this development extends on into adulthood. Other research also argues that the temporal tracking of semantic processes is essential for the hierarchical analysis of speech.[214]

There is no question that the narratively-guided skills of humans far exceed those of other animals. However, it should be clear that narratively-guided attention is not unique to humans. Alex, the African Grey parrot that Irene Pepperberg trained to use vocal sounds as signs, learned to imitate over 150 English words. He used these words both to guide the attention of others and to follow their instructions.[215] When shown a tray of objects Alex could answer questions like "How many blue blocks?" or "How many yellow balls?" He simply could not have answered such questions without using the sounds he heard as referential signs to guide his attention to specific features. When first shown a reflection of himself in a mirror, Alex asked: "What color?" He had never been trained what word to use for the color grey, but he was often asked "what color" in other tasks so he knew how to ask the question. And that is how Alex learned that "grey" was the label for the color of his plumage.

Alex also occasionally invented phrases to describe features he found of interest. For example, he referred to almonds as "cork nuts" to differentiate them from other nuts, and he referred to dried corn seeds, as "rock corn" to differentiate it from the fresh soft corn he sometimes received. Note that these phrases use metaphorical associations to refer to specific details of the object being referenced. In many cases, Alex's sign use was obviously spontaneous. In one popular internet video, fresh corn had just been retrieved from the refrigerator. When Alex ate the corn, he remarked that it was "cold." Later, when he dropped some on the floor, he told Irene to "Go pick up corn." Such spontaneous phrases provide clear evidence that Alex was thinking with signs, and that he expected his partners to use his signs to understand his intentions.

Unlike the vocal apparatus of parrots, the vocal apparatus of non-human primates is not well adapted for making varied sounds. However, several non-human primates, including chimpanzees, gorillas, and orangutans, have been taught to use American Sign Language (ASL) to communicate. ASL is a hand-shape sign language taught to most deaf Americans. In other research programs, primates have been taught to use visual lexigrams on a computer screen to communicate. In fact, the bonobo, Kanzi, arguably the best educated non-human primate on the planet, uses a touch-sensitive computer display with over 400 lexigrams. There are lexigrams for objects, actions, places, and for certain social partners. There are also lexigrams for prepositions like "on" and temporal pointers like "now" or "past". There are even temporal adverbs like "slow". Of course, there are also lexigrams for emotive states such as "good", "bad", "happy", "sorry", "ready", and "surprise".

Like Alex, when Kanzi runs out of primary signs, he combines his signs in metaphorical compounds to describe new features or feelings. When Kanzi is made to wait for something, and then is asked if he is ready, he often responds sarcastically with the lexigrams for "past ready". "Slow lettuce" is the combination he uses to refer to kale because kale is tougher and takes longer to chew. "Potato surprise" was the phrase he invented to refer to what we Americans call potato chips, although the British call them potato crisps. Kanzi doesn't have a separate lexigram for "chip" or "crisp" but it seems clear that, like human speakers, he can invent new combinations when he wants to direct attention to specific features. And, yes, when he could have them, Kanzi obviously enjoyed eating those potato surprises.

To facilitate conversing with humans, Kanzi's computer system is now designed to pronounce the English word associated with a sign whenever a lexigram is pressed. And Kanzi has also learned to recognize many of the spoken words associated with his lexigrams. So while humans become experts in the use of signs for guiding attention, Kanzi and Alex make it clear that other animals share in the basic skills needed for such narrative exchanges using both vocal and visual signs. Pet dogs use gestural signs to tell you when they want to go out, or when they want to be fed. Tom uses gestures to guide my attention, like pointing to the fridge when he wants mayonnaise, or pointing to a specific cabinet when he wants tuna. And in such situations, these gestures come to function much like referential signs.

As this cursory analysis indicates, using acoustic calls, visual signs, or even motor gestures to guide attention is not a uniquely human skill. What is unique about humans is the number of signs that they learn to use in communication and the extent to which human culture depends on signing. Alex learned to use over 150 vocal signs, and he probably partially understood twice that number. Kanzi has learned to use over 400 lexigrams, and including vocal words, he likely understands over a thousand signs. However, human children have been estimated to use some 300 words by two and a half years of age, nearly 5000 words by the age of five, and perhaps as many as 12,000 words by the age of twelve.[216] Thus, when it comes to learning narrative signs, humans clearly exceed the level of sign use found in well-trained animals. And this is where we should recognize Phillip Anderson's insight that *more is different*.[217] The number of distinct signs, and the amount of signing that occurs among adult humans, radically changes human communication.

SELF-NARRATIVE CONSCIOUSNESS

In sender roles, narrative agents use signs to guide the attention of others. In receiver roles, they use signs to follow the attention of others. As language skills grow, conversational exchanges become a routine part of narrative experience. For example, parent-child conversations routinely involve requests from the child, parental replies, and instructions for doing tasks. Some exchanges also involve discipline. In such exchanges, a child is often asked to explain what they have done, and why they did it. In formal education, the process of instructing and questioning becomes even more systematic, while the topics of discussion become more varied. Over years of formal education, narrative agents learn to use question-and-answer dialogues as a standard way of processing ideas and making decisions. These dialogues shape how agents learn to think.

With practice, narrative agents not only learn to converse with others, but they even learn to produce their own instructions and questions. Recall, for example, how Alex told Irene to "Go pick up corn" when he dropped some on the floor, or how he asked "What color" when he saw his reflection in the mirror. It is unlikely Alex could ever have made these narrative exchanges if he had not first been trained to answer questions and to follow instructions.

As narrative exchanges become a prominent part of social interactions, narrative agents learn to alternate between sender and receiver roles in conversations. And once an agent can readily shift between sender and receiver roles in social conversations, it is only a matter of time before they begin to talk with themselves. *Self-narrative consciousness* is the formal label I use to describe how this changes consciousness. More casually, this behavior is often called *self-talk*. Self-talk enables agents to *review their decisions, question their observations, and even respond to their own questions.*

So while sign use begins with intention movements, alerting calls, and deictic signals, once agents learn to use signs to direct and follow the attention of others, they gradually learn to use them to manage attention more generally, even their own attention. Children learn to instruct themselves, question themselves, and even discipline themselves. Sometime soon after self-talk begins, they also learn to talk covertly – that is to talk while holding the brake on vocal output so others cannot hear their self-talk. Running language programs covertly still activates the vocal and auditory planning regions in the brain and still triggers word associations from memory, but it keeps the conversations private. However, the conversational character of the social exchange remains. When we instruct ourselves, we must pause and consider our suggestions. When we admonish ourselves, we must shift our attention to evaluate the criticism.

Those who believe that language is essential for conscious experience have simply failed to understand the bootstrapping nature of the processes that lead to language. Language doesn't make us conscious. We have that part backward. Tracking attention and learning the meaning of words is one of those tasks that we can only accomplish when we consciously attend to words and contexts. We might learn associations between a single word and a repeated event via conditioning in the absence of attention. However, tracking the meanings of words in combination requires ongoing attention and evaluation. And for that to happen words must first be associated with many referent sources of perceptions, actions, and feelings. Only then do words become highly flexible tools for guiding attention.

Over time, conversational dialogues and self-talk dialogues become an integral part of conscious experience. Agents comment on what they observe. They instruct themselves. They even question their own plans. And sometimes they wonder what others are planning. This form of self-narrative consciousness is largely a human process. However, as we have noted, the roots of self-talk grow out of social dialogues. Language-trained animals also engage in social dialogues. They comment on what they observe. They ask spontaneous questions. They sometimes sign to themselves when they are alone. So humans are not unique in this regard. However, only humans have developed a culture of formal education, which over years of training systematically promotes them to use signs routinely to guide their attention, question their experiences, and adopt new signs to extend their internal conversations. In humans, self-dialogues keep developing even well into adulthood and become a routine part of reflection and planning.

CONCLUDING COMMENTS

The importance of emotive signs in conscious communication is largely under-appreciated. Emotive signs make us more aware of our own feelings and communicate our feelings to others. Given that feelings are a core component of conscious experience, this means that emotive signs help prepare others to interpret our communication in the context of feelings. Much of this is accomplished on secondary channels. We constantly accompany our speech with tone-of-voice qualities to guide their interpretation. We add facial expressions, sometimes unconsciously, and sometimes consciously, to guide the interpretation of our messages. In addition, we often learn to use gestures and vocal expressions to make our feelings explicit. In fact, as the use of emojis in messaging illustrates, it seems we can rarely communicate effectively without including emotive signs in our messages.

With the addition of narrative signing, we reach a stage in cognitive processing where the features of conscious experience differ much more between Tom's consciousness and that of our own. Up to this point, the differences have not always appeared that large. Even now, it is clear that Tom shares a common attention architecture and rudimentary elements of deictic and location-based referential signs. However, the extent of narrative signs in humans introduces a new level of control over attention. Tom has a small repertoire of signs and calls to manage my attention and the attention of his peers. He recognizes his name and words for special treats or requests, and he reacts when he hears those words. He even has his own recruiting and pointing signs to gain my attention and to request items. And it seems clear that once Tom points to the tuna cabinet his signing enhances his goal. He does not give up easily.

All this illustrates that Tom can use gestures and signs to guide the attention of others, and sometimes even his own attention. However, the broad range of referential signs available to humans vastly extends the range of concepts to which humans can guide attention. In that sense, human narratives are much different from Tom's. The complexity of human language enables us to direct attention in very precise ways and, in doing so, to develop increasingly complex skills and concepts. These, in turn, may be explored and questioned in social dialogues. Many concepts of modern philosophy and science are defined merely by words and are learned about largely in readings or lectures. Yet people not only learn to think about these concepts, but also how to extend them without ever experiencing them in any more direct way.

It is hard to overestimate the importance of social dialogues in formal education. They play a major role in teaching agents how to analyze problems, how to question their observations, and how to evaluate their decisions. As agents learn to alternate between sender and receiver roles, they soon begin to carry on these conversations with themselves. These self-dialogues add a special dimension to cognition and conscious control. They enable agents to use their conversational skills to guide their actions and even to question their own observations and motives.

However, it is important to recognize that these skills take years to mature. As self-talk becomes a routine part of reflection and planning, it occurs spontaneously even as part of background planning. This is likely why some philosophers believe that language is essential for consciousness. They find themselves thinking in words as they work ideas. There is no question that self-talk can greatly enhance our reflection and planning at times, but ask a jazz musician or a visual artist, and you will get a different impression. Not everyone does their best thinking in words. Further, as we will see in the next chapter, many of our daily conscious activities don't involve constant self-talk.

➢ **Ending Remarks**

If we are to develop robots with human-like awareness they will have to use signs in a similar way as humans. Thus, they will need distinct "curved-bundle" processes that enable them to localize the source of signs, to recognize individual voices, to detect gestures, to react to the emotional valences of signs, and to use these combinations to interpret social interactions. They must learn signs by imitating them and exchanging them with their partners. At first these skills should be used for instructing and questioning them. But over time we should ensure that they can use them to communicate with themselves. Self-talk should be a hallmark of conscious robots, as it is for humans.

10: Dynamic Flow

Conscious experience is fluid; it rarely remains on one topic for an extended period without deviation. Its dynamic nature is illustrated by the experience of mind wandering, in which attention switches from a current task to unrelated thoughts and feelings. ... Examination of the information-processing demands of the mind-wandering state suggests that it involves perceptual decoupling to escape the constraints of the moment, its content arises from episodic and affective processes, and its regulation relies on executive control.– Jonathan Smallwood & Jonathan Schooler, "The science of mind wandering", 2015

> **Introductory Remarks**

Consciousness emerges as perceptual-motor features are bound with life urges in coherent attention. And because attention is focused, only a few features can gain attention at one time. However, new perceptions, actions, and feelings are constantly competing for attention. Thus, consciousness rarely stays at any single focus for long. There is always a dynamic flow of attention.

Over the course of this book we have outlined a number of neural processes that contribute to various aspects of conscious experience. The table below summarizes the primary aspects of consciousness we have described.[218] Consistent with the organization effect, it also points to the supporting neural processes for each,[219] and provides a descriptive label for *the sense of self* that emerges in each process.

Although the categories can be considered a roughly interconnected hierarchy of experiences,[220] this does not imply that the higher levels are always the most important, or even that they usually dominate conscious experience. In fact, the opposite is more often the case. Sensorimotor experiences and feelings are arguably the most important and the most persistent.

Other aspects of experience add novel details to awareness, or new ways of guiding attention, but we don't focus on any one of these details for long. Each focus of attention is metastable and soon morphs into another.[221] Thus, conscious awareness is never fixed. It is always in a state of flow. And yet, these dynamic shifts in attention add to the richness of conscious experience by enabling us to evaluate a situation on multiple levels.

PROTO-CONSCIOUS PROCESSES

Phenomenon:	**Life-Urge Priorities and Orientation Biases**
Sense of Self:	**Proto-Self (Damasio, 1999)**
Characteristics:	**Biases for unconscious aspects of experience.**
Core Systems:	**Life urge feeling and motor networks range from the mid-pontine to hypothalamic regions. Orientation biases begin in the tectum.**

CORE ASPECTS OF CONSCIOUSNESS

Phenomenon:	**Phenomenal Consciousness (Block, 1998)**
Sense of Self:	**Phenomenal Self**
Characteristics:	**The feeling of what happens (Damasio, 1999).**
Core Systems:	**The thalamocortical architecture is key. Absent a cortex, attention and feelings are less distinct. Absent a thalamus, phenomenal experience seems unlikely, although proto-conscious moods may still vary with changes in orientation.**

Phenomenon:	**Spatial Consciousness**
Sense of Self:	**Observer Self**
Characteristics:	**The feeling of where I am.**
Core Systems:	**The cortical eye fields (FEF, SEF, PEF), the pulvinar in the thalamus, and the tectum are all important.**

Phenomenon:	Anticipatory Consciousness
Sense of Self:	Anticipatory Self
Characteristics:	The feeling of what might happen next.
Core Systems:	The extended amygdala, which uses external cues to anticipate changes in feelings, and the cerebellum, which anticipates sequential processing changes all across the brain,

Phenomenon:	Planning Agency
Sense of Self:	Agent Self
Characteristics:	The feeling of being able to change things by planning actions.
Core Systems:	Motor planning activities in the frontal cortex and basal ganglia that come to be learned as anticipatory cues for actions are thought to contribute to a sense of planning.

Phenomenon:	Ownership Agency
Sense of Self:	Owner Self
Characteristics:	The feeling of owning an action or a body part.
Core Systems:	Correlations between action planning, action recognition in the superior temporal sulcus (STS), and feelings in the insula, as summarized in the temporal-parietal junction (TPJ). Body part ownership involves correlations between seeing a part and feelings of touch or movement for that part.

MEMORY-GUIDED CONSCIOUSNESS

Phenomenon:	Reflective Consciousness
Sense of Self:	Reflective Self
Characteristics:	The remembered present (Edelman, 1989).

Core Systems:	Semantic and episodic memory networks.

Phenomenon:	**1. Semantic Reflection**
Sense of Self:	**Familiar or Novel Feelings of the Reflective Self**
Characteristics:	**An awareness of contextual and categorical co-occurrences or their absence.**
Core Systems:	**The parahippocampal region of the medial temporal lobe.**

Phenomenon:	**2. Episodic Reflection**
Sense of Self:	**Re-Experiencing Feelings of the Reflective Self**
Characteristics:	**An ability to explore situational co-occurrences and reactivate selected scenarios of past experience.**
Core Systems:	**The hippocampal region of the medial temporal lobe and thalamic networks that bias attention to memory processing.**

Phenomenon:	**Reflective Agency**
Sense of Self:	**Reflective Agent**
Characteristics:	**The feeling of being able to do what I have done before. This is a hybrid combination of agency and reflective memory.**
Core Systems:	**Motor planning circuits, action ownership correlations in the TPJ, and links from these to declarative networks. These links appear to involve the posterior cingulate cortex.**

ATTENTION-MANAGING CONSCIOUSNESS

Phenomenon:	**Task-Focused Consciousness**
Sense of Self:	**Vigilant Self**
Characteristics:	**The feeling of being alert and focused on**

Core Systems:	events in the immediate situation.
	Certain networks in the thalamus are thought to bias attention to sensorimotor activities while inhibiting memory processing.

Phenomenon:	Memory-Focused Consciousness
Sense of Self:	Recollective Self
Characteristics:	The feeling of re-experiencing memories without a focus on the immediate situation.
Core Systems:	Certain networks in the thalamus are thought to bias attention to memory processing while inhibiting attention to current tasks.

Phenomenon:	Time-Shared Consciousness
Sense of Self:	Multitasking Self
Characteristics:	The feeling of being a multitasking agent.
Core Systems:	Networks in the prefrontal cortex (PFC) appear to be able to shift attention back and forth between various tasks. Connections between the cerebellum and the PFC are thought to facilitate sequential shifts in attention as tasks progress.

Phenomenon:	Exploratory Consciousness
Sense of Self:	Reasoning Self
Characteristics:	The feeling of being able to reason by simulating actions, exploring memories, and engaging feelings. These skills grow as agents learn to manage their planning and memory skills.
Core Systems:	A multitasking ability, largely guided by the PFC, to shift attention back and forth between task planning, evaluating feelings, and memory recall while looking for new opportunities.

Phenomenon:	**Self-Consciousness**
Sense of Self:	**Personal Image-Concerned Self**
Characteristics:	**The feeling of how others may react to me – an enhanced awareness of social reactions when an agent worries about the approval of others. (Note: Mirror recognition appears to be a visual aspect of image concern and yet has little to do with other aspects of self-awareness.)**
Core Systems:	**Social worry may involve a connection between the lateral habenula and the striatum that facilitates pausing when negative consequences are expected. However, many other networks are involved in detecting and evaluating social interactions.**

Phenomenon:	**Sexual Consciousness**
Sense of Self:	**Gender Self**
Characteristics:	**Feelings of socio-sexual identity and sexual attraction.**
Core Systems:	**Sexual identity begins with biological structures and hormones in the first trimester of fetal development. In the third trimester regions in the amygdala take form that interact with later social development to engage feelings of gender identity and partner preference. About 86% of humans in the US declare a general alignment of biological, hormonal, and gender identity, and a preference for hetero partners. For the remaining 14% gender identity and partner preferences may be incomplete or reversed.**

Phenomenon:	**Empathic Consciousness**
Sense of Self:	**Empathic Observer & Imitative Actor**
Characteristics:	**The feeling of what others feel, what they notice, and how they may act.**

Core Systems:	Empathic feelings use the same networks as those for self-feelings and observations. Imitative actions are thought to involve connections between STS temporal movement areas, parietal affordance areas, premotor planning networks, and insular feeling areas. The pTPJ is thought to support shifts between self and other perspectives.

SIGN-GUIDED CONSCIOUSNESS

Phenomenon:	Emotionally Signaled Consciousness
Sense of Self:	Emotive Self
Characteristics:	The feeling of alerting or being alerted about emotive states.
Core Systems:	Emotive signs communicate feelings. Many begin as instinctive signs. However, receivers are often conscious of them and senders may even learn to use them intentionally, e.g., smiles.

Phenomenon:	Narrative Consciousness
Sense of Self:	Narrative Self (Dennett, 1992)
Characteristics:	The feeling of being able to coordinate the thoughts and actions of others with signs. In sender roles signs guide the attention of others. In receiver roles agents use signs to follow attention.
Core Systems:	Deictic and referential signs enhance social communication and reasoning. These signs depend on "curved bundle" connections between areas for social feelings and motor areas for gestures, vocalizations, and signs. Gestures and vocal signs in humans involves Broca's area.

Phenomenon:	Self-Narrative Consciousness
Sense of Self:	Autobiographical Self (Damasio, 1999)
Characteristics:	The feeling of being able to guide self-reasoning and self memories using signs. Self-talk and self-questioning are largely human skills. However, non-human agents raised in a culture of sign use may also acquire these skills.
Core Systems:	Self-narratives emerge from social dialogues as agents learn they can engage in self-talk. That is, that they can reason by commenting, asking questions, and responding to themselves.

Table 10-1: Characteristics of various aspects of conscious experience

In this table I have tried to link my categories of conscious experience to terms proposed by others. However, there are a variety of terms and I do not consider them all.[222] For example, Ned Block distinguishes between *phenomenal consciousness* and *access consciousness*. Phenomenal consciousness basically corresponds to the *feeling of what it is like* to experience something.[223] However, what Block calls *access consciousness* is not a kind of experience, but rather a property of the way the thalamocortical architecture works.[224] However, my categories are experiential, and access consciousness is not an experience. Further, I have no reason to conclude that thalamocortical access occurs in the absence of phenomenal experience.

In a more important experiential distinction, Antonio Damasio distinguishes between *core consciousness,* a category that covers my Core and Learning-Guided categories, and *extended consciousness*. Semantic memories are generally considered to be part of core consciousness, as are emotively signaled consciousness and the spatial aspects of episodic memory.[225] *Extended consciousness* generally encompasses the remaining categories.[226] Gerald Edelman also distinguishes between two major levels of consciousness calling the first level *primary consciousness* and the second *higher-order consciousness*.[227] Because Damasio has popularized the *core consciousness* term, I use it to refer to the first level. However, I prefer the *higher-order consciousness* term for the second level because higher-order consciousness often involves higher-order thalamic relays.

The categories of consciousness I have proposed here are more graded than most of those proposed in earlier descriptions. My goal has been to distinguish among features I believe to be supported by different neural processes, and thus features that may vary in different kinds of agents, or features that may vary in our own consciousness from moment to moment. However, while my categories attempt to tie various aspects of consciousness to supporting brain systems, the very fact that we know the brain represents and re-represents functions in a hierarchy of circuitry, means that even the simplest of experiences may be expanded and enhanced by this multi-level processing. Thus, the core systems proposed in each category are better thought of as starting points for how these experiences are assembled, rather than full mechanisms of expression.

What Is the Nature of the Self?

Given the many aspects of self described in the section above it seems clear that the self cannot be located in any one specific part of the brain. And yet, there are constant reports on the internet that the central agency of the self has been located, or alternately, that it has been proven not to exist. Many of these reports confuse regions of brain activation with sources of function. For example, when people think of themselves, neural activation studies report that the medial prefrontal cortex (mPFC) is always activated. However, lesions studies tell us that patients who lack the mPFC can still think about themselves. Thus, *being able to think about oneself* is not localized in the mPFC.

Andy Clark suggests that the lack of a firm mechanism for self-identity suggests that the self is just a story, a soft coalition of processes of no major importance.[228] Yet the very fact that the self is multi-layered argues that it is a robust coalition of interacting properties that exists on multiple levels. Storms of attention are dynamic systems that experience the world on many levels. They develop along individualized paths depending on their history of experiences. However, their concepts grow incrementally. If you compare the self of one agent with that of another you will discover that each storm of attention has a unique individualized character.

Yes, there are aspects of self that sometimes involve self-talk. Yes, there are even aspects of self that sometimes compose autobiographical stories in which "I" am the central player. But the story is not the self. If you destroy all the networks supporting those aspects of self there is still a robust interconnected sense of self with phenomenal experience, with anticipatory expectations, with a sense of the agency to manage actions. There is still a reflective self who experiences a remembered present, a reasoning self who shifts between memories and planning, an image-concerned self who worries about the approval of others, and an emotive self that signals its feelings to others.

So if the self is truly a dynamic coalition of feeling-bound processes, which processes take control? Those who pose this kind of question assume that all control must be applied by some top-down agency. Now we do know that several kinds of control circuits have evolved to manage cortical processing. For example, we know that a dorsal attention network has self-organized to manage spatial-motor processing, and when spatial-motor tasks are engaged these circuits tend to facilitate those tasks. We also know that when sudden changes in motivation occur, the ventral attention network circuits interrupt the dorsal networks to promote a change in attention.

However, the behavior of most conscious agents makes it clear that a large proportion of their attention is managed by a personal coalition of processes whose interactive skills have been shaped by their developmental history. Thus, the key to understanding the self is to recognize that it truly is a coalition of processes. In short, you are the coalition. Your sense of self is guided by your history of skills, habits, and values. That history is what makes you unique and it is what defines who you are.

What Brain Regions Are Needed for Consciousness?

Questions about what are the minimal brain regions needed for consciousness are even more difficult to answer. Children born with most of their cortex missing, a deficit that would seem to imply they are only capable of a vegetative existence, nevertheless appear to develop some aspects of phenomenal consciousness. They recognize special caretakers. They react to their own names. They show obvious evidence of pleasure and pain. They even develop preferences for certain musical passages and react with apparent joy when they hear them.[229] These observations suggest that some conscious-like processes can operate in the absence of a cortex. It seems likely that this occurs because brainstem life urges can still be bound via thalamic connections to motor regions in the striatum, emotional representations in the extended amygdala, and body-world alignments managed by the brainstem.

However, without a cortex, many higher-order aspects of consciousness would not be possible. These include the enhanced pleasantness of music processed in the anterior insula, facial recognition processed in supplementary visual areas, episodic memories processed in the hippocampus, feelings of action planning processed in the frontal cortex, feelings of action ownership processed in the TPJ, and the feelings of reflective self-agency made possible by links between the TPJ and declarative memories. Some limited aspects of self-awareness may also occur without a cortex. The tectum supports the orientation of an agent, so partial aspects of an observer self may be present. However, the focus of the cortical gaze networks, and their role in guiding attention, would all be missing. These losses would result in a much more limited sense of an observer.

Absent the thalamus to bind disparate features in states of focused attention, it seems unlikely that anything resembling human phenomenal consciousness can occur. However, life urges coordinated by the tectal-periaqueductal orientation complex may engage early states of proto-object awareness. Without the complex feeling-bound processes in the thalamus, there is no known mechanism by which proto-object perceptions can be bound with proto-conscious feelings as they are in agents with an intact thalamus. However, the expression of emotive signals in some cases gives the impression that they are. Given that the extent of the brain deficits in many subjects is often difficult to specify, it seems safest to error on the positive side and to assume that some minimal level of feeling-bound awareness may be present if such reactions occur consistently. Subsequently, tests monitoring patterns of brain activity can then be used to determine whether anything resembling normal brain patterns of consciousness are activated in such situations. However, this is still largely a judgment call.

LOUDER THAN WORDS

It's louder than words. This thing that we do.
Louder than words. The way it unfurls.
It's louder than words. The sum of our parts.
The beat of our hearts. Is louder than words.[230]

Some want to claim that consciousness is the result of self-talk. However, as the categories above illustrate, conscious experience is not limited to one aspect of awareness. There are times when upon being startled we become alerted and orient toward the perceived source of an event. We are aware that something is happening, although we may not be aware of many details. Subsequently, we piece together a context of what just happened and reflect on past associations, or possible causes, to make better sense of the event. But in the initial moment, there is often no clear perceptual focus, no obvious memory associations, and no words to describe what is happening. There is only an awareness of change and the activation of life urges for orientation, vigilance, and self-protection. However, we may be intensely conscious of these reactions and the feelings of risks and uncertainty they produce in the moment.

Similarly, at times, our attention may be captured by a sensory experience, a scenic view or the taste of a new food that engages us in sensory valuing of the experience. Likes and dislikes are valuations, and we can feel such valuations without having to express them verbally. Alternately, our attention may be drawn to emotional states, for example, feelings of grief on the occasion of a loss. The first reaction to such events may be little more than tears and sobbing. Subsequently, we may gain our composure and begin to reflect on the loss in more cognitive terms. We may even try to make sense of such events with narrative explanations, although our narratives may add little more than the unanswered question, "Why?" In such moments, raw emotional values dominate our experience, reason and reflection are largely pushed aside, and narrative summaries lag even farther behind. The point is that the range of conscious experience often shifts among many categories, and words do not manage all these shifts.

In a series of studies ranging over thirty years, Russ Hurlburt and his associates have employed a procedure in which participants are asked to categorize their conscious experience whenever a periodic beeper sounds throughout the day.[231] Because the beeper is not linked to the subject's activities, it provides a random probe into ongoing experience. The method is open to some methodological criticisms. However, Hurlburt has refined the procedure to include a portable random beeper, immediate journaling of the experiences, and critically, a subsequent clinical interview designed to clarify the characteristics of each experience and to categorize them based on objective criteria. The clinical interviews bring an objectivity to the categorization process that otherwise would be missing, and they train subjects to be objective about how they categorize their subsequent descriptions. Subjects report that within a few days it becomes remarkably easy to focus on the moment preceding the beep and categorize the nature of their experiences. Further, within-subject distributions for the types of experiences reported are highly reliable across days, suggesting that subjects have a similar range of experiences every day.

Type of Experience	Frequency
1. Thought in Sensory Images	32%
2. Thought in Inner Speech	31%
3. Thought without Speech or Images	21%
4. Emotional Feelings	24%
5. Sensory Experiences	22%

Table 10-2. The top five categories of experience reported by subjects in Hurlburt & Heavey, 2002.

As an example, the five primary experience categories reported in an early study by Hurlburt and Heavey are shown in Table 8-2. The data in the table are reported as a percentage of the total reports. The total scores exceed 100% because on about one-third of the occasions subjects reported having more than one kind of conscious experience at the same time. Hurlburt's categories do not map directly into the multiple categories of consciousness we have described here. However, it seems likely that his category for emotional feelings involve what we have termed phenomenal consciousness. His category for sensory images would likely involve what we have classed as reflective memories. Sensory experience would likely involve immediate sensing experiences. Anticipatory consciousness could well be a component of either emotional feelings or sensing. Hurlburt notes that subjects often report some difficulty clearly dividing experiences between these two categories.

One category which Hurlburt initially found surprising was the "thought without speech or images" category. However, on 21% of the sampling occasions in this study subjects reported having "thoughts" without having any awareness of either inner speech or sensory images. Some subjects even expressed doubt that such thoughts were common. Nevertheless, upon examination, they concluded that this was the best description. While subjects were surprised by these experiences, it seems worth noting that they are consistent with action planning. Planning involves evaluating different alternatives and assembling a possible motor plan, like deciding to run. However, considering such plans does not require either speech or images.

The rank ordering of experiences found in these studies is not always fixed. Sometimes the percentage of the Inner Speech category slightly exceeds the Sensory Image category, and sometimes Sensory Experiences exceed Emotional Feelings. However, what remains consistent is that large numbers of experiences fitting into all these categories are routinely reported. Note also, that the inner speech category, which would correspond to what we have called self-narrative consciousness, does not dominate these reports. Even for the college students in this study, a full two-thirds of the categories do not involve inner speech. These findings are consistent with the idea that consciousness is normally experienced in multiple and partially separated categories and that sensory, feeling, and action planning experiences may occur alone.

Thus far we have suggested that conscious experience emerges as perceptual and motor activities are bound together in synchronous activity with feelings during attention. We also suggested that this is adaptive because feelings add a context of self-status and reactivity that better enables agents to react to their experiences. Many higher-order aspects of attention summarized in this chapter enable conscious agents to focus on even more specific experiential details. However, as Hurlburt's findings illustrate, and as our own subjective experiences often make obvious, we do not focus on all possible aspects of experience at the same time. In fact, for any situation, it appears that we can only focus on one or two aspects of experience at a time, and that we then supplement that experience with other perspectives by shifting attention to them. In addition, research suggests that ongoing default networks for self-awareness and memory searching are frequently active in the absence of task activity and may even intrude on ongoing tasks. As noted in the opening quote, such extra-task intrusions on attention are sometimes characterized as mind wandering.[232] These observations suggest that conscious mind is often motivated periodically to check its status or consider memories, even in the middle of other tasks.

One question then, is how to make sense of the idea that topics of attention are bound in synchrony with ongoing feelings, but that not all topics are bound together at the same time, and that not all changing topics are even linked to the same task. The simple answer is that feature combinations compete for attention, so not all features are likely to be bound together in the same momentary focus. As we have noted, it is a combination of perceptual features and strong supporting feelings that are most likely to gain attention. These perceptual-feeling links provide an ongoing assessment of our reactions to the world. However, we don't focus on any one perception or feeling for very long. Consciousness is dynamic. Each moment of experience has its own combination of percepts and feelings that naturally branch among different topics. Further, it seems that the flow of task-related attention is routinely interrupted by mind-wandering processes. Some of these may include shifts to check for external risks and some may simply be circuits that monitor ongoing feelings of self. Self-talk may guide some of the task-related experiences, but self-talk is not essential or even involved in many of these experiences. Consciousness is much louder than words.

Concluding Comments

We have noted that various sensory and motor bindings tend to have their own time scales that contribute to the sequential flow of attention. Adding to these time differences there is often a shifting focus on sequential plans as we engage a task. We think about dinner, we consider what we need, and we plan a trip to the store. In each step there are often several subparts. If we are to travel outside the house, we may consider changing into more appropriate clothes or grooming our hair to make ourselves more presentable in public. Before we leave we may check to be sure the house will be locked while we are away. Each of these subtasks takes 300–500 ms to stabilize as a topic of attention and each adds to the ongoing flow of thought.

Given the many steps in even simple tasks, it is a wonder we ever manage to complete longer-term goals. However, it seems clear that we learn to connect activities together in larger plans, and that we are often able to keep plans active, or periodically revisit them until a goal is accomplished. Thus, the normal flow of conscious experience involves a shifting focus of attention between many different perceptions, actions, and feelings. However, it is unlikely that any frame of focus lasts for more than a few seconds. It seems that appreciating an event with a depth of consciousness is one of experiencing it from many perspectives and across many successive moments. Each moment has its own task-related focus and time course, and many tasks have subsets that require their own sequential shifts.

As such, it is amazing that consciousness seems so connected and meaningful. However, I contend that this constant shifting is simply the conscious minds way of compensating for its narrow focus of attention. It paints with a small brush, but the brush keeps moving and blending events together to form a broader picture. And because each shift in attention often shares some elements from the previous focus, the associations and memories tied to one focus are often connected in transition to others. In fact, when we review our experiences in memory, we can often retrace the connected elements and shift our focus of attention so as to re-experience a similar sequence of details in the situation.[233] Conveniently, however, most of the mind wandering side tasks don't get connected in this way. Thus, our memories of the situation are likely to be even better connected than the flow of experience that was occurring as those memories originally took form.

> **Ending Remarks**

If we are to develop a conscious robot we must ensure that it has a similar dynamic focus of attention that constantly switches between perceptions, actions, feelings, and memories as it engages the world. In fact, we should ensure that it also has mind-wandering tendencies that cause it to make periodic vigilant look-around shifts in attention to check for potential risks and ongoing look-inside shifts in attention to update its feelings of self. Of course, our robot will also need the memory resources necessary to blend all these piecemeal moments of attention together in a connected picture. Only then will it have the kind of dynamic experiences of the world that make human consciousness so interesting.

Epilogue: Beyond *Nothing Buttery*

Thus, although each effect is the resultant of its components, the product of its factors, we can not always trace the steps of the process, so as to see in the product the mode of operation of each factor. In this latter case, I propose to call the effect an emergent. It arises out of the combined agencies, but in a form which does not display the agents in action. – George Henry Lewes, *Problems of Life and Mind,* 1875

➤ **Introductory Remarks**

Constructionism is the holistic position that new properties emerge as parts combine and interact in aggregate organizations. This implies that new properties can only be fully understood within these larger organizations. In contrast, reductionism argues that holistic effects all result from the interaction of component parts. Thus, there is nothing more to be explained.

There are two seemingly opposing ways of thinking about the organization of the universe. One is a constructionist approach. The other is a reductionist one. Constructionism argues that new properties emerge within new organizations and that they can only be explained in that context. Reductionism argues that new properties can all be explained based on the properties of component parts. Reductionism has proven to be a highly productive strategy for connecting features across levels in science, to the point that it is sometimes argued that everything can be explained by reductionist theories. Some even go so far as to conclude that reductionism is the more fundamental strategy, and that constructionism is unnecessary or even unscientific. This emphasis sometimes leads reductionists to conclude that all complex phenomena are *nothing but* the interaction of their parts.

This argument was stated most strongly in what Francis Crick called the *astonishing hypothesis.* "That *You*, your joys and your sorrows, your memories and your ambitions, your sense of personal identity and free will, are in fact no more than the behavior of a vast assembly of nerve cells and their associated molecules."[234] In short, that You are *nothing but* the interaction of molecules and neurons. As we have noted, the paradox of this *nothing buttery*[235] argument is that while it seems true in the sense that each emergent organization must necessarily depend on the interaction of its parts, it remains false because an emergent phenomenon can never be explained fully by rules derived only from its component parts. *You* are more than your parts. *You* are a feeling-bound agency with perceptions, feelings, ideas, and skills that only come into existence as you interact with the world.

One reason emergent organizations do not display the properties of their parts is that some interactive properties are engaged in forming the new organization. For example, molecular organizations form by balancing chemical forces. In this process, some chemical forces are bound up forming the molecule, and thus are not active externally. As we noted previously, the strong interactive valences of sodium and chlorine atoms are engaged internally holding the molecule of table salt together. Thus, table salt does not display the noxious reductionist properties of unbound sodium and chlorine. A similar effect occurs when neural activity is bound in synchronous cycles of attention. We do not experience the many interactive forces that filter and bind features in a coherent focus of attention; those processes are tied up selecting what gains attention. We are only consciously aware of the phenomenal experiences that result from the holistic focus of attention.

A second reason that emergent organizations do not display properties like those of their component parts is that some properties depend on the structure of the new organizations they form. These structural properties cannot be explained by the parts, because the structures do not exist at that level. Many complex proteins bend and fold in varied shapes. The shapes themselves can introduce new interactive properties in a living cell. And proteins that fold badly may cause damage. When it comes to minds that can learn and remember, the structures change dynamically over time. Thus, conscious mind cannot be explained simply by pointing to the properties of neurons, because the concepts that guide them are learned through their history of interactions with the world. You are a unique individual because the neural connections that support your ideas and skills depend on your personal history.

Some claim that belief in emergence is incompatible with belief in reductionism. However, what seems to be lost in this argument is the recognition that reductionism and constructionism are contrarian complements. You cannot have one without the other. The value of reductionism is in its ability to connect emergent phenomena with underlying mechanisms. However, reductionist investigations would be of little value if there weren't emergent properties to be explained. To be useful, reductionist explanations first need to be enlightened by the discontinuous properties each new organization introduces. It is only then that attempts can be made to trace emergent properties back to interactions on lower levels. However, reductionism cannot fully explain properties that depend on the structures formed within the new organization.

A common distinction is made between weak and strong versions of emergence.[236] *Weak emergence* is the notion that higher-level phenomena are derived from the fundamental processes of lower-level components. Thus, no new laws of physics are required to explain them. *Strong emergence* is the notion that while higher-level phenomena may be derivable from lower-level processes, when their properties depend on the structure of new organizations they cannot be fully explained by lower-level properties. Thus, new laws are required to explain them.[237]

It seems my version of emergence is best characterized as a probabilistic strong version. Higher-level processes are derived from lower-level properties, and new structures are even *derivable in principle*.[238] As a result, the world is connected; no new laws of physics are required. However, due to the possible variations in new organizations, we cannot predict their discontinuous properties simply by knowing about what parts are involved because we cannot predict how those parts will assemble and how the new combinations will interact. Thus, we must formulate new *summary laws* to describe the higher-order interactions we discover. As Nobel laureate Phillip Anderson succinctly summarized the problem, *more is different*.

> The main fallacy in this kind of thinking is that the reductionist hypothesis does not by any means imply a "constructionist" one: The ability to reduce everything to simple fundamental laws does not imply the ability to start from those laws and reconstruct the universe. .... The behavior of large and complex aggregates of elementary particles, it turns out, is not to be understood in terms of a simple extrapolation of the properties of a few particles. Instead, at each level of complexity entirely new properties appear, and the understanding of the new behaviors requires re-search which I think is as fundamental in its nature as any other.[239]

To summarize the ideas in this section, we need to consider three aspects of emergence. Since the moment of the big bang new organizations have been evolving. However: 1) The new organizations cannot be explained simply based on their parts, because the discontinuous properties of each new organization involve more than their component parts. 2) The claim that new organizations introduce new interactive properties means that as new structures evolve new forces emerge. Natural selection is a major force in living systems, but it does not exist at the chemical level. 3) Emergent structures are connected with their underlying parts. This *emergent interconnectedness* is what makes reductionist analyses helpful at times. However, emergent properties can only be understood fully based on their functions within the organization in which they emerge. Life simply cannot be explained fully in terms of chemical forces. Associative mind cannot be understood fully in terms of living cells. Consciousness cannot be understood using only neural associations.

EMERGENT ORGANIZATIONS AND REDUCTIONIST DEPENDENCIES

The appearance of new levels in this evolution
depends on one critical ability: each new level must
collect and protect resources in a way that outweighs
the increased cost of a more complex structure. If the
seeded aggregate collects resources rapidly enough to
"pay" for the structural complexity, the seed will
spread.[240]

Anderson's note about how new properties appear at different levels of complexity is expanded by John Holland's comments that each emergent level of organization must pay a resource debt to support the costs of its added complexity. When we think about emergent systems, we often refer to them as operating on different levels. For example, we recognize that biological properties emerge from the interactive dynamics of chemical systems. However, because new properties emerge from interactions among supporting systems, it follows that the new properties must be adaptive enough to maintain the integrity of their component parts. Biological systems couldn't continue to exist if they didn't maintain the chemical processes needed for their construction. This same dependency occurs across each new level of organization. We need to put this aspect of emergence in better perspective.

If there is one truth about the universe, it is that its component parts are highly interactive. After the Big Bang, fundamental particles gradually took form and gave rise to simple physical structures like atoms of hydrogen and helium. Clouds of hydrogen and helium were subsequently drawn into larger stellar organizations by gravitational forces. However, it took the interaction of fusion processes within helium-based stars to create intermediate elements like carbon, and nitrogen, and oxygen. It was in this web of physical interactions that the atomic structures needed for organic chemistry gradually evolved. All this organization was based on *thermodynamic selection*, the tendency of physical objects to combine in forms that reduce energy differences.[241] Thermodynamic selection is directional, but it is not adaptive. That is, it does not change how it forms new organizations based on past successes in managing energy flows. However, thermodynamic selection is a fundamental process in nature. As Eric Chaisson has argued, it is effectively the "motor" of all evolution.[242]

Life emerged when thermodynamic processes evolved membrane bound cells that could maintain their organization. A key structure in these cells were ribosomes, chemical collectives that could use RNA codes to guide protein production. This process resulted in a breakthrough beyond thermodynamic controls, because the genetic codes could be used to guide the formation of new organizational copies. It followed from this coding-based reproduction strategy that living agents who succeeded in reproducing would pass on their genetic codes while those that did not reproduce would not. Thus, more successful codes were reproduced more often.

Because genetic coding systems also introduced slight variations from time to time, this scheme allowed living systems with better codes to evolve *adaptively* over generations. We call this evolutionary process *natural selection*. However, living systems were still dependent on their physical components. To be stable they had to support the thermodynamic forces needed to maintain their parts. As it became popular to say, living systems had to pay an *entropy debt* to survive.[243] However, once these new organizations were able to support their parts on a thermodynamic level, *natural selection* was able to introduce emergent properties like reproduction in living systems.

Associative mind emerged when living organizations evolved breakthrough cells specialized, for communicating and coding their workflows. These specialized cells, neurons, used sodium and potassium energy flows through a tubular projection, an axon, to pass signals to other neurons. Receptor cells converted external inputs into neuronal signals. Effector cells used neural inputs to release chemical signals that controlled muscle movement. A key feature of these neural networks was that they could change their signaling patterns based on internal feedback. This coding scheme enabled neural systems to evolve *adaptively* over successive activities. They could learn and remember across experiences. Thus, they could refine and extend their associative processes. However, because the supporting mechanisms of mind depended on living cells they could only be successful if they created living systems that were better able to survive. In effect, in order to succeed associative minds had to pay a *survival debt*. However, once living systems with associative minds were able to compete on a survival level, *associative selection* was able to introduce emergent properties like learning and memory not seen in simpler living systems.

As we have described, consciousness emerged when associative minds evolved a breakthrough architecture that was able to encode momentary assemblies in focused states of attention. A key feature of this architecture was the ability to engage synchronous arrays of associative activity in mutually supporting perceptions and feelings that increased in coherence and intensity due to the recurrent thalamocortical architecture. This coding scheme enabled conscious agents to organize attention based on coherent perceptual and modulatory inputs and to reinterpret neural inputs as qualitative components of attention. If the qualia of conscious experience did not have adaptive effects at the attentional level, they could not pay for the cost of their more complex structure and they would not be maintained. But once they could pay their *associative debt* by enhancing processing at the conscious level, qualia could also introduce higher-order representations like intentions, values, and feelings of self that did not exist at the associative level of neurons.

As conscious agents, we tend to think of conscious mind as a single level of emergent organization. However, conscious minds were much like the neurons that made associative minds possible. Their interactions did more than simply enhance feeling-bound attention. Conscious minds were breakthrough processes whose extensions provided a social bridge for coordinating individual agents. One consequence of this social bridge was the ability to engage other conscious agents in synchronous cycles of activity. Ideas and artifacts could be worked interactively. Individuals could gain status by contributing to this process. Yet the ideas and artifacts formed in this way did not belong fully to any single agent. The incremental products belonged to the larger collective. Still, because cultural minds depended on conscious minds, cultures could only succeed if they made their supporting conscious agents more adaptive. In effect, cultures also had to pay a *consciousness debt*. However, once cultures could support their conscious agents, *cultural selection* could create institutional processes and incremental products that extended well beyond the capacity of individual minds.

The interdependence between emergent processes and their supporting parts often adds to the confusion between constructionist processes and their reductionist dependencies. As we have noted, emergent organizations depend on the interactive processes of their supporting parts to create more complex organizations. There is an upward path of causal organization, but the emergent properties they construct may be largely discontinuous from the supporting parts. Of course, the emergent properties can only succeed if they also maintain the selection prospects of their parts. However, the value of an emergent property can provide a downward path for organization. If it is highly adaptive that will enhance the adaptive value of its parts.

Consider the case of altruism, the tendency of agents to take actions that benefit others even when the agents incur costs to themselves in doing so. The most obvious case of this is the parental care of offspring. Not all animals provide parental care. Animals with precocial young, those requiring little time to mature after hatching or birth, typically leave their offspring to survive on their own. However animals with altricial young, those requiring more time to mature, need to provide parental care to enable their offspring to survive. To support this extended care, these animals have evolved associative mechanisms for recognizing young, sign stimuli that release caring drives, and action patterns for things like cleaning young, providing nourishment, and defending them from predators.

Biologists emphasize that these associative mechanisms are guided by certain genes which have to be maintained to support this behavior. Thus, they claim that the altruistic properties are essentially controlled by the need to pay their genetic survival debt, that is, the passage of parental genes to their offspring. As we have emphasized, emergent properties must support underlying levels of control, so the biological argument that altruism must support gene selection sufficiently well to maintain supporting genes is essentially sound, unless the biologist extends the argument to claim that altruism is nothing but kin selection. This claim is another nothing buttery argument. The reason I make this point is that many of the social behaviors that emerge in this selection process are not limited to functioning only for kin selection. Like other emergent processes they often extend in novel directions.

For example, in addition to feeding-related caring, it is common for parents to come to the defense of their offspring by defending them from predators. However, the emergence of caring feelings on the conscious level do not all map directly back to kin selection. For example, pet dogs are known to defend their extended human families when members of that family are threatened. In the same way, human caretakers, whose pets come to be treated as family members, often defend their pets as if they were their children. These cases of cross-species defense emerge from caring-related processes that often support within species gene selection. However, they result in feelings of caring on a conscious level that extend beyond kin selection. And if strong caring feelings enhance the social status of an agent, that increase in status is likely to add to the value of the genes that make their extended caring possible.

Caring in these situations must still support the genes that promote kin selection at some level, but what should be clear is that when a conscious agent runs into a burning house to save treasured pictures or save heirlooms, they are risking their lives to protect objects they care about. And even though conscious agents must pay a survival debt to the genes that support kin selection, the debts supporting their feelings are not coded in the neural signals that engage the qualia of caring. The conscious feelings that motivate altruistic actions are discontinuous from the biological links that promote kin selection. No one reports that they ran into a burning house to save pets or personal properties because they thought it was good for their genes. Just the opposite, they report that caring made them willing to risk their lives. In effect, the qualia of caring have emergent properties that extend beyond genetic selection.

SOME QUESTIONS ABOUT CONSCIOUSNESS

Earlier we noted that simple life urges are integrated into increasingly complex forms in the brainstem, and are subsequently recombined and prioritized in pre-conscious networks beginning in upper-pontine regions. Many of these preconscious life urges project to the thalamus as modulatory inputs. We argued that those modulatory life urges associated with features that gain attention would have their brainstem arousal enhanced, because part of the return loops from the cortex project back to the brainstem during attention. In addition, we emphasized that some upper-pontine inputs to the limbic thalamus project on to the limbic cortex, effectively creating a separate path for feelings to reach the cortex. Further, we noted that activations in the limbic thalamus also influence subcortical feeling-related processing during attention. These limbic pathways to the thalamus and cortex also contribute to feeling-bound attention. However, these pathways do not explain the qualities of subjective feelings that this circuitry makes possible.

The elemental qualities of conscious experience are referred to as *qualia*. As we have characterized them, qualia are dependent on the neural architecture from which they emerge. Indeed, the architecture ensures that they represent an ongoing focus of attention. Further, neural inputs are often adjusted to influence the saliency of certain qualia, so qualia are not fully independent from their neural sources. However, qualia have discontinuous properties that are not predicted from neural inputs. We do not experience neural firing patterns. We experience images that we can recognize, behavioral intentions that motivate us, and feelings of our ongoing self-status. Some question why these experiences should seem so interesting, but as we have noted, discontinuous properties are better understood within the organizations in which they emerge. Qualia serve to summarize and categorize attention. It is reasonable to assume that those features that win the competition for attention would be considered interesting by the agents who experience them.

One reason we proposed to explain why conscious agents do not experience neural input patterns, is that the conscious agents themselves only emerge in storms of attention. Thus, they are only aware of the qualities of attention they encounter there, not the underlying processes from which those qualities emerge. Another reason proposed for why conscious agents do not experience neural firing patterns is that those patterns involve complex arrays of inputs and intensities. To pay attention to them would be like paying attention to all the pixels in a picture. It would require more time and vastly more resources. However, it would serve little function. Summarizing an array of pixels as an image or feeling is simply more efficient. And because conscious agents can learn and remember, the functions of these summary interpretations can all be acquired that way. In fact, because discontinuous properties cannot be predicted, the only way conscious agents can know about them is to experience them directly and learn what they are like. This is the process by which we come to understand all emergent properties.

When perceptions combine with feelings, we experience a core sense of our self reacting to the world. We termed this experience the phenomenal self. But when we notice how gaze affects our attention, we often experience an *observer self,* a visual agency with a specific orientation. Anticipatory learning results in the experience of an *anticipatory self*, an agency that anticipates changes in perceptions and feelings. Using motor planning as an anticipatory cue, results in an experience of *self-agency*, a sense of being able to change feelings by planning actions. Declarative memories result in a *reflective self,* a self in which memory associations co-occur with ongoing perceptions.[244] As we learn to manage attention, we experience the process as one of a *reasoning self,* an agency that is capable of guiding its own attention to help it perform a task. The use of language leads to the experience of a *narrative self*, an agency who can reason using signs.

In short, the *self* is not a singular phenomenon, but rather a complex composite of internal experiences that influence how agents react to the world. Given that many theorists have difficulty thinking about even the simplest aspects of emergence, it should come as no surprise to discover that there is much confusion about the emergent nature of conscious self. As we have argued, emergent properties occur in all new organizations. Consciousness is not a unique case. Our goal in this chapter is, therefore, to review some common questions about consciousness and to place them in the context of the model of feeling-bound attention that we have developed. The topics are varied and often controversial, and some theorists have taken strong positions that only seem to add to the confusion. However, you won't really feel like you understand conscious mind until you can put these issues in better perspective.

Can Conscious Awareness Be Shared?

When conscious agents interact with each other, they do so by exchanging signs about both their external focus of attention and their internal action plans and feelings. In fact, it is only when conscious minds coordinate their attention with each other in a shared focus on cues, intentions, and feelings that they feel their minds have met.[245]

Qualia are the subjective qualities of experience that emerge as conscious agents interpret the neural patterns that gain their attention as conscious representations. However, there is no reason to believe that other agents make the exact same interpretations you do, even when they encounter the same situation. One reason is that individuals vary due to genetic differences. Because the genes for color vision are on the X-chromosome, human males only get one version. So if there is a defect, males are more likely to have some aspect of color-blindness. In contrast, because females have two X-chromosomes, they are less likely to be color deficient. In fact, because some color genes respond to slightly different color wavelengths, females may have two gene variants for the "same" color. As a result, these females perceive more variations in colors than do normal males or females who lack extra variations in color genes.[246] In fact, some females may have two different color genes for reds, greens, and blues. Having differences in color genes ensures that different people don't all share the same visual qualia.

Even though each individual is different, it is also the case that as members of the same species we all share many of the same neural systems for attention and feelings. We may have slightly different color genes than others in our group, but we use them in a similar way. We also share many basic developmental experiences. And in many cases, we may share similar cultural experiences and values. This means that while we can never understand *exactly* what it is like to be another agent, to the extent we share similar neural systems, developmental experiences, and cultural values we can often empathize as to how we might react in the situations of others. In effect, we can gain insights into the motives and actions of others by interpreting how we would feel in their situation.

Some argue that science must be objective, and then note that conscious experience is largely subjective. Thus they conclude consciousness cannot be studied scientifically. However, this subjective-objective dichotomy is not complete, nor is it unique to consciousness. All complex systems have numerous processes that interact internally, and yet many of those processes are not obvious on an external level. Atoms encounter their own internal "subjective" forces based on things like shared electron shell structures, but we can only partly map out those forces in objective studies. Developing gene networks sense subjective attraction gradients that influence their growth, but we can only partly objectify how that sensing affects them. Neural modules in the brain have many private interactions about which we are rarely aware. However, while we don't know *what it is like* to be an atom, or a gene network, or a neural module, we can nevertheless discover objective laws about how they behave in certain situations.

The fact that many aspects of conscious mind are subjective is really no different. Thus, while the qualia of individual conscious experiences remain partly private and subjective, that doesn't mean we cannot recognize that they occur in a similar way in others. Further, because we have higher-order mappings of *what it is like* experiences in our own consciousness, we can sometimes recognize the effects of similar subjective experiences in other minds. Thus, we actually have the potential for more insight into the behavior of conscious minds than we do for the behavior of atoms or neural modules. We can not only form objective laws about how other minds behave, but to the extent we share similar subjective experiences with them, we can also try to adopt their perspectives, empathize with their situations, and explore how we might behave in similar situations. Following this strategy, we can often gain subjective insights into other minds, and by analogy, share in their perceptual and emotive reactions.

This strategy works even for agents like Tom, because we share similar networks for attention and similar core emotions with him. Of course, subjectively-driven analogies may sometimes be in error. However, objective laws are rarely complete or easily applied in real-world situations. As long as subjective analogies, grounded in our own experience, are compatible with our objective knowledge of a situation they are the best tools we have for improving our understanding of another mind. So while we can never know *exactly what it is like to be another agent*, by attending to what other agents notice and how they react, we can often form cogent analogies for what it would be like for us to be in their situation. And social agents often help each other in this process by exchanging communication signals that make their feelings and intentions more obvious to their partners. This greatly adds to our ability to interpret their feelings accurately.

Some qualia only emerge when we share attention with another agent. When we feel our minds meet in a situation, we feel a bond. When the interactions involve caring, the bonds can be powerful, and the mutual interactions can strengthen friendships, increase trust, and promote mutual understanding. However, even when we share attention with an opponent, there is a degree of mutual recognition and shared understanding. We gain some sense of what he knows. He gains a sense of how we may react. We may even exchange feelings of concern and confidence in the moment. Shared attention is an essential part of bonding with a pet, parenting a child, helping a friend, counseling a client, or even dealing with an adversary. These are emergent aspects of conscious experience that would never occur if we were not able to share aspects of our consciousness with others.

Is Consciousness Merely an Illusion?

> For Dennett, it is not a case of the Emperor having no clothes. It is rather that the clothes have no Emperor.[247]
>
> But that is the beauty of it! In a proper theory of consciousness, the Emperor is not just deposed, but exposed, shown to be a cunning conspiracy of lesser operatives whose activities jointly account for the "miraculous" powers of the Emperor. Banished along with the Emperor are what might be called the Imperial Properties: the two most mysterious varieties being the Qualia Enjoyed by the Emperor and the Imperial Edicts of Conscious Will.[248]

Whereas David Chalmers accepts that there are vivid subjective qualities associated with conscious experience, while claiming they lack any adaptive function, Daniel Dennett argues that the vividness and importance of conscious experiences are merely illusions, nothing but the effects of the nervous system. In fact, Dennett claims that Chalmers' hard problem is just another illusion. As he argues, we, like Chalmers, have been fooled by the illusions of consciousness. We think we experience *qualia*, the subjective qualities of awareness. We think we have conscious control over our actions, *free will* as it is known. However, Dennett claims these seemingly "magical effects" all have mundane explanations that require "no revolutions in physics, no emergent novelties."[249] In this section, we address Dennett's concern about the illusory properties of qualia. We will defer his concern about the illusory properties of free will to the next section.

Less than a hundred years ago, many were convinced that life could not be a property of physical systems. They suggested that an added *vitalistic force* was needed to explain how physical structures could give rise to the seemingly nonphysical property of life. Today, life is still considered a wondrous property, but we no longer feel the need to posit the existence of a separate vital force. We have learned enough about the intricate machinery of the cell, DNA codes, their transcription, and code-guided enzyme and protein production, to understand how a myriad of coding, signaling, and reactive modules can result in interacting cellular organizations with emergent properties. They can manage energy flows, sustain their activity, construct and repair cellular structures, and even reproduce whole new organizations with similar properties. But while life can be understood as an emergent property of interacting coding, signaling, and reacting collectives, no one claims that the interactive properties of life do not exist.

Over time we have come to understand that associative mind depends on the interaction of processes in neural networks. However, that doesn't mean those interactions cannot also have emergent effects. We have now learned enough about the intricate machinery of the neural networks in the brain, and about how neural coding changes its reactions, to understand how a myriad of coding, signaling, and reactive interactions result in dynamic neural processes with emergent properties. They can learn, remember, and react to inputs in adaptive ways. Associative mind is an emergent property of such neurally-guided coding, signaling, and reacting collectives. No one claims that these associative processes cannot emerge in such neural networks. Indeed, we can now simulate neural networks on a computer that can learn to perform specific tasks.

In the previous chapters, we have learned enough about the re-programming made possible by a selective focus of perceptual inputs and life urges, to understand how a myriad of binding, filtering, and synchronous thalamocortical interactions enable vertebrate brains to link perceptions and feelings in a coherent focus of attention that can gain consciousness. We have also seen how many aspects of focused attention contribute to the sense of self. You, and I, and Tom are conscious agents with a phenomenal sense of our own feelings as we react to the world. We have a sense of identity, a sense of personal history, and a sense of self-control. We can even interact to influence those properties in each other's' attention. It makes no sense to claim that these properties of conscious mind do not exist, or that they cannot influence how we think and what we do.

Dennett has argued that the qualia of conscious experience are *nothing but* the interactions of lower-level systems, and thus that their explanation requires "no emergent novelties." But as we have emphasized, when lower-level systems are brought together in dynamic organizations, novel properties emerge. This is the process by which new properties have emerged since the universe began. However, it is important to note that emergent properties must be understood in the context of the organizations that display them, because they only have functions within those organizations. Conscious feelings guide attention and promote adaptive reactions in the body. They even influence likely transitions to new topics of attention, but they can only be understood within dynamic systems of attention.

This is where Dennett misses the point. The fact that the Emperor's clothes and his advice can be attributed to lower-level agents does not prevent the Emperor from having his own ideas and effects on the world. All emperors have subordinates that do much of their work. And while some may claim that this means that an emperor is nothing but a guy with an outlandish wardrobe and clever advisors, his central role in the empire and his ability to make imperial edicts, provides him with a large measure of personal influence. In fact, sometimes he may ignore some of his advisors while favoring others. The processes that lie at the center of attention in vertebrate brains have a similar ability to promote their individual points of view. Thus, it is the conscious agent's ability to favor some goals over other and to coordinate the empire in the pursuit of his preferred goals that endows him with imperial powers.

Dennett notes that while conscious mind is supported by neural advisors, it frequently seems to overleap their advice by creating subjective interpretations that don't follow directly from them. Conscious interpretations thus seem to be subject to errors and illusions. In fact, it is well known that conscious mind often claims ownership of some decisions, when the decisions, or the advice leading to them, originate largely from unconscious advisors. Based on such observations, Dennett concludes that consciousness is largely an illusory process that doesn't map well to reality. However, this conclusion follows from the fact that, as a reductionist, Dennett apparently believes that the properties of consciousness should all map directly back to their component parts. But as we have emphasized, emergent organizations have discontinuous properties that do not map directly back to their component parts. It is this discontinuity that gives new organizations special functions.

The fact that conscious mind reinterprets some of its inputs in discontinuous ways does not prevent those interpretations from being adaptive. The subjective experiences of conscious mind do not come into existence simply to rubber-stamp underlying neural inputs. To make the composite more consistent, conscious mind may even take a few liberties in how it interprets the inputs of its advisors. You instinctively begin reacting to a car veering into your lane some 200 ms before you consciously become aware of the threat. However, you attribute your entire reaction to conscious awareness. And while this may lead some to view consciousness as being an illusion, somehow these "magical" interpretations result in highly adaptive properties. They create an integrated personal sense of self, a sense of agency, a sense of action ownership, and a sense of self-control that extend well beyond the properties of individual advisors.

Do Conscious Minds Have Free Will?

> At the core of the question of free will is a debate about the psychological causes of action. That is, is the person an autonomous entity who genuinely chooses how to act from among multiple possible options? Or is the person essentially just one link in a causal chain, so that the person's actions are merely the inevitable product of lawful causes stemming from prior events, and no one ever could have acted differently than how he or she actually did?[250]

The issue of *free will* was prominently brought into question some thirty years ago when Benjamin Libet noted that the *readiness potential*,[251] an index of the preparatory motor organization in the pre-supplementary motor area (SMA), began some 550 ms before a voluntary action was produced.[252] However, Libet found that subjects were not consciously aware that they were initiating an action until about 350 ms after the readiness potential had started. This suggested to some that the decision to act was made unconsciously. In fact, we have found that it takes some 300–500 ms for inputs to gain consciousness, so the 350 ms delay for action planning to gain consciousness is entirely consistent with these findings. However, this delay implies that early aspects of action planning must necessarily precede conscious awareness of them. Still, because agents become conscious of their plans 200 ms before a motor action starts, and because this delay provides time for conscious agents to inhibit an ongoing action, Libet argued it was consistent with conscious control. However, critics claimed that this kind of control qualified more as a case of *free won't,* rather than one of *free will*.[253] Thus, they questioned whether consciousness could initiate voluntary actions, and, by implication, whether free will really existed.

Because processing in the left motor cortex controls action on the right side of the body, and processing in the right motor cortex controls action on the left side of the body, it is possible to use the side of the dominant readiness potential to predict which hand a subject will use to respond in these studies. Most people are right-handed and generally initiate actions via activity in the left SMA, even if they subsequently switch to the right SMA to produce outputs with their left hand. However, experimenters watching the readiness potential can detect which hand a subject will use prior to their action. Again, this seems to degrade the idea that the subjects have conscious control. However, if subjects are instructed to press with their right hand, it is the left SMA that becomes most active immediately prior to responding. If they are instructed to press with their left hand, then right SMA activity precedes their actions. Thus, the very SMA activity that brought conscious control into question can apparently be influenced by prior instructions. Subjects never report that they have difficulty preventing the non-instructed hand from taking control. This implies that SMA activity provides a marker for action planning, but that it is not the source of conscious control.

In a previous chapter we noted that simply looking at a cup, or thinking about the taste of coffee, can bias our decision to reach for a coffee cup. Thus, the fact that reaching programs are largely assembled unconsciously, does not mean that we cannot consciously influence them during planning, or even before background planning begins. Hence it is not surprising that we often interpret such actions as due to conscious planning. However, the fact that we sometimes reinterpret such events in discontinuous ways, does not prevent those emergent representations from being adaptive. Research has shown that when a subject believes he does *not* have conscious control, he is less likely to notice and respond to errors.[254] In fact, his readiness potential in the SMA is reduced some 200 ms before he takes action.[255] This implies that a belief in self-control actually changes neural activity. Belief in self-control makes an agent more intent on taking action, more sensitive to errors, and more likely to correct them.

Despite such findings, some continue to believe that determinism cannot be compatible with free will. This philosophical position is known as *incompatibilism*. A common argument, one that we have encountered before, is that there are no emergent processes in mind, all mental activity is determined by lower-level neural processes. Thus, there is no way for conscious awareness to influence choices. Those who subscribe to nothing buttery arguments or those who believe that consciousness is merely an epiphenomenon, generally adopt this position. In contrast, others argue that consciously-guided determinism is essential for free will. They argue that determinism is not fixed to a single path. It can be influenced by conscious attention. This view of free will is commonly known as *compatibilism*. Given what we know about the interconnections between physical and mental processes, there is every reason to assume that a number of deterministic mental processes sometimes bias decisions. In fact, the idea that mechanisms on multiple levels determine actions, and that some of these mechanisms may be guided by conscious awareness is consistent with the laws commonly used to attribute responsibility for actions. Consider what happens when someone is suspected of having caused the death of another.

> If the evidence suggests that the suspect planned to cause the death, then the subject will be charged with premeditated murder … an action guided by conscious planning. If there is evidence that the suspect was aware of the possibility of serious injury but acted more on impulse … then he or she is likely to be charged with second-degree murder, an act in which the outcome was less clearly considered. If the suspect was not aware that he or she had put another at risk but acted in careless disregard of the possible consequence of the action, then the subject will usually be charged with manslaughter, an action for which the outcome should have been considered ahead of time, but was not. However, if the suspect was acting with due care and was unaware that his or her actions were putting another at risk, then the death will be ruled accidental, not intentional, and the suspect will not be charged at all.[256]

Legal rules of this sort attribute responsibility for actions to the extent that the consequences of acting were consciously considered ahead of time and less so when the consequences were not well considered. If attorneys were philosophers, then it seems likely that every defense attorney would be a confirmed *incompatibilist*. He would start each trial with an argument that his client did not have free will and, therefore, even if you could prove he did something, it would be unjust to punish him for making decisions he had no control over. In contrast, the prosecutor would likely be an aggressive *compatibilist*. She would argue that the suspect not only had free will, but that he planned his actions well ahead of time and, therefore, that he is responsible for their consequences. This compatibilist position is closer to the general stance on free will and responsibility found in most modern legal systems. In general, the more evidence there is that an agent consciously planned and considered his behavior before acting, the more he is considered to have exercised his will, and the more responsible he is considered to be for his actions.

It is true that an agent may be guided by strong instinctive motives at times, and thus may not fully consider her action. In such cases, her guilt may be excused due to the passion of the moment. However, even when an action is not well planned, a person may still recognize its negative consequences and inhibit it. Sometimes these inhibitory reactions occur as an agent logically considers the physical consequences of an action. Sometimes they occur as a person recognizes the action may lead to social rebuke. Sometimes they are merely based on vague emotional feelings. However, the more different causes an agent may be guided by; the less well her behavior can be explained based on any single cause. Thus, simply by changing her focus of attention to one preferred source of control, rather than another, the agent may be able to change her decision. Free will in this scenario does not mean that the agent acts in the absence of deterministic causes, rather it means that a conscious agent may influence what deterministic causes she chooses to guide her decisions.

These ideas follow directly from the model of consciousness we have proposed in this book. As we have argued, a key to managing conscious control is the ability to influence what cues gain attention. We cannot attend to all sources of control at the same time, only to a few. Thus, it is possible to influence what cues we attend to when making a decision. *By selectively attending to those cues that are more important to us, we can bias our attention to them, even when other deterministic forces are competing for attention.*

By following this strategy, a conscious agent can overcome instinctive reactions, learned habits, and emotional dispositions. In fact, as Richard Dawkins proposed, at times he may even be able to rebel against the tyranny of his own selfish genes. Following this logic, the more sources of deterministic control a conscious agent has to choose among, the more *degrees of freedom* she has for biasing her decisions. Her decisions are still among deterministic forces, but her goals and values can influence what forces she considers. Using personal goals and values to make a decision is the essence of free will.

Can Qualia Have Effects in the Physical World?

Qualia are not themselves causal, and to assume otherwise would go against the laws of physics.[257]

Many authors have suggested that consciousness itself is causal. But consciousness accompanies particular brain

events and is not a material entity. Instead, it is a process
that is entailed by those material events. Those events are
part of the physical world, and that world is causally closed;
only matter energy can be causal.[258]

Another issue in which the emergent properties of consciousness commonly result in confusion is the question of whether conscious experiences can have effects in the physical world. The quotes above are from Gerald Edelman, a Nobel laureate. He claims that conscious qualities cannot be causal because the idea that subjective feelings can produce effects in the physical world would violate the laws of physics. This conclusion is related to the comment by Dennett earlier, when he suggested that revolutions in physics would be needed for qualia to influence the physical world. But why does the idea that subjective feelings can have effects in the physical world seem so challenging for these theorists? It seems the primary reason is that many theorists subscribe to a strong dualistic separation between subjective mind and physical matter. Thus, they see no mechanism by which the experiences of mind can affect the physical world. Their logic is categorical. Causal mechanisms are physical. Subjective experiences are not. Therefore, subjective experiences cannot be causal.

Dualism can be largely traced back to Descartes. Descartes argued that mind and body were composed of different kinds of substances. However, Descartes also suggested that when mind and body were bound together in a living agent, they were capable of bidirectional interactions. In fact, he proposed that the pineal gland served as the seat of the soul in the human brain. In that function, he argued that the *animal spirits* of the body could interface with the associative components of mind in the pineal. Further, he argued that mental processes in the pineal could interface with the rest of the brain by exerting forces on the central ventricles of the brain. Descartes noted that this strategy of mental control was indirect, similar to how the force of wind on a ship's sails influences its path. However, his analogy clearly implied that mental processes could be causal.[259]

Descartes' interactionist ideas lost favor as it became clear that his model for interactive control was flawed. There was no evidence the body sent *animal spirits* to the pineal. There was no evidence that the pineal gland produced associative waves in the ventricles. It was not that many theorists didn't assume that interactions between mind and body could still occur, but the mechanisms by which those interactions were implemented were not obvious. As a result, Descartes' dualistic separation between mind and body continued to dominate thought, while his interactionist position was largely ignored. Following this line of thinking, many modern theorists like Chalmers, Dennett, and Edelman believe that subjective experiences are epiphenomena. An *epiphenomenon* is a philosophical concept invented to support dualistic thinking. It assumes that phenomenal experiences can exist, while denying they have any function in the physical world. However, simply inventing such a concept does not mean that epiphenomena really exist.

Like Descartes, others believe that while mind and body have partly different properties, they can nevertheless interact. Further, some of us also recognize that nothing buttery arguments are incomplete. Simply reducing emergent organizations to the interaction of their parts does not mean that all the properties of a new substance can be explained away. All the major physical organizations in the universe emerged after the Big Bang, and yet we do not deny that atoms, stars, or galaxies exist, or that they have discontinuous properties that add to the forces of the universe. We even accept that the emergent properties of physical organizations can be causal, because we believe that, at some level, their properties are derived from connections with fundamental forces. However, many reject the idea that the emergent properties of consciousness can have effects in the physical world, because they don't see how conscious feelings are connected with physical matter and its forces.

As scientists have looked for mechanisms supporting the functions of mind, their focus has been drawn to the neural organization of the brain. Neural networks can learn and remember. Some activate arousal systems that increase the activity of other systems. Some even motivate actions. But neural networks are not disconnected from the physical world. They depend on physical changes that influence connectivity at specific neural nodes. We can even simulate these physical processes on a computer. Yet somehow, when it comes to consciousness, many theorists suddenly choose to abandon the idea that there can be causal links between the qualia of experiences in conscious mind and the physical world.

The fact that emergent properties are partially dependent on their parts, as proposed at the start of this chapter, means that mind and matter are not disconnected. In fact, emergent interconnectedness means that mind and matter can never be disconnected. Ascending neural information enables reflexive reactions to be integrated into more complex life urges in brainstem proto-self regions that support life. Projections from these regions to thalamic attention networks enable these life urges to influence what features are likely to gain attention. And those life urges that come to be bound with the topics of attention introduce yet other emergent properties. They are experienced as concepts and feelings that can influence mental decisions. But as noted, there are also downward dependencies between the properties of conscious awareness and the neural systems that support them.

Thus as conscious decisions are made, the interconnections that are prioritized enhance activity in underlying neural systems. In particular, the life urges that gain attention have their reactive effects in the body intensified. And when conscious decisions involve actions, these downward effects activate motor networks that release acetylcholine to cause muscles to contract. Having interconnections between conscious processing and underlying neural networks, and from neural networks on to motor cells, means that the mind doesn't have to violate the laws of physics to produce effects in the world. Anything that can gain conscious attention can influence decisions that engage motor actions.

Is Consciousness Merely Information Integration?

According to integrated information theory (IIT), consciousness is determined by the causal properties of any physical system acting upon itself. That is, consciousness is a fundamental property of any mechanism that has cause-effect power upon itself.[260]

[IIT] predicts that consciousness is graded, is common among biological organisms and can occur in some very simple systems. Conversely, it predicts that feed-forward networks, even complex ones, are not conscious, nor are aggregates such as groups of individuals or heaps of sand. Also, in sharp contrast to widespread functionalist beliefs, IIT implies that digital computers, even if their behaviour were to be functionally equivalent to ours, and even if they were to run faithful simulations of the human brain, would experience next to nothing.[261]

The information integration theory (IIT) of consciousness was introduced by Guilio Tononi in 2004 and later expanded in conjunction with Christoph Koch.[262] Tononi's model grew out of his analyses of the patterns of thalamocortical activity that occurred in studies of consciousness with Gerald Edelman.[263] He concluded that thalamocortical activity needed to reach a high level of coherent processing, a score he termed *phi*, before people reported conscious awareness. Earlier in this book, I noted that Tononi's analysis provided insight into why conscious awareness was a delayed aspect of attention. As the research suggested, it took some 300 ms or more before there was sufficient coherence in thalamocortical processing for conscious experience to emerge.

The model of consciousness that we have proposed here depends on the thalamocortical architecture. Phenomenal consciousness is proposed to emerge from processing in this architecture when life-urge dispositions are bound with perceptions in coherent thalamocortical cycles of attention. However, Tononi's mathematical model for calculating *phi* is not dependent on the thalamocortical architecture, it is a measure of the dynamic coherence of mutually integrated activity within a system. Thus, as Tononi formally extended the model, he argued that consciousness need not even be limited to brains, any system that has some coherent degree of cause-effect power on itself, even a set of complex XOR gates, could show high phi scores and be "conscious".

In effect, IIT proposes that there is a simpler kind of "consciousness", what I will call here, *integrative sentience*, that depends only of high levels of information integration. IIT accepts that this integrative sentience may be graded from the simple integration of living cells to the more complex integration of human consciousness. Further, IIT does not claim that simple integrative sentience results in human-like phenomenal experience, only that it must be adaptive in the sense of better fitting its systemic interactions with environmental variations. As the quote above suggests, this kind of integrative organization is likely to be a property of all living systems and even a property of some complex non-living organizations.

My concern with describing all integrative organizations that show high *phi* scores as conscious is that this completely redefines what we usually mean by consciousness. As proposed earlier, I believe Tononi's analysis of the degree of thalamocortical coherence needed for conscious awareness was an important insight into why conscious attention is slow to take form. However, it seems to me he has let his mathematical algorithm for calculating coherence take control of his definition of consciousness. The thalamocortical architecture is unique for several reasons. First, it provides an organization that drives synchronous processing toward a focus of attention. IIT does not address attention. Second, this architecture enables life urges to be experienced as feelings of self during attention. Feelings and the sense of self are not addressed in the IIT model.

The brainstem-thalamocortical architecture proposed in our model results in the amplification of features at the focus of attention, binds perceptions with feelings, and sets the stage for the emergence of subjective qualia that interact with higher-order constructs of attention during consciousness. These higher-order interactions are essential for the subjective experience of consciousness and self. However, IIT is not concerned with phenomenal experience. Thus, it concludes that consciousness is simply a fundamental property of any mechanism that has cause-effect power upon its own activities.

Information integration is part of the process that leads to consciousness, but without an architecture to drive attention and engage subjective feelings the IIT claim that integration results in conscious experience is hopelessly incomplete. In order to have anything resembling what humans call consciousness an agency must be 1) self-aware, that is, aware of its own status, 2) self-modifying, that is, able to exert cause-effect changes on itself, and 3) self-maintaining, that is, motivated to select actions that maintain or improve its status.

So how do we fit information integration into the organization of mind? To answer this question, we need to put the emergence of mind in yet a larger framework. *Panpsychism* is the philosophical position that assumes all matter, even simple particles like electrons and quarks, have some basic kinds of inner experience that share in the universal "consciousness" of the universe. If by *consciousness* here we mean that matter is sensitive to fundamental forces in the universe, then this idea is generally considered to be true. We can even term these experiences as *subjective*, if by subjective we mean they involve internal processes within the dynamic systems that organize that element of matter. However, if by *consciousness* here we mean that matter is aware of itself in a way that is separate from the fundamental forces that compose it, then there is no reason to believe that fundamental particles can be conscious. Self-awareness requires representations that are separate from the forces that hold an object together.

Formal models of IIT go to great lengths to argue that information integration is not merely panpsychism.[264] They emphasize that there is always an element of systemic cause-effect coordination in organizations with high *phi* scores. This cause-effect coordination is considered to result in potentially higher-order interactions. IIT models do not claim that life is essential for information integration in these systems, only that they have these added cause-effect interactions. As such, structures with integrative information appear to be more like the components from which living systems might be assembled. For example, the ribosome structures within living cells are not considered to be living, but they have sentient-like information integration properties. They can "read" RNA instructions and construct proteins.

Early in this book, we introduced the idea that novel organizations emerge from interactions at lower levels and that there are often interfaces between levels. In addition, in major transitions we noted that there are coding systems that guide the assembly of higher-order structures. Life emerged when assemblies of membrane-bound physical structures were able to use codes to guide their construction. Ribosomes were integratively sentient structures in this process. They built proteins based on sequences in RNA molecules. These sentient structures were essential for the emergence of life. Many stages of integratively sentient organization and coding strategies had to evolve before living cells could combine into multicellular organizations. I believe that IIT may be useful in describing the self-assembly processes by which ribosomes lead to the emergence of living cells, but this does not mean that ribosomes are conscious.

Associative mind began when special cells in those organizations, neurons, evolved to form integratively interactive neural networks. These networks could learn and remember by coding sequences of firing patterns as changes in the synaptic nodes that guided the flow of neural information in larger assemblies. Conscious mind emerged when the thalamocortical organization for attention resulted in dynamic neural structures that could bind perceptions and feelings together in a synchronous focus of integrative sentience. The codes were the input assemblies that were bound together in each successive moment. But as these assemblies gained coherent attention they were re-interpreted as the qualia of experience. Patterns of visual inputs were interpreted as images, objects, and social partners. Patterns of limbic inputs were interpreted as drives and goals. Patterns of motor action were interpreted as intentions and decisions.

Integrative sentience was, and still is, a part of all these transitions. The integrative information needed for the emergence of life involved sentient processes that coordinated physiochemical reactions within a cell. The integrative information needed for the emergence of associative mind involved sentient processes that coordinated the flow of activity in neural networks. The integrative information needed for the emergence of conscious mind involved sentient processes that coordinated the binding of synchronous assemblies within the thalamocortical architecture. The integrative information needed for the interpretation of qualia as subjective experiences involved sentient processes that summarized neural inputs as conceptual qualities of attention.

Based on these observations, I see integrative information as an organizing process in the construction of living systems, in the formation of associative minds, and in the transition from neural inputs to conscious awareness. However, while sentient integration results in the construction of emergent organizations, it doesn't define what emerges. The substances that are integrated in each new organization shape what kinds of properties emerge on each new level. Thus, while I consider IIT to be a model for explaining the emergence of integrative organization, I find the claim that IIT provides a functional account of consciousness to be an oversimplification. Conscious mind is more than simply information integration. It is a dynamic system that combines its perceptual experiences of the world with its internal feelings of self so as to be aware of how its perceptions influence its status and how its actions may be able to change how it feels. IIT does not provide that level of integration.

Is There a Global Workspace?

> We then propose … a global neuronal workspace. This framework postulates that, at any given time, many modular cerebral networks are active in parallel and process information in an unconscious manner. … The long-distance connectivity of these `workspace neurons' can, when they are active for a minimal duration, make the information available to a variety of processes including perceptual categorization, long term memorization, evaluation, and intentional action. We postulate that this global availability of information through the workspace is what we subjectively experience as a conscious state.[265]

The global workspace theory of consciousness grew out of Barnard Baars ideas that consciousness resulted from interactions among short-term working memories using a visual-spatial buffer for visual semantics, a phonological buffer for linguistic regularities, and an episodic buffer for long term memory processing.[266] Baars later extended this model, suggesting that a central workspace could help integrate brain functions that were otherwise processed in separate memory maps.[267] However, the nature and locus of this workspace were vague. While Baar's model never had a strong following, it was re-invigorated when Stanislas Deheane and Lionel Naccache termed the enhancement of thalamocortical activity during consciousness as the result of central global neuronal workplace activity.[268]

The apparent impetus for Deheane and Naccache to suggest that consciousness involved a global neuronal workplace was because at the times agents reported conscious experience there was a broad increase in the intensity of cortical activity.[269] This increase was suggested to account for the finding that conscious mind seemed to be able to access an extensive array of possible topics. A phenomenon sometimes referred to as access consciousness.[270] However, there is a conflict between the assumption that consciousness emerges as a narrowing focus of attention gains coherence and the assumption that consciousness increases the global accessibility of features.

According to the model presented in this book, the global range of possible ideas that may reach consciousness results from the fact that almost all the sensorimotor signals projecting to the cortex pass through the thalamus. Thus, all are possible candidates for inclusion in the assemblies that compete for attention. It is the combined arousal of inputs in each assembly that determines which assembly outcompetes the other. The thought is that this strategy evolved because assemblies with the most joint arousal are more likely to be adaptive in the moment.

Yet, as we have noted, as an assembly of features gains conscious attention it becomes more focused and more intense. This suggests that conscious *experience* does not simply result from the global availability of features, as Deheane and Naccache suggest above, but rather it results from the intensity of processing that is engaged as the focus of attention grows more coherent. In earlier chapters, we suggested that coherently focused attention likely engages the *communication-through-coherence* phenomenon that Pascal Fries has reported.[271]

However, there may be a way that consciousness adds to the processing of more global features. As we have noted, consciousness does not dwell on one topic for long. It constantly shifts and flows. Deheane and Naccache note that after some minimal duration the enhancement of arousal often extends from one central focus to include regions for perceptual categorization, or long term memory, or self-evaluation, or intentional action. Thus, when activation spreads to these regions during one moment of attention, some of those features are likely to become part of a new assembly that gains attention in the next. In this way, the flow of conscious attention takes on a more varied character, although each moment of attention would still be focused only on a few features.

In addition to the intensity of conscious arousal, our model proposes that conscious processing is coordinated by synchronous return loops from the cortex back to the thalamus and on to supporting brainstem regions. It seems likely that the neurons in these return loops correspond to what Deheane and Naccache referred to as long-distance "workspace neurons". This implies that the global workspace results from ongoing cycles of synchronous thalamocortical-brainstem activity that change dynamically as new assemblies gain the focus of attention. Thus, to answer the opening question, the thalamocortical-brainstem connectivity supports a wide range of possible interactions—so it could be called a global workspace. However, it is synchronous coordination of attention within this workspace that engages conscious processing. The global workspace model has nothing to say about the mechanisms that result in synchronous attention and coherent processing.

As we have proposed, the neural coordination that leads to consciousness begins with synchrony and is enhanced as attention becomes more coherent. However, we have also noted that the coherence of neural processing is extended across subsystems operating on different time frames via harmonic coupling.[272] These extensions are necessary to coordinate rapidly changing networks for perceptions with slower operating feelings of self. This linkage of perceptions and feelings is consistent with Antonio Damasio's argument the consciousness involves an object-organism integration.[273] Recent work also suggests that there is a dynamic macroscale brain circuit that alternates between default mode networks for internal processing and dorsal attention networks for external processing. In humans, the interruption of this alternating circuitry results in unresponsiveness and an apparent loss of consciousness.[274]

As we have noted, a conscious sense of self emerges as we categorize internal processes as different from external events, and this sense of self is expanded with a sense of ownership as we detect synchronous dependencies between internal networks and subsequent actions or somatic inputs. In fact, we come to experience the self as an agency that can react to varied topics of attention. But the self is not a global agency. So while consciousness may emerge within a process of synchronous coordination, and while topics of attention may be selected from a global set of features and reactions, the subjective interpretations of conscious experience in each moment requires a focused synchrony between specific events and feelings. The global workspace model has no focus.

Are There Metaphorical Constructs In Thought?

> For young children, subjective (nonsensorimotor) experiences and judgments, on the one hand, and sensorimotor experiences, on the other, are so regularly conflated – undifferentiated in experience – that for a time children do not differentiate between the two when they occur together. … During the period of conflation, associations are automatically built up between the domains. Later, during a period of *differentiation*, children are then able to separate out the domains, but the cross-domain associations persist.[275]

As we have described them, conscious minds are storms of attention that grow with experience. However, what is not often recognized is that new skills and concepts tend to develop incrementally by building on earlier skills and concepts. Further, the brain circuits for the earlier skills often become founding parts of the newer skills. Theorists George Lakoff, a linguist, and Mark Johnson, a philosopher, provide some instructive insights into how these extensions take form. They argue that many of the constructions of mind are grounded in primary sensorimotor experiences, that is, in the perceptions, actions, and feelings associated with early sensorimotor activities. These early experiences, they argue, contribute to thinking about later more complex experiences because they frequently come to be cross-connected with them in learning situations. As noted in the quote above, the authors refer to the process of forming these cross-connected associations with more fundamental experiences as *conflation*.

Lakoff and Johnson go on to propose that cross-mappings between domains help a developing agent to conceptualize experiences by linking the properties of earlier and better understood experiences, *source domains*, with those encountered in later more complex situations, *target domains*. In fact, they argue that this cross-mapped linkage comes to affect how we conceptualize the target domain. For example, the early experiences of affection tend to be associated with being held against a warm body. Thus, metaphorical connections with both closeness and warmth are conflated with affection. The cross-mapped linkages even influence how we talk about affection. As the authors note, we actually have difficulty describing the quality of a relationship without resorting to metaphors involving *warmth* and *closeness*. ""Recently, our relationship has cooled and we've been drifting apart." Such descriptions seem so natural that we are not usually aware of their conflated origins.

As Lakoff and Johnson note, the linkage of source domains with target domains results in a metaphorical extension in which the target is partly understood in the context of the source experiences. However, unlike literary metaphors, in which a likeness between two experiences is called to conscious attention with words, these primary metaphors are formed by the sensorimotor conflation of related experiences without the need for verbal comparisons. Thus, they result in largely unconscious links in which more complex experiences are interpreted based on the role of earlier developmental experiences. Similarly, unconscious links also form when early sensorimotor actions and goals are later conflated with more complex plans and goals.

> Consider an infant who begins her sensorimotor development by investigating objects within her reach. Initially she must learn to coordinate her gaze with her grasp. Over time, she will then learn to locate, grasp, and hold onto nearby objects. However, as she becomes more mobile, crawling, walking, climbing, her concept of what is within reach will change. She will learn to find paths that help her change her position and bring more distant objects within reach. As she grows older and visits far-away places, what she will consider within her reach will be expanded again. Later she may see a foreign journalist on the nightly television news and decide that is a career *within her reach*. This concept of reach extends well beyond the arm-reach grasp, and yet the core experience of grasping contributes to the meaning of the higher-level concept as she *reaches* toward her new career choice. She understands that she must *position* herself correctly to reach her new goal. She looks for educational *paths* that will bring her goal nearer. These ideas seem so natural that the young lady will probably fail to notice that the meanings of position and path have also been metaphorically extended as she interprets her attempt to gain her goal as an extended kind of reach.[276]

The idea that concepts build up in layers of sensorimotor relationships also helps to explain why thought is often expressed with spontaneous gestures, motor actions that we are often only partially aware of performing. If new concepts are built on previous sensorimotor concepts, then it should not be surprising to find that when we speak about grasping an idea, we may find ourselves making subtle grasping motions as we speak. Similarly, when we talk about rejecting an idea, we may find our hands in front of us making push-away gestures. The objects to grasp or push away are not even present, and the actions we make are largely incomplete. Yet they provide obvious evidence that thinking about grasping an idea partially activates thoughts of grasping an object, and that thinking about rejecting an idea partially activates thoughts of pushing something away. Yet while these gestures seem superfluous, it turns out they serve a function. Because if other agents have similar cross-feature mappings with early sensorimotor experiences, they are more likely to interpret your arguments in a similar way, if your gestures cause them to think about similar primary sensorimotor experiences as they think about your arguments.

In these examples, we have tried to show how lower-level processes are conflated with higher-level processes to illustrate the incremental nature of thought. However, when new ideas come to be built unconsciously on prior experiences, we don't always recognize how our early experiences influence our later ideas. For example, in other works, Lakoff has gone on to show that our thinking about governmental authority and laws are logically conflated with thinking about early experiences with our parents and their rules. As a result, aspects of political beliefs and values come to be influenced by our experience with strategies of parental caring and control.[277] It seems the values of conservative constituents are often conflated with strict parental strategies of child caring, whereas the values of liberal constituents are more often conflated with supportive parental child caring. These differences result in different political values for agents that grow up in families with different parental patterns of child care, although the agents are usually unaware of why they adopt those political values. It is not my goal to explore these political differences in more detail here. However, Lakoff's analysis makes it clear that thoughts may be cross-linked with unconscious source domains that nevertheless have profound influences on later concepts.

Lakoff's point that early experiences have fundamental effects on how we think about the world should not be that surprising. It is a natural consequence of reusing established skills, concepts, and motivational dispositions in new combinations as we adapt to new situations.[278] Lakoff and Johnson suggest that these primary cross-mappings, which they term the *cognitive unconscious,* account for about 95 percent of all thought. That number is of course merely an estimate. Such relationships are difficult to quantify. However, it seems clear that many aspects of metaphorical thinking are influenced by sensorimotor cross-mappings and that cross-mappings guide thought and language production in largely unconscious ways.

Because developmental hierarchies occur in all animals, conflated learning and unconscious cross-mappings can be expected to occur in animals too. In ethology, animal gestures are commonly referred to as *intention movements*. The idea is the gestures reveal cross-mappings that influence underlying motives. Not surprisingly, I often find that when my cats need something they sometimes approach, reach toward me, and make pulling gestures. They want to bring me closer. Over time, I have come to recognize that those pulling movements mean they want my help. And those simple gestures have a marked effect on how much I want to help them.

Lakoff has largely focused his analysis on thought in human minds. However, he and his students have also applied these ideas to the process of creating computer programs that think like humans. Lakoff notes the when metaphorical cross-mappings influence the organization of thought they also influence the connectivity of thoughts in language. Given that language is considered to be a hallmark of higher-order thought, it becomes hard to dismiss the importance of Lakoff's layered conceptual architecture for both unconsciously guided bottom-up associations and consciously guided top-down comparisons. Lakoff's analysis makes it clear that metaphorical connections are essential for understanding mental organization on multiple levels of thought and in all kinds of minds. And if we want to build a conscious robot, we need to take advantage of this metaphorical hierarchy and even make sure our robot uses supporting gestures when they communicate with us.

In Chapter 6 we described the planning and decision structures in the basal ganglia (BG) and introduced a master-apprentice architecture that could learn concepts incrementally. That architecture was based on Ann Graybiel's thinking that the cortex, striatum, and pallidum have come to function as a massive three-layer learning network in which the middle layer, the striatum, learns to map cortical inputs to output drivers in the pallidum, with dopamine providing the critical learning signal for both the striatum and the sequential planners in the PFC.[279] Graybiel's idea is that because the striatum receives motor and dopamine feedback as actions are assembled, it can learn to treat the ongoing feedback as part of the input pattern it uses to engage subsequent actions in larger chunks. And because the decisions in the BG feed back to the cortex, this enables the cortex to plan in larger concepts.

Because we know that cholinergic signals from the basal nucleus of Meynert/ magnocellularis (BNM) project to the cortex and influence cortical reorganization,[280] I included the BNM in the master-apprentice architecture as a mechanism to promote conceptual growth in the cortex. In addition, I realized that metaphorical extensions could be assembled using the same architecture. If metaphorical extensions are cross-linked in the cortex, then this linkage should result in the cortex passing a motor reach plan to the BG but then shifting to a new grasp plan for a new kind of contact. At first the striatum would treat these as two plans, but if this sequence keeps repeating the striatum would begin chunking parts of the two plans together, so that over time they become a single extended reach plan. In this way, part of the core "reach" motor information would still be activated in the metaphorically extended reach.

Does Social Contagion Lead to Cultural Consciousness?

> It is commonly believed that information spreads between individuals like a pathogen, with each exposure by an informed friend potentially resulting in a naive individual becoming infected. However, empirical studies of social media suggest that individual response to repeated exposure to information is far more complex. ... The likelihood an individual will spread information increases monotonically with exposure, while explicit feedback about how many friends have previously spread it increases the likelihood of a response.[281]

In addition to the extension of thought via metaphors, conscious thought is also expanded by what is best called *social contagion*. We develop within a cultural world in which our own ideas and values are continually drawn into synchronous interactions with those of other social agents. These interactions release social neural modulators that reinforce attention for socially promoted concepts. Thus, many individual ideas and values are shaped by inputs from social partners, especially when the partners are valued or when their ideas are often repeated. This tends to bring the ideas of a group together. The breakthrough mechanism for sharing ideas was language. However, while language was, and still is, essential for sharing ideas, the number of people that can be reached by language at one time is limited. Thus, over time cultures have evolved additional tools for storing ideas and sharing them more broadly. Writing has long been a powerful tool for sharing ideas with more people. In recent times, electronic tools for transmitting talk or written material have greatly expanded this process.

Sharing ideas and feelings in a group is often beneficial. Activities are more efficient when agents recognize the intentions of others and cooperate on tasks. As noted earlier, if one individual discovers a solution to a particular problem, then the solution can be saved and shared with others. Tools and social conventions are also refined in this manner across time. Consider how the tools for mathematical calculation have changed. An early tool for addition was the abacus, a structure in which small stones, in Latin, *calculi*, were placed in columns to represent numerical values. Stones on the right side represented integer numbers, stones in each column to the left represented values that were ten times the values on the left. When two numerical values were added on the abacus, sometimes the value in one column exceeded the number of places in that column and a stone needed to be *carried* to the next left column to represent the overflow. We now use numerical symbols rather than stones for representing mathematical values, but we still keep the symbols in columns of times-ten value. Further, when adding numbers to one column exceeds its level of representation, we are taught to metaphorically *carry* the excess value to the next left column.

This group-level working of ideas and conventions is such a common part of modern human experience that we rarely consider it as an independent thought process. However, in a real sense, group thinking is the product of another kind of mind. The ideas and tools worked in this way don't belong to a single individual. They are the cumulative effects of many minds shared in cultural systems of representation that are maintained and extended across time. And to complete our example, note that the professional abacus users were known in Latin as *calculatores*, stone movers. And today, we call our electronic tools for doing such mathematical processes calculators. It seems concepts for tools and conventions may be metaphorically sourced to earlier activities, even in cultures.

There are several parallels between the processes of individual minds and those of cultural minds that may be useful to consider here. Individual consciousness is guided by feelings, and involves sharing activations among neural systems for attention. When adjacent neurons in attention networks fire at roughly similar frequencies, they provide mutual stimulation to each other. This tends to draw groups of neurons into synchronous rhythms. Such rhythms enhance mutually aligned signals and diminish signals with competing rhythms. During attention these rhythms may even propagate in traveling waves to other parts of the brain and enhance related neural activities.

And just as the behavior of individual mind cannot be fully explained simply by looking at their neurons, the behavior of cultural mind cannot be fully explained simply by looking at individual minds. The attention of cultural mind can coordinate individual minds in shared values. When social agents engage similar states of arousal, their mutual excitement tends to draw the group members together into synchronous states of activity. This promotes group agendas and social values while inhibiting competing ones. Sometimes the waves even spread activation across the social collective in recurrent cycles of debate and resolution as an issue is worked and refined by the group. These mutual forces can have a formidable impact on cultural decisions.

Interestingly, the role of attention in individual consciousness suggests a likely direction for the evolution of cultural minds. Individual consciousness emerged when thalamocortical circuits began using synchronous algorithms to bind features together with feelings in states of attention. In this process, feelings made the topics of attention more salient and linked perceptions with reactive dispositions. Cultural consciousness began taking form when cognitive agents began coding ideas in shared systems of signs. Recurrent processes of culturally-directed social contagion bind features together with social values in cultural attention. In this process, social values make the topics of group attention more salient and link them with reactive dispositions within social groups.

However, individual minds gradually evolved higher-order processes that helped them to expand conscious awareness beyond feelings and to coordinate attention for task-related goals. To be truly productive, cultural consciousness will also need a steering committee to guide its attention in more productive ways. An independent press has emerged in many modern cultures as a tool for promoting topics to group attention. When promoted by trusted journalists these can be powerful. However, not all news sources are independent or well-intended. How a more independent prioritizing and attention focusing process may emerge is not yet clear. The appearance of social networks, blogs, and hashtag links that not only track issues, but keep interested members connected, informed, and motivated is one strategy. Still, the voices of various causes will need to be integrated into group opinions that can raise concerns, set priorities, and motivate social agendas. They must also be robust enough to resist being overtaken by groups with devious motives, and this may be a formidable task.

To improve the decisions of cultural mind, we need processes that rate information for accuracy and prioritize it around important topics. News sites should be valued for the quality of their information, not just for promoting popular topics or allowing clickbait links to masquerade as news. Deliberately promoted fake news is even more damaging. Still, better information will not fix all the variations in cultural mind. Cultures are known to go through phases of changing values as new attitudes take form. Generally, these processes change gradually. However, times of crisis or terrorism may promote sharp changes in cultural mood. And if such problems persist, defensive dispositions and actions may become increasingly confrontational. Inspiring leaders may help counter such changes in mood. However, devious agents may take advantage of them to promote their own agendas. Thus, cultural mind is likely to follow many sidetracks as it evolves.

Where Do the Qualia of Consciousness Come From?

> A constructionist analysis of the organizations in which consciousness emerges explains why qualia must exist. They are the stuff of conscious experience. Just as the microlaws for chemistry cannot fully explain the properties of life, the microlaws of neural networks cannot fully explain how experience is implemented in the brain, or why conscious minds feel experience as they do. Qualia only come into existence within storms of attention, and they can only be fully understood within that context. They are the categorical tags and valences which guide the attention of conscious agents so as to make their experiences interpretable. Without qualia, there would be no *feeling of what happens*.[282]

Qualia are generally defined as the subjective qualities of "what it is like to experience" something.[283] However, taking a reductionist approach, Daniel Dennett suggests that the concept is not really needed to explain consciousness.[284] He claims that a sufficiently detailed physical and functional account of how experience is implemented in the brain would leave nothing more to be explained. David Chalmers, in contrast, "knows" that qualia exist because he experiences them.[285] However, he agrees that reductionist mechanisms within the brain do all the work of mind, and he suggests that qualia may simply be epiphenomena, experiences that run in parallel with physical interactions but have no function. The fact that experience is disconnected from function, he claims, is why explaining qualia is such a hard problem.

We have already noted that qualia are connected with functional systems in the brain, so Chalmer's claim that qualia lack function need not concern us. However, we are now at a point where we can propose an explanation for why qualia have an experiential character. As we have characterized them, qualia serve to provide summary representations of the neural assemblies that gain attention. They do not map to the objective details of sensory inputs, or the many properties of associated motor plans, or the feelings that support them. They map to the functional concepts that gain attention. Summarizing interconnected arrays of inputs as images, feelings, or actions is simply more efficient than trying to remember the combinatorial inputs that the qualia represent. Functional summaries are easier to remember.

So how are these summaries assembled? MIT neuroscientist Ann Graybiel proposed a chunking model to explain the growth of cognition.[286] Her idea was that because the cortex receives feedback as action plans are assembled in the striatum, it can learn to treat the summary feedback as larger planning units. Because the basil nucleus of Meynert (BNM) promotes cortical reorganization, I added it to Graybiel's model. This effectively results in a *master-apprentice architecture* – an arrangement that incrementally reorganizes perceptions and actions into larger chunks. The cortex, as the master, promotes plans in sequences. However, over trials the striatum, as the apprentice, learns to connect common sequences and returns its action strategies to the master as larger units. The BNM provides cholinergic learning signals that encourage the cortex to use these new units as larger action plans.

Lakoff and Johnson argue that higher-order concepts often develop as extensions of sensorimotor experiences that begin in childhood.[287] Thus, the core sensations, motives, and feelings of early sensorimotor actions are the foundations of experiential feelings. And because new concepts develop as metaphorical extensions of previous concepts, the qualia of later experiences are grounded in simpler child-like experiences. That is how qualia grow.

When actions are extended as the striatum learns to plan in sequential patterns, we can describe this as chunking, as Graybiel did. However, when the actions are extended as cross-connections of simpler sensorimotor experiences, as Lakoff and Johnson propose, the cortex must initially plan with more complex inputs, but new concepts can be assembled in the same master-apprentice architecture. Chunking and metaphorical extensions are ways to form larger actions, and as the cortex learns this, it can plan in larger concepts.

So qualia have a function, summarizing features of attention. And the master-apprentice architecture enables qualia to grow incrementally. And because the primary components of new skills are grounded in childhood sensorimotor tasks, qualia link new concepts with individual child-like feelings. This happens because, when they are expressed, the new concepts and skills partially activate the foundational concepts and feelings they are built on. And because these early experiences are personal and subjective, the extended concepts are likely to feel more meaningful. This is how incremental learning and metaphorical extensions expand actions and feelings in personal ways.

Some may question whether child-like cognition and feelings are really a primary part of later qualia. However, if you follow George Lakoff's analyses of cognition and language you will understand how strongly sensorimotor actions and feelings are embedded in later cognition. Neuroscience has largely neglected metaphorical thinking because there has not been an obvious neural mechanism for metaphorical cognition. However, the master-apprentice architecture provides a neural mechanism for incremental growth that links cortical reorganization and growth with metaphorical extensions of cognition and language. No neural model of consciousness would be complete without such a mechanism.

Along the way, the qualia of conscious experience summarize many aspects of self. The observer self, the agent self, the reflective self, and the narrative self all link back to early sensorimotor experiences. We all have a history, but we never outgrow our individual histories — we simply extend them in new directions. And when attention engages conscious experience the intensity of those subjective feelings is also enhanced. Thus, the features assembled in higher-order qualia are always likely to be linked with interesting foundational concepts and feelings. It's not a hard problem, a child can do it.

Concluding Comments

Conscious mind emerges in an architecture that enables adaptive feelings to guide attention and add to subjective experiences. When we build a robot with its own proto-feeling networks that contribute to a similar architecture for attention, it too will be a dynamic storm of attention with its own emergent skills, beliefs, and values, all of which will expand with its experiences. The argument that our robot will be *nothing* but the programming modules we provide to guide its development will be as vacuous as the argument that our children are *nothing but* the modules our genes provide them. Individual minds depend on inherited modules but their path of development is shaped in layers of metaphorical experience and social contagion. It is time to abandon the *nothing buttery* thinking that denies emergent properties to the very conscious agents who think about them. The phenomenal properties of individual conscious minds are just as real and causal in conscious agents as the interactive properties of individual atoms, stars, and galaxies are in the physical universe.

> **Ending Remarks**

Consciousness cannot be dismissed as *nothing but* the interaction of nerve cells and molecules. Yes, it emerges from such an organization. However, like all emergent organizations, it introduces discontinuous properties that do not exist at the parts level. Each conscious agency changes as it develops.

The qualia of consciousness are subjective and cannot be shared directly. However, to the extent agents share similar brain structures and developmental experiences their qualia should have similar qualities. And the more you share the topics of your attention and feelings with others, the better they can map your descriptions to their qualia and the more they feel they understand you.

Consciousness involves experiences that do not exist at the neural level. And while this leads some to view

consciousness as being an illusion, somehow its "magical" interpretations of neural states can have highly adaptive properties. It creates an integrated sense of self, a sense of agency, a sense of action ownership, and a sense of self-control that extend well beyond the sense of its neural advisors.

We cannot attend to all sources of control at the same time, only to a few. Thus, it is possible to influence what cues we attend to when making a decision. By selectively attending to cues that are more important to us, we can bias our attention to them, even when other deterministic forces are competing for attention. Using personal goals and values to make a decision is the essence of free will.

The emergent interconnectedness between conscious qualia and underlying associative networks, and between associative networks and motor control cells, and between motor cells and actions in the world means that the mind doesn't have to violate the laws of physics to produce effects in the world. Anything that can gain attention can influence motor actions.

Information integration is part of the process that leads to consciousness, but without an architecture to drive attention and engage subjective feelings the claim that it results in conscious experience is hopelessly incomplete. To have anything resembling what humans call consciousness, an agency must be self-aware, self-modifying, and self-maintaining.

Conscious processing is engaged by circuitry within the brainstem-thalamocortical architecture. This architecture has been called a global neuronal workspace. However, the assembly of features that gain consciousness must be highly focused. This means that consciousness is not a result of the global availability of features, but rather a result of the intensity of processing that is engaged as attention reaches a coherent focus. However, the global architecture ensures that a wide range of experiences can interact during consciousness.

Mental processing has an underlying metaphorical structure, because new skills and concepts tend to develop incrementally by building on earlier skills and concepts. In fact, the earlier skills often become founding parts of the newer skills. Lakoff and Johnson propose that this happens developmentally when cross-domain associations are bound together in conflated experiences.[288] Ann Graybiel has proposed a cortico-striatal chunking model to explain how concepts grow incrementally.[289] The master-apprentice architecture described earlier provides a mechanism that explains how both of these models can be implemented.

Modern cultures are conscious. They are self-aware, self-modifying, and self-maintaining. Individual consciousness emerged when thalamocortical circuits began using synchronous algorithms to bind features together with feelings in states of attention. In this process, feelings made the topics of attention more salient and linked perceptions with reactive dispositions. Cultural consciousness began when cognitive agents began coding ideas in shared systems of signs. Recurrent cycles of culturally-directed social contagion bind features together with social values in cultural attention. In this process, social values make the topics of group attention more salient and link them with reactive dispositions within social groups.

Qualia are subjective interpretations of neural inputs that gain attention as functional units of experience. Given that they can be learned and remembered, summarizing neural input patterns as units of experience is simply more efficient than trying to hold on to the detailed firing patterns that bring that experience together. In effect, like words, qualia are units of thought. And because the primary components of new qualia are grounded in childhood experiences, qualia link new concepts with subjective child-like feelings.

Appendix: Evolving Core Consciousness

> When core consciousness began, millions of years and many species ago, we were very far from the current sophistication of modern consciousness, very far from the ease with which we can describe, using language, the reasons behind our actions, past or intended. However, when core consciousness began, we were on the right track and we transcended the critical threshold. We were telling ourselves, without using any words, the answer to the question we never asked, that yes, there was an individual perspective to our percepts, and yes, there was an individual ownership of images, and yes, it was all tied to life. – Antonio Damasio, "Investigating the biology of consciousness", 1998

> ➤ **Introductory Remarks**

Descartes claimed humans were conscious. They had feelings, they reasoned, they willed, they imagined, and they acted in the absence of obvious physical causes. Animals, he concluded, reacted to physical triggers and mechanical forces, but lacked the spontaneous feelings, reasoning, will, and imagination that the spiritual substance of mind made possible.

We began this book by describing René Descartes' thinking about animal minds. Descartes drew an analogy between the automatons in the royal gardens of Saint-Germain-en-Laye and the workings of the body. Following this analogy, he argued that mechanical forces could explain the actions of the body. However, lacking an equivalent mechanistic account of mind, Descartes concluded that conscious mind was essentially a different category of substance.[290] It was spiritual and did not require a physical form for existence. He claimed humans had such a substance, a soul. They were conscious, they had feelings and they acted in the absence of obvious physical causes. Animals, he concluded, reacted to physical triggers and mechanical forces, but they lacked the spontaneous feelings, reasoning, will, and imagination that occurred in conscious agents.

Although many modern theorists have adopted contrary positions since Descartes proposed this division between human and animal minds, there are still those who subscribe to his view. A primary reason for this is that a clear account of the mechanisms underlying consciousness has yet to reach consensus. In the absence of such an account, almost any hypothesis is given credence by some, and Descartes' hypothesis is the historical standard. Our goal here has been to provide an account of the mechanisms that lead to consciousness, and thus to remove part of this confusion. Still, because consciousness involves feelings, and feelings are largely personal experiences, some deny that it is possible to know about the consciousness of other minds. However, most of these theorists are willing to accept the verbal reports of others about conscious experiences, as long as those reports resonate with their own personal experience. Not surprisingly, this leaves their thinking about consciousness neatly endorsing Descartes' dualism, because they do not credit animals with the ability to comment on their subjective experiences.

In another version of dualism, some theorists claim that consciousness can be experienced, but that it has no function, and thus that it cannot be measured.[291] In these accounts, the experience of conscious mind is considered to be an epiphenomenon, an experience that occurs in parallel with processes in the nervous system, but one that has no effect in the physical world. Any physical effects that occur are attributed to the nervous system, not to the experience. However, even if we accept that our nervous system has real effects on our actions and conscious feelings simply run along in parallel, why conscious feelings don't also run in parallel with animal nervous systems is not clear. When scientists ask non-human animals to report about their experiences behaviorally, they find that animals are aware of different feeling states.[292] Other reports indicate that animals even experience visual illusions.[293] What could be more subjective than illusions?

Other theorists anchor their dualism to the intentionality provided by language and then argue that non-human animals cannot be conscious because they lack language. Perhaps the strongest version of this position is proposed by Peter Carruthers.[294] He argues that consciousness involves second-order intentionality and that second-order intentionality requires language. Further, as Derek Browne notes, Carruthers proposes a distinction between two aspects of phenomenal subjectivity.

> These are ... worldly-subjectivity' and 'mental-state-
> subjectivity'. Equivalently, he distinguishes two different
> kinds of phenomenal properties: "phenomenal properties of
> the world ... and phenomenal properties of the subject's

experience of the world". Worldly-subjectivity is constituted by what the world is like for the organism. Mental state-subjectivity is constituted by what the organism's experience of the world is like for the organism.[295]

Curiously, Carruthers' distinctions are not so different from those proposed in our model of how conscious feelings come to be represented in vertebrate brains. As we have suggested, many first-order life urges arrive via the sympathetic and parasympathetic inputs to the brainstem. These are then re-represented in a number of second-order summary networks for somatic status, like the parabrachial nucleus (PBN), and adjacent midbrain networks for emotional dispositions and reactions, like the periaqueductal gray (PAG). However, while these second-order life-urge networks integrate somatic status and reactivity states, their processing is still unconscious. As we have argued, it takes a higher-order representation of life urges in the context of attention to create the *object-organism integration* that occurs in consciousness.[296]

This object-organism integration is comparable to what Carruthers refers to as *mental state-subjectivity* – how the experience of the world is linked to the experience of the organism. We have explained this level of re-representation as a higher-order integration that occurs as life urges are synchronously bound with perceptions in states of attention. However, Carruthers is convinced that language is the only means by which mental state-subjectivity can occur. In fact, he takes his dualistic stance to an extreme position denying that we should even be morally concerned about the apparent suffering of animals, or brutes as his alignment with Descartes leads him to call them. Without language, Carruthers claims that animals cannot even be conscious of their suffering.

> In the case of brutes: since their experiences, including their pains, are nonconscious ones, their pains are of no immediate moral concern. ... Neither the pain of the broken leg itself, nor its further effects upon the life of the dog, have any rational claim upon our sympathy. ... Not only is it possible that this should occur — after all, the history of mankind is replete with examples of those who have eradicated all feelings of sympathy even for members of other races, by telling themselves that they are not 'really human' — but it is a moral imperative that it ought to.[297]

However, Carruthers' explanation in this quote betrays his underlying motivation. There is no evidence to prove that dogs cannot feel pain. On the contrary, even Caruthers describes what the dog feels as *pain*. Further, Caruthers acknowledges that humans are capable of denying feelings and of suppressing sympathy, even for other humans when they are considered inferior. Yet Caruthers argues that it is a moral imperative to deny feelings to animals, as if we must do so to defend our superiority. This is a sad commentary.

It seems unlikely that those who are locked into this dualistic position will ever be able to overcome their belief that animals require language to feel pain. However, for those of us who have not committed to such an extreme position, the model of consciousness proposed in this book provides a framework that unites mind and body without language. Life urges are not separate from the mind; rather they are sensing-reacting dispositions of the body. And when they gain attention they are experienced as conscious feelings. To put this description of consciousness in better perspective, we need to review our model of how life urges become feelings.

FROM SENTIENCE TO CONSCIOUSNESS

Life began as adaptive sensing-acting dispositions took form in membrane-bound chemical collectives. These adaptive dispositions are what we have termed *life urges*. They correspond to what Fred Keijzer has described as forms of biologically embodied cognition.[298] Life urges enable an organism to detect changes in its world and react in constructive ways. Without adaptive life urges, no living organism could survive for long.

In cells as simple as the *Escherichia coli* bacteria, life urges involve chemical sensors and connected reactive effects that change the behavior of the cell. For example, in these bacteria, receptor regions that detect potential food sources have chemical links that activate flagella movements. These movements engage swimming runs as food gradients increase, and tumbles that change direction, when food gradients decrease.[299] Cells in which food sensing is linked with positively directed motor actions are better able to survive. This directional link between sensing and acting is the essence of sentient knowledge. The road to consciousness begins with adaptive sentience.[300]

Adaptive sentient life urges also occur in plants. They seek light, water, and nutrients and avoid toxins, but without motor systems their reactions depend largely on differential growth processes and are slower. However, plants can detect environmental stressors and can communicate internally to react to them. In addition, it seems that plant roots may even communicate chemically with adjacent plant roots regarding stressors. Thus, plants not only have sensing-reacting dispositions, they can communicate about them socially.[301]

Animals have evolved faster acting sensing-reacting processes based on neural signaling. Simple combinations result in reflexes and directional movements toward or away from sensed events. However, neural signaling is not limited to these reactions. Sensing and reactive information in animals is often passed on for further processing. Bilateral worms have a segmented body plan. Each segment has its own ganglion nerve center and these nerve clusters centers are connected across segments. Aspects of sensing in one segment are passed on to adjacent segments, so the information is partly shared and passed on to brain regions.

Insects evolved from bilateral worms, and thus both worms and insects have similar strategies for integrating sensory and effector processes across segments. However, insects tend to have larger brains and likely have more sophisticated life urges. Some intelligent insects, honeybees and cockroaches, have brains with around one million neurons. These insects have complex saliency, orientation, and urgency dispositions, and can learn surprisingly complex tasks. However, their "attention" is managed by a sparse filtering process in structures known as mushroom bodies.[302] Greater urgency makes a motive more likely to dominate the sparse filtering process, but there is no evidence insects have the kind of feeling-bound attention process that would make them aware of their own urgency.

Colin Klein and Andrew Barron have proposed describing the coordinated saliency, orientation, and urgency dispositions found in insects as a "primary" consciousness – a basic awareness of the world without further reflection on that awareness.[303] Their arguments for highly coordinated life-urge dispositions in insects are well formed. However, I prefer to describe this level of awareness as *urgency-prioritized sentience,* not as a form of consciousness. The term *primary consciousness* was first defined by Gerald Edelman in 1989, to refer to the phenomenal state of human consciousness that included reflection. He would never have considered insect awareness to be equivalent to primary consciousness.[304] I, therefore, restrict *conscious sentience,* at a minimum, to the capacity of cognitive agents to reflect on self-feelings as they react.

In vertebrates, coordinated saliency, orientation, and urgency dispositions are integrated and expanded in the brainstem, which contains a thousand times more neurons than a complex insect brain.

One region, the parabrachial nucleus (PBN) summarizes somatic status inputs broadly from all across the body. Connected to the PBN, the periaqueductal gray (PAG) extends into the midbrain and manages urgency-related emotional action patterns. Other pontine regions provide core motor and arousal life urges. The midbrain tectum uses internal motor processes to orient sensory receptors toward external events, effectively distinguishing between inputs from the self and the world. However, none of these structures have networks that are capable of being simultaneously aware of their self-feelings as they react. As Antonio Damasio has argued, an added *object-organism* integration is essential for conscious awareness.[305] In the preceding chapters, we have argued that this object-organism integration emerges as perceptions are bound together with feelings during synchronous states of attention.

Still, some authors note that because complex cephalopods, octopuses, squids, and cuttlefish, have evolved aspects of intelligent learning and memory, they should be considered conscious. Intelligent reactions may cause human observers to attribute conscious awareness to agents showing such reactions. However, not all intelligent reactions are based on feeling-bound attention. My criterion for concluding an animal is capable of conscious awareness is evidence of an architecture that supports the synchronous integration of perceptions and feelings. This is what causes the *feeling of what happens* in vertebrate minds. I do not see that architecture in cephalopods.

I admit that animals with urgency-prioritized sentience, even many insects, react to injuries with sensory searches and may even identify possible sources. Bees may attack presumed predators by stinging. Caterpillars react to predators by attempting to avoid them. In fact, their reactions sometimes invoke empathic feelings in human observers, because such reactions are typically correlated with human feelings. However, urgency reactions or intelligent behaviors do not provide evidence that an animal experiences the kind of synchronous object-organism integration that occurs during feeling-bound attention.

My criterion for concluding an animal is capable of conscious awareness is evidence of a recurrent attention architecture that binds perceptions and self-feelings into coherent feature assemblies during attention. The feeling-bound attention architecture that engages conscious awareness evolved in vertebrate brains. I do not see anything comparable to that recurrent architecture in cephalopods or insects. I admit that animals with urgency-prioritized sentience, sometimes even insects, react to injuries with sensory searches and may even identify possible sources. Bees may attack presumed predators by stinging. Caterpillars react to predators by attempting to avoid them. In fact, their reactions sometimes invoke empathic feelings in human observers, because such reactions are typically correlated with human feelings. However, urgency reactions or intelligent behaviors do not provide evidence that an animal experiences the synchronous object-organism integration that occurs during conscious attention.

To be clear, I consider urgency-prioritized sentience and reactions to be aspects of higher sentience. Similar forms of urgency-prioritized actions occur in vertebrates when strong instinctive action patterns take control in times of high priority. In such cases, even human agents do things impulsively without considering them consciously first. So perhaps it would be appropriate to consider urgency-prioritized sentience to be a stage of *proto-consciousness*. This would partly fit the emphasis that Klein and Barron have placed on it. However, just as I do not consider life urges that project from proto-self regions in the human to be conscious feelings until they are bound together with perceptions in attention, it is my argument that while adaptive urgency-prioritized dispositions have a proto-conscious character, they cannot qualify as conscious feelings unless they result in an awareness of self and world bound together in attention. In agents with feeling-bound attention, impulsive proto-conscious actions are often reviewed and subsequently placed in a feeling-bound context. Impulsive actions may even come to be regretted after review. However, I know of no evidence that this sort of reflective review ever occurs in insects and cephalopods.

Other theorists have proposed accounts for explaining how consciousness might have evolved. However, these accounts have varied widely due to the absence of an agreed-upon model of how consciousness is implemented, and thus a clear idea of what mechanisms are needed for conscious experience. Deriving models under such constraints is a formidable undertaking. Our goal will therefore not be to critique the details of these models, but rather to look for common themes in them. One common theme is the idea that sensing and spatial-motor control in support of movement played a role in shaping the evolution of mind. Rodolfo Llinás made this point in his book on consciousness, using the sea squirt's tadpole stage as an example of how *motility* contributed to the emergence of mind.[306] There is obviously something special about the mental abilities of mobile agents. They have to react quickly as their environment changes.

Michael Trestman has extended this point suggesting that a cognitive toolkit of skills, with elements of spatial orientation, object sensing, body awareness, and action control, was needed to manage mobile articulated bodies.[307] Trestman links the emergence of this toolkit to the changes in motility that began in the Cambrian explosion. However, Andrew Parker argues that it was largely the emergence of eyes that drove the development of mind in the Cambrian.[308] In yet another analysis, Simona Ginsburg and Eva Jablonka suggest that associative learning was a major impetus in advancing the Cambrian mind.[309] Orientation, visual awareness, body awareness, action control, and associative learning all, no doubt, contributed to the emergence of a more complex mind. However, neither Trestman, Parker, nor Ginsburg and Jablonka provide a clear marker for when, why, or how consciousness emerged in this process.

HOW DID CONSCIOUS SENTIENCE EMERGE?

So what evolutionary forces drove animals toward a conscious sense of self? Bjorn Merker suggests that vertebrate "consciousness arose as a solution to problems in the logistics of decision-making in mobile animals with centralized brains."[310] Further, he suggests that the transition to terrestrial life may have been an impetus for evolving this level of awareness. Consistent with Merker's thinking about the importance of the transition to terrestrial life, Michel Cabanac has proposed that the emotional feelings involved in reward and punishment are central to the emergence of consciousness. Cabanac suggests that feelings are linked to changes in the dopamine reward and punishment systems that emerged in early terrestrial vertebrates.[311]

However, Marcus Stephenson-Jones and colleagues argue that the dopamine pathways in the vertebrate basal ganglia have been largely conserved since the time of the lamprey.[312] This suggests that the transition to land may not have resulted in as big a change in dopamine systems as Cabanac postulated. Still there is evidence of limbic changes in terrestrial vertebrates. Ann Butler and William Hodos note that regions of the medial pallium are enlarged in amniotes and receive "so-called higher-order inputs of an associational nature" from limbic relays in the dorsal thalamus.[313] Thus, it seems that expanded emotional and limbic networks, although not necessarily dopaminergic pathways, probably began playing a larger role in the decisions of terrestrial animals.

Influenced by Jaak Panksepp's emphasis on the role of brainstem and mesencephalic networks in consciousness, Derek Denton and colleagues also emphasize a role for core emotions in consciousness.[314] However, these authors note that core emotions are phylogenetically ancient. Thus they emerged well before the vertebrate transition to land. In fact, they suggest that emotions are essentially the subjective components of instincts.

> It is hypothesized that early in animal evolution complex reflex mechanisms in the basal brain subserving homeostatic responses, in concert with elements of the reticular activating system subserving arousal, melded functionally with regions embodied in the progressive rostral development of the telencephalon. This included the emergent limbic and paralimbic areas, and the insula. This phylogenetically ancient organization subserved the origin of consciousness as the primordial emotion, which signaled that the organism's existence was immediately threatened.[315]

This account from Denton and colleagues contains several elements of the organization supporting feeling-bound consciousness that we have proposed in previous chapters. Although the emphasis on basal forebrain emotions minimizes the role of life urges in the upper-pontine networks and overlooks their role in promoting features to attention, these authors also cite work by Damasio showing that mesencephalic and brainstem areas are largely involved in supporting emotions.[316] Thus, it seems we are growing closer to a consensus about the importance of brainstem and mid-level life urges in supporting conscious feelings. Both Cabanac and Denton see instinctively motivated emotions as underlying processes for bringing feelings to consciousness, and many of those emotions are thought to begin in upper pontine life-urge regions. This link between instincts and emotions is an interesting insight. In fact, this idea fits compellingly with the description of instincts proposed by William McDougall in 1923.

> Absorption of the organism in any particular task or mode of activity is what we call in ourselves "attention;" and that general excitement whose indications we observe in the animals, when their instincts are strongly excited, is what we call in ourselves "emotion." We may therefore define "an

instinct" as any innate disposition which determines the organism to perceive (to pay attention to) any object of a certain class, and to experience in its presence a certain emotional excitement and an impulse to action which finds expression in a specific mode of behavior in relation to that object.[317]

McDougall's characterization of instincts as activities guided by attention to cues and associated emotions, largely parallels the model of core consciousness we have presented here. To be clear, simple instinctive reactions managed in the brainstem do not require attention. The tectal-periaqueductal complex can produce orientations and reactive emotion-like dispositions without the support of attention. However, the more complex instincts that McDougall was describing often involve a thalamic focus of attention on feelings and stimuli that engaged action patterns managed by the basal ganglia for output.

The model of consciousness that we have proposed here argues that vertebrate brains adopted the strategy of using life urges to prioritize their attention. This is effectively how instincts coordinated by the thalamus prioritize attention. Thus, it seems likely that phenomenal consciousness began as the emotive dispositions of instinctive reactions came to guide thalamocortical attention. This is what we have called *feeling-bound attention*.

A consequence of using the feeling-bound attention architecture to expand instincts was the higher-order integration of changes in feelings with changes in perceptions. As we have proposed, the binding of feelings with perceptions during attention would have resulted in what Damasio called an ongoing *feeling of what happens*.[318] A coherent focus of attention would enhance adaptive reactions to cues and feelings. This would make instincts more focused and adaptive. And because feelings become part of the features that gain attention the agent would be aware of its changing feelings as it perceived and acted. This feeling-bound attention architecture is well elaborated in modern vertebrates, and feelings now prioritize attention beyond instinctive actions.

In fact, once this feeling-bound attention process evolved, other brain processes soon began to rely on it. It seems that many cases of perceptual recognition, and the concepts they support, could not be assembled without the selective attention needed to bind multiple features together in perceptual units. Even learning processes as simple as trace eye-blink conditioning do not appear to be possible without attention to memory processes that can bridge the gap in time between cues and when the reactions to them should occur.[319] Thus, the thalamocortical attention network provided a framework within which other aspects of awareness could be bound with feelings. And once this framework took form, feeling-bound attention was soon recruited in support of action planning, learning, memory processing, and even for expanding the feelings of higher-order emotions.

A TIMELINE FOR FEELING-BOUND ATTENTION

It is now time to consider our framework for consciousness in the context of the evolution of the vertebrate brain. As Antonio Damasio noted, the brain regions that support the feelings of core consciousness are "among the phylogenetically older structures of the brain".[320] Jaak Panksepp echoed this position arguing that the feeling networks are not only old but that their organization is highly conserved across vertebrate brains.[321] We know that modern vertebrates, like the domestic cat, have much of the same core architecture for feelings and attention that we do. In fact, recently Zamora-Lopez and colleagues have even shown that in fMRI studies cats have cortical connectivity hubs that are similar to those found in macaque monkeys and humans.[322] Obviously, if we are going to gain more insight into the evolution of conscious mind, we need to consider the time frame in which neural structures essential for consciousness appear in vertebrate evolution.

Multicellular organisms emerged with the evolution of neural networks during the Cambrian period beginning some 570 million years ago (MYA). The Chordata, the phylum that includes all vertebrate animals, was one of several evolutionary lines to emerge in this period. Chordates are characterized by a dorsal rod of dense cartilage, the notochord, which stiffens the body and resists compressions when muscles contract, and a dorsal nerve cord that runs along the notochord. Neurons in this dorsal nerve cord enabled rapid communication between receptors and muscles in the body and the cognitive networks in the brain. The notochord and the dorsal nerve structures are precursors of the bony spine that stiffens the trunk of modern vertebrates and the central spinal cord that connects the body with the brain.

The earliest chordates, sea squirts and larvaceans, are grouped in a subphylum known as the urochordates. This group is estimated to have emerged in the mid-Cambrian some 544 MYA. The sea squirt begins life as a swimming tadpole-like larva. It has a notochord, a dorsal nerve cord, pharyngeal slits, and a post-anal tail. However, it soon finds an appropriate home site where it attaches to the substrate and takes on an immobile polyp form. The polyp then absorbs its nervous system for mobility and feeds on what its tentacles contact. It will never swim again. The larvaceans, however, retain the swimming tadpole form throughout their lives. If we had to pick one design as the prototype of early vertebrates, it would be this tadpole form. The larvaceans have a "brain" ganglion in the head region which contains fewer than 70 neurons. This control structure has about 30 olfactory and taste cells near the mouth, a small middle region with a few hormonal cells, and a posterior motor ganglion for managing tail movement.[323] It's a very efficient design. Olfaction and taste provide some degree of substance recognition and guidance. Mid-brain sensitivity and hormones adjust behavioral dispositions depending on internal needs. And the tail movements enable the larvaceans to swim.

By 520 MYA a more advanced chordate variation, the cephalochordates, had taken form. The best-known modern descendants of this group are lancelets. The notochord in lancelets extends into the head, thus, the prefix "cephalo" referring to the head region. Later vertebrates would develop bony heads to surround the top of their nerve cord. However, the lancelets hadn't gotten that far. They were small filter-feeding organisms that rarely grew to be as much as eight centimeters in length. They didn't have true eyes, only simple light-sensitive clusters of pigment cells, and their total brain was composed of only about 300 neurons. Brain development hadn't even resulted in a swelling in the head end. However, the brain cells were differentiated in forms that presaged the structure of later vertebrate brains.

Lancelets have eye spots and olfactory cells connecting to the front of their brain. They have cell structures that appear to be homologous to the tectum in the middle of their brains. This region receives some inputs from the light-sensitive eye clusters like the tectum of modern vertebrates does. Lancelets have a central lamellar body region that includes a light-sensitive pineal-like structure and a primitive hypothalamus that connects with hormone-producing cells, an arrangement typical of the hypothalamus and pituitary in modern vertebrates. The lamellar body is capable of monitoring temperature, light, and internal needs, and of motivating actions based on those states.[324] Lancelets also have a primitive motor center just posterior to the tectum, suggestive of the location of brainstem motor nuclei in modern vertebrates.

The transition to more vertebrate-like fishes occurred with the evolution of eel-like jawless fishes around 500 MYA. The modern representatives of these animals are hagfishes and lampreys. Like the lancelets, jawless fishes have primitive light-sensitive eye clusters under their skin, but they lack object-focusing mechanisms for vision. They also lack a segmented and calcified vertebral column, like full vertebrates, but their notochords are partially calcified. Thus, they are considered the earliest vertebrates. Modern sea lampreys are parasites that attach themselves to fish and rasps away tissue with a keratinized tongue. Some lampreys may reach over a meter in length. Modern hagfish average about a half meter in length. They have paddle-like tails and are good swimmers. Behaviorally, they tend to burrow in mud awaiting the odor of food and then swim along the odor gradient to find their meal. Lacking jaws and teeth they also feed using a raspy tongue.

There is another interesting behavior found in hagfish. When threatened, they secrete mucous that covers them in copious amounts of slippery slime. Thus, they are commonly called slime eels. The slime clogs the gills of predatory fish, often causing them to choke and release their catch. This probably accounts for how an active hunter, like the hagfish, managed to survive relatively unchanged for nearly 500 million years. Surprisingly, hagfish have evolved a fixed action pattern for removing the slime from their own bodies. They tie themselves in a knot just below their head and then slide the knot down their body. The knot catches the slime and pushes it away as it moves. This is important because the slime also interferes with respiration in the hagfish, so if a hagfish could not clear the slime away, its respiration would be degraded and it could suffocate.

When we examine the brain of the hagfish, we find that, compared to the lancelets, the change in neural structure is nothing short of stunning. Although their brain is only about a centimeter in length, most of the major components of the modern vertebrate brain, or homologous versions of them, are evident. There is a clear telencephalon (olfactory region, septum, and striatum), a diencephalon (hypothalamus, habenula, and hormonal center), a mesencephalon (midbrain tectum and tegmentum), and a complexly innervated hindbrain. Even more significantly, the diencephalon and telencephalon are connected by a thalamus with multiple nuclei. Tracer studies indicate that these connections are reciprocal, although they do not appear to be well differentiated.[325] There are also reciprocal connections between the thalamus and the tectum and between the thalamus and the mesencephalic gray. These latter regions are areas that in higher vertebrates serve as preconscious life-urge feeling centers. Thus, the thalamic connections needed for feeling-bound awareness appear to have been taking form in the hagfish, although well-developed top-down controls to the thalamus were not yet apparent.

Adding to the surprising appearance of modern brain structures in jawless fish, all the basic components of the basal ganglia are present in the hagfish and lamprey.[326] The structure of the basal ganglia is still primitive, but it is obviously sufficient to manage the fixed action pattern needed for slime cleaning in hagfish. In addition, a well-developed peripheral nervous system is present. Homologous forms of five cranial nerves, modern vertebrates have twelve, are evident in hagfish. And while the hagfish lacks a cerebellum, the lamprey has an early cerebellar structure. All this suggests that the modern vertebrate brain was beginning to take form in jawless fish some 500 MYA.

Still, the jawless fish were primitive. They lacked a fully calcified spine. Their eye clusters were only capable of light/dark detection and lacked mechanisms for focusing vision. Their hearing was limited. And their telencephalon was dominated by olfactory and taste inputs, a plan that we primates tend to consider rather primitive. However, jawless fish had a thalamus with connections to primitive midbrain life-urge regions. This arrangement marks the beginning of the architecture that in modern vertebrates supports phenomenal consciousness.

Given that the Cambrian extended to 485 MYA, this suggests that a primitively conscious brain architecture was emerging in vertebrates before the end of the Cambrian. Todd Feinberg and Jon Mallatt also propose that consciousness emerged functionally in the Cambrian, but they do not specify a critical brain architecture for tracking its development.[327] However, the relatively rapid change in brain development between lancelets and the jawless fish suggests that cognitive skills were becoming increasingly important in the competition for survival. Indeed, that competition continued.

Several lines of jawed fish appear in the fossil record beginning around 440 MYA, and by this time all the core brain regions needed for binding life urges with attention and well-formed top-down connections from the telencephalon to the thalamus were present. Thus, there is every reason to conclude that jawed fishes had feeling-bound attention. Jawed fish have a multisensory tectum for spatial coordination and a cerebellum for temporal coordination. Critically, they have a thalamus with robust life-urge inputs and a number of functionally distinct nuclei projecting to the telencephalon. Indeed, both collothalamic and lemnothalamic pathways are present.[328] In addition to an enhanced thalamocortical architecture, jawed fish have object-focusing eyes and several brainstem nuclei to manage eye movement.

The earliest jawed fish were the placoderms. They had large heads, a primitive hinged jaw, large eyes thought to be capable of color vision, cartilaginous skeletons, and bony plaques protecting their head. Placoderms lacked teeth and instead used razor-edged jaw bones to tear their food apart. This design was initially successful. However, amid the competition among later jawed fish, placoderms became extinct within about 50 million years. Their successors were cartilaginous fish, early sharks with better-articulated jaws and real teeth. These fishes gave rise to a persistent line of cartilaginous fish that today includes modern sharks and rays.

Two later lines of jawed fish with bony skeletons subsequently appeared around 420 MYA. One of these lines was the ray-finned fishes. These fishes developed fins that were stiffened by rod-like bones. This line of fishes has been immensely successful. Approximately half of all modern vertebrates are ray-finned fish. The other line of bony fish, the lobe-finned fish, developed thicker fleshy fins without spines. The lobe-finned fish were less prolific. Today, they account for only about one percent of all modern fishes. However, the decedents of bony fishes, the sharks, the ray-finned fishes, and the lobed-fin fishes, all began their evolutionary journey with the feeling-bound attention architecture of core consciousness.

The Transition to Land

It seems that some bony fish developed lung-like structures to supplement their oxygen intake. These structures subsequently evolved into swim bladders in ray-finned fish. However, in lobed-finned fish the supplemental lungs better adapted them for life in shallow tidal pools, marshes, and lagoons with stagnant waters, thus extending their habitats. To assist their locomotion, the lobe-finned fishes also evolved longer fleshy "fins" that made it easier for them to crawl through thick vegetation and sometimes even to scuttle across muddy areas to adjacent pools. This set the stage for the transition of vertebrates to land.

We know that something like this occurred because a fossil skeleton of a 380 million-year-old Gogonasus fish found in Western Australia had large holes for breathing air through the top of its snout.

It also had muscular front fins with well-formed bones connected in an arrangement resembling that of the modern humerus, ulna, and radius of the vertebrate forelimb.[329] A slightly more advanced fish dating to about 375 MYA even shows the beginning of a wrist and bony digits supporting webbed paw-like front fins.[330] Thus, many of the adaptations needed for the transition to life on land began as changes that helped lobe-finned fish maneuver through shallow brackish waters.

Evolution doesn't seek goals. However, it does take advantage of adaptive opportunities, and terrestrial habitats were a big opportunity. Once lobe-finned fish could snort air and scuttle across mudflats, it wasn't long before some of them began scuttling farther beyond the shoreline to take advantage of the rich supply of shore-based plants and insects that swimming fish could not reach. This is estimated to have occurred some 365 MYA. And as these shore feeders evolved stronger appendages and more efficient lungs, they began staying on land for extended time periods. These were the first vertebrates to invade the land. Their descendants are modern amphibians. However, although they could stay on land for extended time periods, they needed to keep their skin moist. Similarly, their gelatin-covered eggs could only survive in water. And in a case of ontogeny recapitulating phylogeny, their hatchlings began life as swimming tadpoles that looked much like their larvacean ancestors. It was only after tadpoles developed legs that a young amphibian could leave the water. Thus, amphibians could never be wholly terrestrial animals.

However, the transition to a terrestrial body plan complete with four articulated appendages had begun. By about 300 MYA, some of these early land invaders formed legs before they hatched, and had evolved a tough scaly skin to conserve water. They had also developed a water-resistant membrane, the amnion, to keep their eggs from drying out on land, and they soon added a shell to make their eggs more resistant to damage. These primitive reptiles were the first fully terrestrial animals and soon diverged into two groups, sauropsid amniotes and synapsid amniotes. The sauropsid line gave rise to the evolution of modern reptiles, dinosaurs, and eventually birds. The synapsid line gradually took a less reptilian form and evolved to form monotremes, marsupials, and placental mammals. However, these two lines already shared many common aspects of brain organization.

In modern mammals, the cortical projection areas are the six-layered tissue we call the neocortex, whereas in avians the homologous projection areas are nuclear rather than layered. However, modern avian brains follow the same general plan of sensory projections through the thalamus,[331] use the same genes to guide striatal and cortical development,[332] use dopamine in a similar way for motor learning,[333] and show similar patterns of slow wave sleep as do modern mammals.[334] Further, current research suggests that the nuclear cortices of avians have as many neurons, and sometimes even more, than the layered cortices of comparable-sized mammals.[335] In fact, recent evidence has found that avian and mammalian forebrains are homologous, and show similarities in connectivity and function down to the cellular level, including laminar cross-connections.[336]

As Husband & Shimizu, 2001 note:

> Both the mammalian and avian systems are characterized by major thalamic input to the telencephalon (e.g., layer IV in mammals; the core ectostriatum in birds) which is then relayed to overlying areas (layer IV projections to layers II and III in mammals; core ectostriatum projections to peri-ectostriatal belt and overlying neostriatum in birds). Additionally, in mammals, there are descending projections from layers II and III to layers V and VI, from which output is directed to the tectum. From the intermedial, lateral neostriatum in birds there are descending projections to the archistriatum, which in turn is a source of projections to the tectum. The comparisons of cortical layers with the nuclear groupings of birds noted above indicate a similar pattern of information processing in amniote brains.[337]

In addition, there are also comparable higher-order thalamic relays in avians and mammals. For example, the avian nucleus rotundus, and its surrounding shell region, has a higher-order visual attention function like that of the pulvinar nuclei in mammals.[338] Further, regions comparable to the higher-order limbic regions of the mammalian thalamus, the midline nuclei, mediodorsal nuclei, and the intralaminar nuclei have also been identified in avians.[339] These higher-order visual and limbic regions are thought to play a role in managing cortical-cortical associations via the thalamus. Avians also appear to have evolved an executive control region, the nidopallium caudolaterale (NCL), in the bird forebrain. Similar to the PFC, the NCL is a center of multimodal integration, connects with higher-order sensory, limbic, and motor structures, and is densely innervated by dopaminergic fibers.[340] As these findings suggest, although the ancestors of modern avians and mammals diverged some 300 MYA, they still share a similar cognitive architecture.

The transition to land involved modifications in the limbs, muscles, and brain structures needed for terrestrial locomotion, and the physical changes needed for reproducing out of water. No doubt, many new cognitive processes supporting these activities evolved during this transition. But the changes were gradual. Modern mammals are arguably smarter than their amphibian and reptile ancestors. In fact, on average, their brains are six times larger than the brains of early tetrapods of comparable body size. Much of this increase involves the expansion of the forebrain, including limbic regions in the basal forebrain. It seems likely that these changes resulted in a more sophisticated sense of motor agency and motivational feelings in terrestrial animals. However, both cartilaginous and bony ray-finned fishes, anamniote lines that never moved onto land, were evolving along their own trajectories. So a few additional comments on the evolution of fishes seem in order.

Revisiting Fishes

In early jawed fish, the telencephalon of the brain expanded during fetal development by a process called *evagination*. During evagination, the upper lateral walls of the developing forebrain vesicle expand faster than the bottom layers. This causes the lateral walls to bulge upward and then fold around inside the skull to form the common dome shape of the cerebral hemispheres. This developmental plan is retained in later cartilaginous fish, in lobed-fin fish, and in all terrestrial vertebrates, including humans.

However, for some reason, ray-finned fish adopted a slightly different developmental plan. For these fish, the middle and bottom layers of the forebrain vesicle expand faster during development than the upper lateral walls and top. This pattern of expansion causes the bottom-most layers of the forebrain vesicle to push down and spread around to the side leaving the original lateral regions more centrally located as they develop. This developmental process is called *eversion*. It is not known what led to the different expansion of brain development in ray-finned fish. However, the differences in relative location of comparable brain regions between other vertebrate brains and ray-finned fish brains slowed comparative work for many years because functional regions discovered in evaginated brains were not in a corresponding location in everted ray-finned brains.

However, homologous regions have gradually been located, and it seems that the switch from shaping the brain by evagination to shaping it by eversion has more to do with the final topology of ray-finned fish brains than with their functions. Ray-finned fish appear to have all the same functional regions, just in different relative locations.[341] Thus, the early assumption that modern fishes lack brain functions comparable to those of birds and mammals is going away. In fact, recent work suggests that the cognitive abilities of many modern ray-finned fish are well developed. They learn new skills, have good spatial memories, and they remember what they learn for long time periods. There are even cases of "tool" use in fishes. The archer fish, for example, uses a jet of water to knock down insects perched above the water. Gouramis and wrasses have been observed using water jets to manipulate objects, and others of this group have been observed carrying scallops and urchins to rock sites and throwing them against the rocks to break them open.[342] Some fish also exhibit surprisingly advanced social behaviors. For example, some gouramis and wrasses cooperate in searches for food.[343] And guppies appear to choose cooperative partners for tasks and retain those partnerships in later life.[344]

Despite the many similarities among the learning and social faculties of modern fishes, birds, and mammals, there is one topic that has raised continued controversy. Some authors have concluded that because fish do not have the same neocortical structures involved in pain perception as mammals do, that they cannot experience pain consciously.[345] In fact, Brian Key has argued that for fish to feel pain they must have a laminated cortex like humans.[346] He dismisses all nociceptive reactions by fish as irrelevant by claiming that the feelings in those reactions are unconscious.

However, there is no evidence that a laminated cortex is required for consciously feeling anything. In fish and avians, the thalamocortical architecture involves connections from the thalamus to regional nuclear targets in the pallial cortex rather than to laminated neocortical regions. So if fish cannot feel pain, this implies that avians cannot feel pain either. The argument that only a layered neocortex will work for pain perception is specious. There is broad evidence for similar functional connections between the thalamus and the nuclear cortex for other senses. Birds and fish do not have a laminated visual cortex either, but there is no evidence they are not conscious of what they see.[347]

The conclusion that fish cannot feel pain also does not fit well with the insights of those researchers who work with fish.[348] In fact, Culum Brown has addressed this issue in some detail.[349] Some key points of his argument are:

- The pain receptors in all vertebrates are conserved structures derived from an early fish-like ancestor.
- It is unreasonable for evolution to separate the detection of pain from cognitive and emotional responses to it, since they are so clearly part of an integrated system that evolved to reduce the chances of injury.
- Rapid reflexive responses to pain do not rule out the likelihood that fish also learn to use pain to alter their cognitive reactions to the world. Mammals also have rapid reflexive responses to pain.
- Studies using fMRI have shown that when suffering from pain, there is significant activity in the fish forebrain which is similar to increased activity observed in the human forebrain during pain.[350]
- Further evidence that fish respond to pain in a cognitive sense is that when fish are in pain, they suffer from attention deficits. They simply fail to notice stimuli that they otherwise would notice.
- The application of analgesic drugs reduces the deficits caused by pain in fish, just as it does in humans.[351]
- In addition to Brown's points, other work has identified laminar cross-connections within parts of both fish and avian cortices which support a pattern of cortical information flow similar to the mammalian cortex.[352]

The model of consciousness proposed in this book argues that life urges guide and become part of the cues that gain attention. Thus, evidence that pain interferes with shifting attention to novel stimuli is just what would be expected if pain was biasing attention to other cues. From an evolutionary standpoint, pain is one of the earliest adaptive life urges to evolve. It facilitates learning that avoids injury. If feelings enhance attention and promote more vigorous adaptive reactions, as proposed here, then there is no way that evolution would prevent fish from using pain to guide their attention when all the necessary support networks for feeling pain have been in place in fish for hundreds of millions of years. The parallels with mammalian vertebrates are obvious. Fish brains have all the major components of modern terrestrial brains, including connections from brainstem life-urge regions to the thalamus. Fish react to pain in ways similar to how terrestrial vertebrates react. Denying conscious pain to fishes and avians because they lack a laminated cortex, is no more convincing than Carruthers' claim that dogs do not experience pain because they lack language.

CONCLUDING COMMENTS

Biologically embodied "cognition" occurs on many levels in living organisms, from protists, to plants, and onto animal minds.[353] These embodied processes are what we have termed *life urges*. We have proposed that phenomenal consciousness began as vertebrates adopted the strategy of using life urges to prioritize attention. The brainstem-thalamocortical architecture that manages vertebrate attention is unique. Sensorimotor information is passed through the thalamus to the cortex. Brainstem inputs to the thalamus help prioritize attention. Return loops from the cortex project back to the thalamus and these loops also branch on to the brainstem. This algorithm focuses within 350-500ms and reaches an enhanced level of neural processing when attention gains consciousness.

The simple beginnings of this brain architecture are evident in the jawless fish that evolved some 500 MYA, although jawless fish only have rudimentary parts for some of the necessary architecture. However, all the core brain regions needed for binding life urges with attention and well-formed top-down connections from the telencephalon to the thalamus were present by the time jawed fishes evolved some 440 MYA. The idea that prioritizing attention with feelings marked the path to core consciousness may not leap out as a satisfactory explanation for modern consciousness. However, paraphrasing Damasio's opening quote: When core consciousness began, we were on the right track. We were telling ourselves that there was an individual perspective to our attention and that it was all tied to life. Sensory inputs passing through the thalamus, life urges directed to the thalamus, and an attention architecture capable of binding life urges with perceptions during attention were the primary neural processes needed for the emergence of core consciousness.

Some authors argue that because complex cephalopods, octopuses, squids, and cuttlefish, have evolved aspects of intelligent learning and memory, they should be considered conscious. However, not all intelligent reactions involve feeling-bound attention.

My criterion for concluding that an animal is capable of consciousness is evidence of an architecture that supports the synchronous integration of perceptions and feelings in a focused architecture that enhances neural processing. This is what engages the *feeling of what happens* in vertebrate minds. I do not see that architecture among invertebrates so I do not consider them to have *conscious sentience*. I do see evidence of what I called *urgency-prioritized sentience* in cephalopods, octopuses, squids, cuttlefish, and even in some insects. They react to injuries and take on defensive stances. However, urgency reactions do not provide evidence that an animal experiences the kind of object-organism integration that occurs when feeling-bound attention engages conscious sentience.

> **Ending Remarks**

As best we know conscious sentience evolved in jawed fishes some 440 MYA and has been retained in vertebrates since that time. I see no evidence that there is a comparable feeling-bound attention architecture among invertebrates.

Notes and References

Introduction: Minding Consciousness

1 The fountains, waterworks, and water-driven automata in the gardens and grottoes at Saint-Germain-en-Laye were designed by the Florentine hydraulics engineers Tommaso Francini and his younger brother Alessandro Francini.

2 Descartes did have a mechanistic account of how the soul interfaced with the body. This was based on the flow of animal spirits managed by the pineal gland. It is easy to see the flow of animal spirits as related to modern accounts of mind as resulting from the flow of neural signals. However, this flow was obviously not needed for the soul to carry on ideas after death. A position that Descartes accepted. Thus, Descartes mechanistic account of mind was largely incomplete. See Lokhorst, 2014, for several variations of Descartes' thinking on these issues.

3 See Radner & Radner, 1996, for an interesting analysis of Descartes' thinking on animal consciousness. The authors suggest that Descartes occasionally considered the possibility that there may be a non-reasoning form of consciousness in animals.

4 Descartes appears to have been careful not put his work in the position of challenging contemporary religious ideas and bringing discredit on himself. See Lokhurst, 2014.

5 See Griffin 1976–2000 for his books on this topic and some influential papers.

6 Damasio, 1994, 1999, 2010. Damasio's emphasis on the role of feelings in conscious mind, especially as developed in his 1999 book, was my inspiration.

7 See Sherman & Guillery, 2006.

8 Lucas, 2011, Emergence, Mind, and Consciousness.

9 See Craig, 2002, 2010; Damasio, 1994, 1999.

10 See Crick & Koch, 2003; Edelman, 1998, 2003; and Llinás, 2001.

11 Sherman & Guillery, 2006.

12 Lucas, 2011.

13 Tononi, 2008.

14 Fries, 2015.

15 See Dehaene & Nacche, 2001; Dehaene, 2014.

16 Middleton & Strick, 2000.
17 Graybiel, 2008. I first discuss this model in Chapter 16 of Lucas, 2011 and propose my master-apprentice architecture there.

Craig A. D. (2002). How do you feel? Interoception: The sense of the physiological condition of the body. *Nature Reviews Neuroscience*, 3, 655–666.

Craig A. D. (2010). The sentient self. *Brain Structure and Function*, 214, 563–577.

Crick, F. & Koch, C. (2003). A framework for consciousness. *Nature Neuroscience*, 6, 119–126.

Damasio, A. R. (1994). Descartes' Error: Emotion, Reason, and the Human Brain. New York: Avon Press.

Damasio, A. R. (1999). The Feeling of What Happens: Body and Emotion in the Making of Consciousness. New York: Harcourt Brace & Co.

Damasio, A. R. (2010). Self Comes to Mind: Constructing the Conscious Brain. New York: Pantheon Books.

Deco, G. & Kringelbach, M. L. (2016). Metastability and coherence: Extending communication through the coherence hypothesis using a whole-brain computational perspective. *Trends in Neurosciences*, 39, 125–135.

Dehaene, S. (2014). Consciousness and the Brain: Deciphering How the Brain Codes Our Thoughts. City of Westminster, London: Penguin Books.

Dehaene & Naccache, (2001). Towards a cognitive neuroscience of consciousness: Basic evidence and a workspace framework. *Cognition*, 79, 1–37.

Edelman, G. M. (1989). The Remembered Present: A Biological Theory of Consciousness. New York: Basic Books.

Edelman, G. M. (2003). Naturalizing consciousness: A theoretical framework. *Proceedings of the National Academy of Sciences (USA)*, 100 (9), 5520-5524.

Fries, P. (2015). Rhythms for cognition: Communication through coherence. *Neuron*, 88, 220–235.

Graybiel, A. M. (2008). Habits, rituals, and the evaluative brain. *Annual Review of Neuroscience*, 31, 359–387.

Griffin, D. R. (1976). *The Question of Animal Awareness: Evolutionary Continuity of Mental Experience*. Rockefeller University Press (second edition: 1981).

Griffin, D. R. (1978). Prospects for a cognitive ethology. *Behavioral and Brain Sciences*, 4, 527–538.

Griffin, D. R. (1984). *Animal Thinking*. Harvard, University Press.

Griffin, D. R. (1992). *Animal Minds: Beyond Cognition to Consciousness*. University of Chicago Press.

Griffin, D .R. (1995). Windows on animal minds. *Consciousness and Cognition*, 4, 194–204.

Griffin, D. R. (2001). *Animal Minds: Beyond Cognition to Consciousness*, 2nd Ed. University of Chicago Press.

Llinás, R. (2001). *I of the Vortex: From Neurons to Self*. Cambridge, MA: Bradford/MIT Press.

Lokhorst, G-J. (2014). Descartes and the pineal gland. In: Edward N. Zalta (Ed.), *The Stanford Encyclopedia of Philosophy* (spring 2014 Edition), URL = <http://plato.stanford.edu/archives/spr2014/entries/pineal-gland/>.

Lucas, G. A. (2011). Emergence, Mind, and Consciousness: A Bio-Inspired Design for a Conscious Agent. Bloomington, IN: iUniverse.

Middleton, F. A. & Strick, P. L. (2000). Basal ganglia output and cognition: Evidence from anatomical, behavioral, and clinical studies. *Brain and Cognition*, 42, 183–200.

Miller, M. & Clark, A. (2017). Happily entangled: Prediction, emotion, and the embodied mind. *Synthese*, doi:10.1007/s11229-017-1399-7.

Radner, D & Radner, M. (1996). *Animal Consciousness*. Amherst, NY: Prometheus Books.

Sherman, S. M. & Guillery, R. W. (2006). *Exploring the Thalamus and its Role in Cortical Function*. Cambridge, MA: MIT Press.

Tononi, G. (2008). Consciousness as integrated information: A provisional manifesto. *Biological Bulletin*, 215, 216–242.

1: ATTENTION, MIND, AND SELF

18 The story about Tom requesting my help and its subsequent discussion was adapted rather directly from the Introduction in Lucas, 2011. Unfortunately, Tom has now passed away, but features of his mind live on forever in these memories.

19 Descartes, 2008, p. 117.

20 See Lokhorst, 2014. As Lokhurst notes, Descartes' thinking varied at times, and there are several varying interpretations of how best to characterize his ideas about the connection between mind and

body. However, as in the quote from the Meditations, at times Descartes clearly suggested that mind and body could intimately interact. This makes him an interactionist.

21 Damasio, 1999.

Chalmers, D. J. (1997). Facing up to the problem of consciousness. *Journal of Consciousness Studies*, 4(1), 3–46.

Damasio, A. R. (1999). The Feeling of What Happens: Body and Emotion in the Making of Consciousness. New York: Harcourt Brace & Co.

Descartes, R. (2008/1641). *Meditations*. (Trans. John Veitch.) New York: Cosimo, Inc.

Lokhorst, G-J. (2014). Descartes and the pineal gland. In: Edward N. Zalta (Ed.), *The Stanford Encyclopedia of Philosophy* (Spring 2014 Edition), URL = <http://plato.stanford.edu/archives/spr2014/entries/pineal-gland/>.

Lucas, G. A. (2011). Emergence, Mind, and Consciousness: A Bio-Inspired Design for a Conscious Agent. Bloomington, IN: iUniverse.

2: FROM LIFE URGES TO PROTO-FEELINGS

22 See Damasio, 1999, 2010; Craig, 2002, 2009, 2010; and Panksepp, 1998, 2005.

23 See Panksepp 1998, chapter 3.

24 In Lucas, 2011 I referred to all these inputs as kinds of interoceptions. However, interoception is more commonly used to refer only to sensory inputs from the body. Arousal and motor reactivity sources are not interoceptive in that sense. Thus, here I have adopted Damasio's characterization of these early inputs as *life urges* and I refer to the brain regions that manage life urges more generally as *limbic* regions. My intent is that life urges, as broadly defined here, should be seen as anchoring limbic networks to status sensations, action dispositions, and arousal states.

25 See Craig, 2002, 2003, for a detailed description of sympathetic and parasympathetic inputs to the brainstem.

26 Interesting, Damasio & Carvalho, 2013, note that both early

sympathetic and parasympathetic inputs are largely transmitted by unmyelinated fibers. They suggest that because these fibers are not insulated by myelin sheaths they may be more sensitive to extracellular states of passage and thus more likely to synchronize via ionic bonds.

27 Damasio, 1999, cites the tectum, the cingulate gyrus, and certain thalamic nuclei, in particular, the intralaminar nuclei of the thalamus, as secondary regions where object-organism relationships may be bound together.

28 Gloveli et al., 2023.

29 Ferguson et al., 2022.

30 Damasio, 1996.

31 Moruzzi & Magoun, 1949. The source of ascending cholinergic neurons comes largely from the pedunculopontine tegmental nucleus and the laterodorsal tegmental nucleus. Ascending norepinephrine neurons come from the locus coeruleus. Ascending serotonin neurons arise from the raphe nuclei along a central brainstem. Apparently, having major sources of ascending arousal controlled from a few localized sites makes it easier to manage the timing of the arousal signals.

32 Fuller et al., 2011.

33 See Damasio, 1999 chapter 8, for a detailed account of the effect of brainstem lesions. See also Parvizi and Damasio, 2003.

34 Craig, 2003, 2009. Craig, 2010, emphasizes that the opponent processes of the sympathetic and parasympathetic inputs are retained in the cortex.

35 Critchley et al., 2003.

Craig A. D. (2002). How do you feel? Interoception: The sense of the physiological condition of the body. *Nature Reviews Neuroscience*, 3, 655–666.

Craig A. D. (2003). Interoception: The sense of the physiological condition of the body. *Current Opinion in Neurobiology*, 13, 500–505.

Craig A. D. (2009). How do you feel - now? The anterior insula and human awareness. *Nature Reviews Neuroscience*, 10, 59–70.

Craig A. D. (2010). The sentient self. *Brain Structure and Function*, 214, 563–577.

Critchley, H.D., et al. (2003). Human cingulate cortex and autonomic control: Converging neuroimaging and clinical evidence. *Brain*, 126(10), 2139–2152.

Damasio, A. R. (1996). The somatic marker hypothesis and the possible functions of the prefrontal cortex. *Philosophical Transaction of the Royal Society of London. B*, 351, 1413–1420.

Damasio, A. R. (1998). Investigating the biology of consciousness. *Philosophical Transaction of the Royal Society of London. B*, 353, 1879–1882.

Damasio, A. R. (1999). The Feeling of What Happens: Body and Emotion in the Making of Consciousness. New York: Harcourt Brace & Co.

Damasio, A. R. & Carvalho, G. B. (2013). The nature of feelings: Evolutionary and neurobiological origins. *Nature Reviews Neuroscience*, 14, 143–152.

Ferguson, M.A. et al. (2022). A neural circuit for spirituality and religiosity derived from patients with brain lesions. *Biological Psychiatry*, 91 (4), 330-331.

Fuller, P.M., Sherman, D., Pedersen, N.P., Saper, C.B. & Lu, J. (2011). Reassessment of the structural basis of the ascending arousal system. *Journal of Comparative Neurology*, 519(5), 933–956.

Gloveli, N. et al. (2023). Play and tickling responses map to the lateral columns of the rat periaqueductal gray. *Neuron,* https://doi.org/10.1016/j.neuron.2023.06.018.

Lucas, G. A. (2011). Emergence, Mind, and Consciousness: A Bio-Inspired Design for a Conscious Agent. Bloomington, IN: iUniverse.

Moruzzi, G. & Magoun, H. W. (1949). Brainstem reticular formation and activation. *Electroencephalography and Clinical Neurophysiology*, 1(4), 455–473.

Panksepp, J. (1998). Affective Neuroscience: The Foundations of Human and Animal Emotions. New York: Oxford University Press.

Panksepp, J. (2005). Affective consciousness: Core emotional feelings in animals and humans. *Consciousness and Cognition*, 14, 30–80.

Peelle, J.E. & Davis, M.H. (2012). Neural oscillations carry speech rhythm through to comprehension. *Frontiers in Psychology,* 3: 320.

Perdikis, D., Huys, R., & Jirsa, V. K. (2011.) Time scale hierarchies in the functional organization of complex behaviors. *PLoS Computational Biology*, 7(9): e1002198.

Raizada, R. D. & Grossberg, S. (2003). Towards a theory of the laminar architecture of cerebral cortex: Computational clues. *Cerebral Cortex*, 13, 100–113.

Salinas, E. & Sejnowski, T. J. (2001). Correlated neuronal activity and the flow of neural information. *Nature Reviews Neuroscience*, 2, 539–550.

Sherman, S. M. & Guillery, R. W. (2006). *Exploring the Thalamus and its Role in Cortical Function*. Cambridge, MA: MIT Press.

Steriade, M., Contreras, D., Amzica, F. & Timofeev, I. (1996). Synchronization of fast (30-40 Hz) spontaneous oscillations in intrathalamic and thalamocortical networks. *Journal of Neuroscience*, 16, 2788–2808.

Siebenhühner, F. et al., 2020. Genuine cross-frequency coupling networks in human resting-state electrophysiological recordings. *PLoS Biology*, 18(5): e3000685.

Tononi, G. (2004). An information integration theory of consciousness. *BMC Neuroscience*, 5:42.

Tononi, G. (2008). Consciousness as integrated information: A provisional manifesto. *Biological Bulletin*, 215, 216–242.

Tononi, G., Boly, M., Massimini, M., & Koch, C. (2016). Integrated information theory: From consciousness to its physical substrate. *Nature Reviews Neuroscience*, 17, 450–461.

Trageser, J. C. & Keller, A. (2004). Reducing the uncertainty: Gating of peripheral inputs by zona incerta. *Journal of Neuroscience*, 24, 8911–8915.

Zhu, F., Elnozahy, S., Lawlor, J. et al. (2023). The cholinergic basal forebrain provides a parallel channel for state-dependent sensory signaling to auditory cortex. *Nature Neuroscience,* 26, 810–819.

3: ASSEMBLING CONSCIOUS ATTENTION

36 The role of the thalamocortical architecture in attention has broad support. See Crick & Koch, 2003; Dehaene, Sergent, & Changeux, 2003; Di Lollo, Enns, & Rensink, 2000; Edelman, 2003; Edelman & Tononi, 2000; Lamme & Roelfsema, 2000; Llinás, 2001; Llinás & Ribary, 2001; Llinás, Ribary, Contreras, & Pedroarena, 1998; Raizada & Grossberg, 2003.

37 The comment regarding Crick and Koch's use of transient coalitions can be found in Edelman, 2003. For earlier works describing the dynamic core see Edelman 1987; 1989; 1992; and Edelman & Tononi, 2000.

38 Edelman, 2003.

39 Koch, C., Winograd, T., & Moravec, H. (1992). What is

consciousness? *Discover (November 1992)*, p. 96.
40 Sherman & Guillery, 2006.
41 Craig, 2002.
42 Groh et al., 2014; Trageser & Keller, 2004
43 Damasio, 1996.
44 Halassa, et al., 2014.
45 Jones, 2001, 2006.
46 Edelman & Tononi, 2000.
47 Tononi, 2004; 2008.
48 Tononi et al., 2016.
49 See Fries, 2005; Kopell et al., 2000; Palva, Palva, & Kaila, 2005; Salinas & Sejnowski, 2001.
50 Gollo et al., 2015.
51 Sensory bindings generally involve higher frequencies, such as those in the gamma (30–60 cps) and high-gamma (80–200 cps) range, while beta frequencies lie (13–30 cps), alpha (8–12 cps), and theta (4–7 cps) rhythms.
52 Gollo et al., 2015. Recent research suggest that both phase-amplitude couplings and cross- frequency phase synchrony may contribute to this harmonic synchrony, see Siebenhühner, et al., 2020.
53 Fries, 2005; Izhikevich, 2006. In a large scale simulation of the thalamocortical system Izhikevich & Edelman, 2008, demonstrated how this architecture, and its emergent interactions, appear to fit the time scales of conscious processing.
54 Peelle & Davis, 2012. See also the analysis of handwriting by Perdikis, Huys, & Jirsa, 2011.
55 Chaudhuri et al., 2015, p.1.
56 Fries, 2015.
57 Dehaene, 2014.
58 Dehaene, 2014, has focused on the consciousness of visual attention. While his work follows largely from earlier thalamocortical studies of consciousness, he has come to characterize his model as a neural version of the global workspace model. I generally consider his descriptions of how features reach global access to be highly informative. However, I do not assume that global access always requires the activation of the PFC as he seems to suggest, although I agree this may often happen with strong global activations.
59 Fuller et al., 2011. Fuller et al. also suggest that ascending arousal from the locus coeruleus/pre-coeruleus region contributes to BNM arousal and that this path is important for activating memory

processing during consciousness
60 Kuenzel et al., 2011.
61 Berg et al., 2005; Munn et al., 2021; Oswald et al., 2022; Zhu et
    al., 2023.
62 Damasio, 1999.
63 Gollo et al., 2015.
64 Huang et al., 2020, 2021.
65 Blanke, 2012; Ionta et al., 2014.
66 Damasio, 1998, p. 1882.
67 Damasio, 1999.
68 Craig, 2010; Panksepp, 2005.
69 See Crick & Koch, 2003, Edelman, 2003, and Llinás, 2001.
70 Sherman & Guillery, 2006.
71 Fries, 2005, 2015.

Berg, R.W., Friedman, B., Schroeder, L.F. & Kleinfeld, D. (2005).
    Activation of nucleus basalis facilitates cortical control of a brain
    stem motor program. *Journal of Neurophysiology*, 94(1), 699-711.
Blanke, O. (2012). Multisensory brain mechanisms of bodily self-
    consciousness. *Nature Reviews. Neuroscience*, 13(8), 556–571.
Chaudhuri et al. (2015). A large-scale circuit mechanism for
    hierarchical dynamical processing in the primate cortex. *Neuron*:
    http://dx.doi.org/10.1016/j.neuron.2015.09.008.
Craig A. D. (2002). How do you feel? Interoception: The sense of the
    physiological condition of the body. *Nature Reviews
    Neuroscience*, 3, 655–666.
Craig A. D. (2010). The sentient self. *Brain Structure and Function*,
    214, 563–577.
Crick, F. & Koch, C. (2003). A framework for consciousness. *Nature
    Neuroscience*, 6, 119–126.
Damasio, A. R. (1996). The somatic marker hypothesis and the
    possible functions of the prefrontal cortex. *Philosophical
    Transaction of the Royal Society of London. B*, 351, 1413–1420.
Damasio, A. R. (1998). Investigating the biology of consciousness.
    Philosophical Transaction of the Royal Society of London. B, 353,
    1879–1882.
Damasio, A. R. (1999). The Feeling of What Happens: Body and
    Emotion in the Making of Consciousness. New York: Harcourt
    Brace & Co.
Dehaene, S. (2014). Consciousness and the Brain: Deciphering How
    the Brain Codes Our Thoughts. City of Westminster, London:
    Penguin Books.

Dehaene, S., Sergent, C., & Changeux, J-P. (2003). A neuronal network model linking subjective reports and objective physiological data during conscious perception. *Proceedings of the National Academy of Sciences (USA),* 100 (14), 8520–8525.

Di Lollo, V., Enns, J. T., & Rensink, R. A. (2000). Competition for consciousness among visual events: The psychophysics of reentrant visual pathways. *Journal of Experimental Psychology: General,* 129, 481–507.

Edelman, G. M. (1987). Neural Darwinism: The Theory of Neuronal Group Selection. New York: Basic Books.

Edelman, G. M. (1989). The Remembered Present: A Biological Theory of Consciousness. New York: Basic Books.

Edelman, G. M. (1992). Bright Air, Brilliant Fire: On the Matter of the Mind. New York: Basic Books.

Edelman, G. M. (2003). Naturalizing consciousness: A theoretical framework. *Proceedings of the National Academy of Sciences (USA),* 100 (9), 5520-5524.

Edelman, G. M. & Tononi, G. (2000). *A Universe of Consciousness: How Matter Becomes Imagination.* New York: Basic Books.

Fries, P. (2005). A mechanism for cognitive dynamics: Neural communication through neural coherence. *Trends in Cognitive Sciences,* 9, 474–480.

Fries, P. (2015). Rhythms for cognition: Communication through coherence. *Neuron,* 88, 220–235.

Fuller, P.M., Sherman, D., Pedersen, N.P., Saper, C.B. & Lu, J. (2011). Reassessment of the structural basis of the ascending arousal system. *Journal of Comparative Neurology,* 519(5), 933–956.

Gazzaniga, M. S. (2010). Neuroscience and the correct level of explanation for understanding mind. *Trends in Cognitive Sciences,* 14, 291–292.

Gollo, L. L., Zalesky, A., Hutchison, R. M., van den Heuvel, M., & Breakspear, M. (2015). Dwelling quietly in the rich club: brain network determinants of slow cortical fluctuations. *Philosophical Transactions of the Royal Society B,* 370: 20140165.

Groh, A., Bokor, H., Mease, R.A., Plattner, V.M., Hangya, B., Stroh, A., Deschenes, M., & Acsády, L. (2014). Convergence of cortical and sensory driver inputs on single thalamocortical cells. *Cerebral Cortex,* 24(12), 3167–3179.

Halassa, M. M. et al. (2014). State-dependent architecture of thalamic reticular subnetworks. *Cell,* 158, 808–821.

Huang, Z., Tarnal, V. et al. (2021). Anterior insula regulates brain network transitions that gate conscious access. *Cell Reports,* 35(5), 109081.

Huang, Z., Zhang, J., Wu, J., Mashour, G. A., & Hudetz, A. G. (2020). Temporal circuit of macroscale dynamic brain activity supports human consciousness. *Science Advances*, 11: eaaz0087.

Ionta, S., Martuzzi, R., Salomon, R., & Blanke, O. (2014). The brain network reflecting bodily self-consciousness: A functional connectivity study. *Social Cognitive and Affective Neuroscience*, 9(12), 1904–1913.

Izhikevich, E. M. (2006). Polychronization: Computation with spikes. *Neural Computation*, 18, 245–282.

Izhikevich, E. M. & Edelman, G. M. (2008). Large-scale model of mammalian thalamocortical systems. *Proceedings of the National Academy of Sciences (USA)*, 105, 3593–3598.

Jones, E. G. (2001). The thalamic matrix and thalamocortical synchrony. *Trends in Neurosciences*, 24, 595–601.

Jones, E. G. (2006). *The Thalamus Revisited*. Cambridge, U. K.: Cambridge University Press.

Koch, C., Winograd, T., & Moravec, H. (1992, November). What is consciousness? *Discover*, p. 96.

Kopell, N., Ermentrout, G. B., Whittington, M. A. & Traub, R. D. (2000). Gamma rhythms and beta rhythms have different synchronization properties. *Proceedings of the National Academy of Sciences (USA)*, 97, 1867–1872.

Kuenzel, W.J., Medina, L., Csillag, A., Perkel. D.J., & Reiner, A. (2011). The avian subpallium: New insights into structural and functional subdivisions occupying the lateral subpallial wall and their embryological origins. *Brain Research*, 18, 1424:67-101.

Lamme, V. A. & Roelfsema, P. R. (2000). The distinct modes of vision offered by feedforward and recurrent processing. *Trends in Neurosciences*, 23, 571–579.

Llinás, R. (2001). *I of the Vortex: From Neurons to Self*. Cambridge, MA: Bradford/MIT Press.

Llinás, R. & Ribary, U. (2001). Consciousness and the brain: The thalamocortical dialogue in health and disease. *Annals of the New York Academy of Sciences*, 929, (1), 166–175.

Llinás, R., Ribary, U., Contreras, D., & Pedroarena, C. (1998). The neuronal basis for consciousness. Philosophical Transactions of the Royal Society of London B, 353, 1841–1849.

Munn, B.R., Müller, E.J., Wainstein, G. et al. (2021). The ascending arousal system shapes neural dynamics to mediate awareness of cognitive states. *Nature Communications,* 12, 6016.

Oswald, M.J., Han, Y., Li, H. et al. (2022). Cholinergic basal forebrain nucleus of Meynert regulates chronic pain-like behavior via modulation of the prelimbic cortex. *Nature Communications,* 13, 5014.

Palva, J. M., Palva, S. & Kaila, K. (2005). Phase synchrony among neuronal oscillations in the human cortex. *Journal of Neuroscience*, 25, 3962–3972.

Panksepp, J. (2005). Affective consciousness: Core emotional feelings in animals and humans. *Consciousness and Cognition*, 14, 30–80.

Peelle, J.E. & Davis, M.H. (2012). Neural oscillations carry speech rhythm through to comprehension. *Frontiers in Psychology,* 3: 320.

Perdikis, D., Huys, R., & Jirsa, V. K. (2011.) Time scale hierarchies in the functional organization of complex behaviors. *PLoS Computational Biology*, 7(9): e1002198.

Raizada, R. D. & Grossberg, S. (2003). Towards a theory of the laminar architecture of cerebral cortex: Computational clues. *Cerebral Cortex*, 13, 100–113.

Salinas, E. & Sejnowski, T. J. (2001). Correlated neuronal activity and the flow of neural information. *Nature Reviews Neuroscience*, 2, 539–550.

Sherman, S. M. & Guillery, R. W. (2006). *Exploring the Thalamus and its Role in Cortical Function.* Cambridge, MA: MIT Press.

Steriade, M., Contreras, D., Amzica, F. & Timofeev, I. (1996). Synchronization of fast (30-40 Hz) spontaneous oscillations in intrathalamic and thalamocortical networks. *Journal of Neuroscience*, 16, 2788–2808.

Siebenhühner, F. et al., 2020. Genuine cross-frequency coupling networks in human resting-state electrophysiological recordings. *PLoS Biology*, 18(5): e3000685.

Tononi, G. (2004). An information integration theory of consciousness. *BMC Neuroscience*, 5:42.

Tononi, G. (2008). Consciousness as integrated information: A provisional manifesto. *Biological Bulletin*, 215, 216–242.

Tononi, G., Boly, M., Massimini, M., & Koch, C. (2016). Integrated information theory: From consciousness to its physical substrate. *Nature Reviews Neuroscience*, 17, 450–461.

Trageser, J. C. & Keller, A. (2004). Reducing the uncertainty: Gating of peripheral inputs by zona incerta. *Journal of Neuroscience*, 24, 8911–8915.

Zhu, F., Elnozahy, S., Lawlor, J. et al. (2023). The cholinergic basal forebrain provides a parallel channel for state-dependent sensory signaling to auditory cortex. *Nature Neuroscience,* 26, 810–819.

4: SUBJECTIVE EXPERIENCE

72 See Lucas, 2011, Chapter 1 for more details on my view of emergence.
73 See Lucas, 2011, p. 9. Note, Arthur Koestler, Clive Staples Lewis, and Donald M. MacKay have all been credited with the phrase "nothing buttery" to describe this class of arguments.
74 Anderson, 1972, p. 393.
75 Anderson, 1972.
76 Lucas, 2011, p. 319.
77 Damasio, 2003, p. 227.
78 Damasio, 1999, p.170. Emphasis in the original.
79 Llinás, 2001, p. 126.
80 Edelman, 2003, p. 5523.
81 Chalmers, 1995.
82 Fuller et al., 2011.
83 Kuenzel et al., 2011.
84 Bjordahl, Dimyan & Weinberger, 1998; Kilgard & Merzenich, 1998; Kilgard et al., 2002.
85 Deco & Kringelbach, 2016.
86 Graziano, Guterstam, Bio, & Wilterson, 2020.
87 Wilterson & Graziano, 2021.

Anderson, P. W. (1972). More is different. *Science*, 177, 393–396.
Bjordahl, T. S., Dimyan, M. A. & Weinberger, N. M. (1998). Induction of long-term receptive field plasticity in the auditory cortex of the waking guinea pig by stimulation of the nucleus basalis. *Behavioral Neuroscience*, 112, 467–479.
Chalmers, D. J. (1995). Facing up to the problem of consciousness. *Journal of Consciousness Studies*, 2(3), 200–219.
Chalmers, D. J. (1997). Moving forward on the problem of consciousness. *Journal of Consciousness Studies*, 4(1), 3–46.
Damasio, A. R. (1999). *The Feeling of What Happens: Body and Emotion in the Making of Consciousness.* New York: Harcourt Brace & Co.

Damasio, A. R. (2003). Mental self: The person within. *Nature*, 423, 227.

Deco, G. & Kringelbach, M. L. (2016). Metastability and coherence: Extending communication through the coherence hypothesis using a whole-brain computational perspective. *Trends in Neurosciences*, 39, 125–135.

Edelman, G. M. (2003). Naturalizing consciousness: A theoretical framework. *Proceedings of the National Academy of Sciences (USA)*, 100 (9), 5520–5524.

Fuller, P.M., Sherman, D., Pedersen, N.P., Saper, C.B. & Lu, J. (2011). Reassessment of the structural basis of the ascending arousal system. *Journal of Comparative Neurology*, 519(5), 933–956.

Graziano, M.S.A., Guterstam, A., Bio, B.J., & Wilterson, A.I. (2020). Toward a standard model of consciousness: Reconciling the attention schema, global workspace, higher-order thought, and illusionist theories. *Cognitive Neuropsychology*, 37, 155-172.

Kilgard, M. P. & Merzenich, M. M. (1998). Cortical map reorganization enabled by nucleus basalis activity. *Nature Neuroscience*, 1, 727–731.

Kilgard, M. P., Pandya, P. K., Engineer, N. D. & Moucha, R. (2002). Cortical network reorganization guided by sensory input features. *Biological Cybernetics*, 87, 333–343.

Kuenzel, W.J., Medina, L., Csillag, A., Perkel. D.J., & Reiner, A. (2011). The avian subpallium: New insights into structural and functional subdivisions occupying the lateral subpallial wall and their embryological origins. *Brain Research*, 18, 1424:67-101.

Llinás, R. (2001). *I of the Vortex: From Neurons to Self*. Cambridge, MA: Bradford/MIT Press.

Lucas, G. A. (2011). Emergence, Mind, and Consciousness: A Bio-Inspired Design for a Conscious Agent. Bloomington, IN: iUniverse.

Wilterson, A.I., & Graziano, M.S.A. (2021). The attention schema theory in a neural network agent: Controlling visuospatial attention using a descriptive model of attention. *Proceedings of the National Academy of Sciences (USA)*, 118.

88 Desimone & Duncan, 1995.
89 The initial section of this chapter reworks ideas from Lucas, 2011, Chapter 12 to make them more accessible.
90 Quote from Hiram Powers, an American neoclassical sculptor (1805-1873).
91 Cohen & Andersen, 2002.
92 Baker, Donaghue & Sanes, 1999.
93 Kodaka et al., 1997; Leszczynski, et al., 2023.
94 The pulvinar shares many input regions with the lateral posterior complex, a spatial processing region found in less visual mammals like the rat (see Kamishina et al., 2008, 2009). In less visual animals the pulvinar is generally considered part of the lateral posterior complex. In primates the pulvinar stands out as a largely independent complex in all likelihood because visually-guided attention is more important in these animals. Homologous visual functions in avians are managed by the nucleus rotundus complex in the avian thalamus.
95 Sherman & Guillery, 2006.
96 Rod receptors lack differential color detecting pigments, so they only perceive a gray-scale view of the world. This is the big-picture view that reaches the tectum in birds and mammals. However, in fishes cone cells, which are sensitive to color differences, also reach the tectum. So fishes have a colored big-picture view.
97 Given that the brain is bilaterally symmetrical, all the brain structures discussed in this chapter actually occur in pairs. There are two eyes, two frontal eye fields, two tecta, two sides to the thalamus, etc. To avoid constantly speaking in plurals, I will simply refer to the connections on one side of the brain. However, the fact that all these networks are duplicated, even to the point that the two sides of the brain sometimes support different representations, should not be overlooked.
98 Webster et al., 1994.
99 Coe et al., 2002.
100 In macaques this region corresponds to the lateral intraparietal region, often abbreviated as LIP. In humans, these functions are located above the intraparietal landmark and thus have been given a more functional label.
101 Duhamel, Colby & Goldberg, 1992.
102 Colby, Duhamel & Goldberg, 1996; Kodaka et al., 1997.
103 Shipp, 2004, p. 224.

104 Crick, 1984.

105 Corbetta, Patel & Shulman, 2008; Vossel, Geng, & Fink, 2014.

106 Friedman-Hill, Robertson & Treisman, 1995.

107 Friedman-Hill et al., 2003.

108 See Pylyshyn, 1994, 2001. Damasio proposes that there are proto-feeling processes that lead to feelings. Pylyshyn proposes that there are proto-object processes that enable perceptual features to gain attention as objects. Thus, it seems that attention for both feelings and objects is a multistage process.

109 Adapted from Table 12-1 in Lucas, 2011.

110 Alan Leslie and colleagues, 1998, proposed the term *sticky indexes* to note that indexes were capable of binding features together.

111 Koch & Tsuchiya, 2007 and Lamme, 2003, argue that consciousness (at least, some evidence for awareness) can be dissociated from top-down (cortically controlled) attention. However, in our model feeling-bound awareness does not require top-down attention. Bottom-up attention is quite sufficient to create robust feelings. Thus, conscious feelings are never fully dissociated from attention in our model.

112 Darwin & Hukin, 1998.

113 Mitrofanis, 2005.

114 Trageser & Keller, 2004.

115 Trageser et al., 2006.

116 Urbain & Deschenes, 2007.

117 Groh et al., 2014; Trageser & Keller, 2004

118 León-Domínguez et al., 2013; Schiff et al., 2013; Mair et al., 2015; Saalmann, 2014.

119 Izquierdo & Murray, 2010. These functions involve connections with the basal ganglia, the amygdala, the orbital PFC, and the anterior cingulate cortex (ACC).

120 The dorsally located paraventricular and paratenial nuclei project to the ACC and to limbic subcortical structures, in particular, to the amygdala and nucleus accumbens, where they are thought to be important for coordinating both positive and negative affective states. This circuitry is thought to be involved in an emotional saliency hub in the cortex, see Seeley et al., 2007. In this role, paraventricular fibers terminate more heavily in the basal nucleus of the stria terminalis, the central and basal nuclei of the amygdala, and the hypothalamus than do paratenial connections. However, both these nuclei have broad connections with the ACC, see Vertes et al., 2015. The affective connections of

paraventricular nucleus also influence the sleep/wake networks in the hypothalamus, see Calavito et al., 2015.

121 Vertes et al., 2015; Cholvin, et al., 2013.

122 Redinbaugh et al., 2020.

123 In Chapter 3 we noted that synchrony among planning, actions, and proprioceptive feedback detected in the TPJ was treated as evidence for self-ownership for actions.

124 The anterior intralaminar group is composed of the central medial nucleus, the paracentral nucleus, and the central lateral nucleus. This groups is considered part of the oculomotor thalamus. The posterior intralaminar group is composed of the centromedian nucleus and the parafascicular nucleus. This group is extensively connected to the frontal cortex, the posterior cingulate, and the temporal-parietal area. See Hudetz, 2012; Saalmann, 2014; Van der Werf et al., 2002.

125 Buckner, Andrews-Hanna, & Schacter, 2008; Greicius et al., 2009.

126 Saalmann, 2014.

127 Wilkinson et al., 2010.

Baker, J. T., Donaghue, J. P., & Sanes, J. N. (1999). Gaze direction modulates finger movement activation patterns in human cerebral cortex. *The Journal of Neuroscience*, 19, 10044–10052.

Buckner, R. L., Andrews-Hanna, J. R., & Schacter, D. L. (2008). The brain's default network: Anatomy, function, and relevance to disease. *Annals of the New York Academy of Sciences*, 1124 (1), 1–38.

Cholvin, T., Loureiro, M., Cassel, R., Cosquer, B., Geiger, K., De Sa Nogueira, D., Rain-gard, H., Robelin, L., Kelche, C., Pereira de Vasconcelos, A., & Cassel, J. C. (2013). The ventral midline thalamus contributes to strategy shifting in a memory task requiring both prefrontal cortical and hippocampal functions. *Journal of Neuroscience,* 33, 8772–8783.

Coe, B., Tomihara, K., Matsuzawa, M., & Hikosaka, O. (2002). Visual and anticipatory bias in three cortical eye fields of the monkey during an adaptive decision-making task. *The Journal of Neuroscience*, 22(12), 5081–5090.

Cohen, Y. E., & Andersen, R. A. (2002). A common reference frame for movement plans in the posterior parietal cortex. *Nature Reviews Neuroscience, 3, 553–562.*

Colavito, V., Tesoriero, C., Wirtu, A. T., Grassi-Zucconi, G., & Bentivoglio, M. (2015). Limbic thalamus and state-dependent behavior: The paraventricular nucleus of the thalamic midline as a node in circadian timing and sleep/wake-regulatory networks. *Neuroscience and Biobehavioral Reviews, 54*, 3–17.

Colby, C. L., Duhamel, J. R., & Goldberg, M. E. (1996). Visual, presaccadic, and cognitive activation of single neurons in monkey lateral intraparietal area. *Journal of Neurophysiology, 76*, 2841–2852.

Corbetta, M., Patel, G., & Shulman, G. L. (2008). The reorienting system of the human brain: From environment to theory of mind. *Neuron 58*, 306–324.

Crick, F. (1984). Function of the thalamic reticular complex: The searchlight hypothesis. *Proceedings of the National Academy of Sciences (USA), 81*, 4586–4590.

Darwin, C., & Hukin, R. (1998). Perceptual segregation of a harmonic from a vowel by interaural time difference in conjunction with mistuning and onset asynchrony. *Journal of the Acoustical Society of America, 103*, 1080–1084.

Desimone, R., & Duncan, J. (1995). Neural mechanisms of selective visual attention. *Annual Review of Neuroscience, 18*, 193–222.

Duhamel, J. R., Colby, C. L., & Goldberg, M. E. (1992). The updating of the representation of visual space in parietal cortex by intended eye movements. *Science, 255*, 90–92.

Friedman-Hill, S. R., Robertson, L. C., & Treisman, A. (1995). Parietal contributions to visual feature binding: Evidence from a patient with bilateral lesions. *Science, 269*, 853–855.

Friedman-Hill, S. R., Robertson, L. C., Desimone, R., & Ungerleider, L. G. (2003). Posterior parietal cortex and the filtering of distractors. *Proceedings of the National Academy of Sciences (USA), 100*, 4263–4268.

Greicius, M.D., Supekar, K., Menon, V., & Dougherty, R.F. (2009). Resting state functional connectivity reflects structural connectivity in the default mode network. *Cerebral Cortex, 19*, 72–78.

Hudetz, A. G. (2012). General anesthesia and human brain connectivity. *Brain Connections, 2*, 291–302.

Izquierdo, A., & Murray, E. A. (2010). Functional interaction of medial mediodorsal thalamic nucleus but not nucleus accumbens with amygdala and orbital prefrontalcortex is essential for adaptive response selection after reinforcer devaluation. *Journal of Neuroscience, 30*, 661–669.

Kamishina, H., Yurcisin, G. H., Corwin, J. V., & Reep, R. L. (2008). Striatal projections from the rat lateral posterior thalamic nucleus. *Brain Research, 1204*, 24–39.

Kamishina, H., Conte, W. L., Patel, S. S., Tai, R. J., Corwin, J. V., & Reep, R. L. (2009). Cortical connections to the rat lateral posterior thalamic nucleus. *Brain Research*, 1264, 39–56.

Koch, C., & Tsuchiya, N. (2007). Attention and consciousness: Two distinct brain processes. *Trends in Cognitive Sciences*, 11, 16–22.

Kodaka, Y., Mikami, A., & Kubota, K. (1997). Neuronal activity in the frontal eye field of the monkey is modulated while attention is focused onto a stimulus in the peripheral visual field, irrespective of eye movement. *Neuroscience Research*, 28, 291–298.

Krout, K. E., Belzer, R. E., & Loewy, A. D. (2002). Brainstem projections to midline and intralaminar thalamic nuclei of the rat. *Journal of Comparative Neurology*, 448, 53–101.

Krout, K.E., & Loewy, A.D. (2000). Parabrachial nucleus projections to midline and intralaminar thalamic nuclei of the rat. *Journal of Comparative Neurology*, 428, 475– 494.

Lamme, V. A. F. (2003). Why visual attention and awareness are different. *Trends in Cognitive Sciences*, 7, 12–18.

León-Domínguez, U., Vela-Bueno, A., Froufé-Torrex, M., & León-Carrión, J. (2013). Achronometric functional sub-network in the thalamo-cortical system regulates the flow of neural information necessary for conscious cognitive processes. *Neuropsychologia* 51, 1336–1349.

Leslie, A. M., Xu, F., Tremoulet, P. D., & Scholl, B. J. (1998). Indexing and the object concept: Developing 'what' and 'where' systems. *Trends in Cognitive Sciences*, 2, 10–18.

Leszczynski, M. et al. (2023). Saccadic modulation of neural excitability in auditory areas of the neocortex. *Current Biology*, 33, 1185–1195.

Lucas, G. A. (2011). Emergence, Mind, and Consciousness: A Bio-Inspired Design for a Conscious Agent. Bloomington, IN: iUniverse.

Mair, R. G., Miller, R. L. A., Wormwood, B. A., Francoeur, M. J., Onos, K. D., & Gibson, B. M. (2015). The neurobiology of thalamic amnesia: Contributions of medial thalamus and prefrontal cortex to delayed conditional discrimination. *Neuroscience and Biobehavioral Reviews,* 54, 161–174.

Mitrofanis, J. (2005). Some certainty for the "zone of uncertainty"? Exploring the function of the zona incerta. *Neuroscience*, 130, 1–15.

Pylyshyn, Z. W. (1994). Some primitive mechanisms of spatial attention. *Cognition*, 50, 363–384.

Pylyshyn, Z. W. (2001). Visual indexes, preconceptual objects, and situated vision. *Cognition*, 80, 127–158.

Redinbaugh, M. J. et al. (2020). Thalamus modulates consciousness via layer-specific control of cortex. *Neuron*, 106, 1–10.

Saalmann, Y. B. (2014). Intralaminar and medial thalamic influence on cortical synchrony, information transmission and cognition. *Frontiers in Systems Neuroscience*, 8, 83.

Schiff, N. D., Shah, S. A., Hudson, A. E., Nauvel, T., Kalik, S. F., & Purpura, K. P. (2013). Gating of attentional effort through the central thalamus. *Journal of Neurophysiology*, 109, 1152–1163.

Seeley, W.W., Menon, V., Schatzberg, A..F, Keller, J., Glover, G.H., Kenna, H., Reiss, A.L., & Greicius, M.D. (2007). Dissociable intrinsic connectivity networks for salience processing and executive control. Journal of Neuroscience, 27, 2349–2356.

Sherman, S. M., & Guillery, R. W. (2006). *Exploring the Thalamus and its Role in Cortical Function.* Cambridge, MA: MIT Press.

Shipp, S. (2004). The brain circuitry of attention. *Trends in Cognitive Sciences*, 8, 223–230.

Silva, A. de M., et al., (2014). Serotonergic fibers distribution in the midline and intralaminar thalamic nuclei in the rock cavy (*Kerodon rupestris*). *Brain Research*, 1586, 99–108.

Trageser, J. C., & Keller, A. (2004). Reducing the uncertainty: Gating of peripheral inputs by zona incerta. *Journal of Neuroscience*, 24, 8911–8915.

Trageser, J. C., Burke, K. A., Masri, R., Li, Y., Sellers, L., & Keller, A. (2006). State-dependent gating of sensory inputs by zona incerta. *Journal of Neurophysiology*, 96, 1456–1463.

Trick, L. M., & Pylyshyn, Z. W. (1994). Why are small and large numbers enumerated differently? A limited capacity preattentive stage in vision. *Psychological Review*, 10, 1–23.

Urbain, N., & Deschenes, M. (2007). Motor cortex gates vibrissal responses in a thalamocortical projection pathway. *Neuron*, 56, 714–725.

Van der Werf, Y. D., Witter, M. P., & Groenewegen, H. J. (2002). The intralaminar and midline nuclei of the thalamus. Anatomical and functional evidence for participation in processes of arousal and awareness. *Brain Research Reviews*, 39, 107–140.

Vertes, R. P., Linley, S. B., & Hoover, W. B. (2015). Limbic circuitry of the midline thalamus. *Neuroscience and Biobehavioral Reviews*, 54, 89–107.

Vossel, S., Geng, J. J., & Fink, G. R. (2014). Dorsal and ventral attention systems: Distinct neural circuits but collaborative roles. *The Neuroscientist*, 20(2), 150–159.

Webster, M. J., Bachevalier, J., & Ungerleider, L. G. (1994).
Connections of inferior temporal areas TEO and TE with parietal
and frontal cortex in macaque monkeys. *Cerebral Cortex*, 4, 470–
483.
Wilkinson, A., Mandl, I., Bugnyar, T., & Huber, L. (2010). Gaze
following in the red-footed tortoise (Geochelone carbonaria).
Animal Cognition, 13, 765-769.

6: PLANNING AND REASONING

128 Libet, 1985.

129 Middleton & Strick, 2000. Brain region abbreviations are those
used in this article.

130 Humphrey, 1976; Dunbar, 1998.

131 Stephenson-Jones et al. 2013. Note, while this path may be
involved in social worry it was discovered in the lamprey, so it
appears that worry was an early addition to the vertebrate brain
plan. It seems likely that it evolved to inhibit actions leading to
other kinds of negative outcomes and later came to be used for
evaluating social outcomes.

132 Graybiel, 1998, 2008.

133 Bjordahl, Dimyan & Weinberger, 1998; Kilgard & Merzenich,
1998; Kilgard et al., 2002.

134 Fuller et al., 2011.

135 Berg et al., 2005; Munn et al., 2021; Oswald et al., 2022; Zhu et
al., 2023.

136 See Lakoff & Johnson, 1999.

137 See the Lucas, 2023, Epilogue, "Are There Nested Patterns in
Conscious Thought?"

138 Edelman, 1989.

139 Damasio, 1999.

140 Sherman & Guillery, 2006.

141 Fuster, 1989.

142 Koechlin & Summerfield, 2007; O'Reilly et al., 2002; Petrides,
1994. The term "working memory" is used in a number of
contexts. Baddeley (2003) used it to refer to the short-term
auditory and visual memory buffers. These short-term sensory
memories limit how much information you can integrate at one
time. However, a much more important kind of working memory

results from task-related memory configurations learned in the PFC. These are not short-term buffers.

143 According to Onur Güntürkün, 2005, the NCL is a multimodal integration center, connects with higher-order sensory, limbic, and motor structures, and is densely innervated by dopaminergic fibers. However, it does not appear to be homologous to the PFC. Rather, it appears to have resulted from convergent evolution.

144 Lara & Wallis, 2015.

145 Wimmer et al., 2015.

146 Wolters & Raffone, 2008.

147 O'Reilly et al., 2002.

148 The *working hypothesis* term is my addition. O'Reilly does not use it.

149 Note that O'Reilly and colleagues have extended their network model to show how executive control might come to include hierarchical biases. See O'Reilly & Frank, 2006; Reynolds & O'Reilly, 2009.

150 Corbetta & Shulman, 2002; Wen et al., 2012.

151 Doricchi et al., 2022.

152 Piaget, 1977.

153 Soutschek et al., 2016.

154 Blanke, 2012; Decety & Sommerville, 2003; Ionta et al., 2014; Karnath & Baier, 2010.

155 See Decety & Lamm, 2007; Lenggenhager, Smith, & Blanke, 2006; Vogeley & Fink, 2003. The networks that contribute to self and other action attribution appear to be assessed in the temporal parietal junction.

156 Middleton & Strick, 2000.

157 Edelman & Tononi, 2000.

158 See Libet, 1985.

159 In fact, there is evidence that rapid perceptual movements that never reach conscious awareness may nevertheless be relayed on to parts the dorsal stream motor-planning cortex by inputs from the tectum. See Sperling & Carrasco, 2015.

Baddeley, A. (2003). Working memory: Looking back and looking forward. *Nature Reviews Neuroscience*, 4, 829–839.

Berg, R.W., Friedman, B., Schroeder, L.F. & Kleinfeld, D. (2005). Activation of nucleus basalis facilitates cortical control of a brain stem motor program. *Journal of Neurophysiology*, 94(1), 699-711.

Blanke, O. (2012). Multisensory brain mechanisms of bodily self-consciousness. *Nature Reviews. Neuroscience*, 13(8), 556–571.

Bjordahl, T. S., Dimyan, M. A. & Weinberger, N. M. (1998). Induction of long-term receptive field plasticity in the auditory cortex of the waking guinea pig by stimulation of the nucleus basalis. *Behavioral Neuroscience*, 112, 467–479.

Corbetta, M. & Shulman, G. L. (2002) Control of goal-directed and stimulus-driven attention in the brain. *Nature Reviews Neuroscience*, 3, 201–215.

Damasio, A. R. (1999). The Feeling of What Happens: Body and Emotion in the Making of Consciousness. New York: Harcourt Brace & Co.

Darwin, C. (1871). *The Descent of Man and Selection in Relation to Sex (Vol.1)*. London: John Murray. <http://darwin-online.org.uk/contents.html#books>

Decety, J. & Lamm, C. (2007). The role of the right temporoparietal junction in social interaction: How low-level computational processes contribute to meta-cognition. *Neuroscientist*, 13(6): 580–593.

Decety, J. & Sommerville. J. A. (2003). Shared representations between self and other: A social cognitive neuroscience view. *Trends in Cognitive Sciences*, 7, 527–533.

Doricchi, F., Lasaponara, S., Pazzaglia, M., & Silvetti, M. (2022). Left and right temporal-parietal junctions (TPJs) as "match/mismatch" hedonic machines: A unifying account of TPJ function. *Physics of Life Reviews*, 42:56-92.

Dunbar R. I. M. (1998). The social brain hypothesis. *Evolutionary Anthropology*, 6, 178–190.

Edelman, G. M. (1989). The Remembered Present: A Biological Theory of Consciousness. New York: Basic Books.

Edelman, G. M. & Tononi, G. (2000). *A Universe of Consciousness: How Matter Becomes Imagination*. New York: Basic Books.

Fuller, P.M., Sherman, D., Pedersen, N.P., Saper, C.B & Lu, J. (2011). Reassessment of the structural basis of the ascending arousal system. *Journal of Comparative Neurology*, 519(5), 933–956.

Fuster, J. M. (1989). *The Prefrontal Cortex*. New York: Raven.

Graybiel, A. M. (1998). The basal ganglia and chunking of action repertoires. *Neurobiology of Learning and Memory*, 70, 119–136.

Graybiel, A. M. (2008). Habits, rituals, and the evaluative brain. *Annual Review of Neuroscience*, 31, 359–387.

Güntürkün, O. (2005). The avian 'prefrontal cortex' and cognition. *Current Opinion in Neurobiology*, 15, 686–693.

Humphrey, N. K. (1976). The social function of intellect. In: P. Bateson & R. Hinde (Eds) *Growing Points in Ethology, (pp. 303–317).* Cambridge: Cambridge University Press.

Ionta, S., Martuzzi, R., Salomon, R., Blanke, O. (2014). The brain network reflecting bodily self-consciousness: A functional connectivity study. *Social Cognitive and Affective Neuroscience,* 9(12), 1904–1913.

Karnath, H.O. & Baier, B. (2010). Right insula for our sense of limb ownership and self-awareness of actions. *Brain Structure and Function,* 214(5–6), 411–417.

Kilgard, M. P. & Merzenich, M. M. (1998). Cortical map reorganization enabled by nucleus basalis activity. *Nature Neuroscience,* 1, 727–731.

Kilgard, M. P., Pandya, P. K., Engineer, N. D. & Moucha, R. (2002). Cortical network reorganization guided by sensory input features. *Biological Cybernetics,* 87, 333–343.

Koechlin, E. & Summerfield, C. (2007). An information theoretical approach to prefrontal executive function. *Trends in Cognitive Sciences,* 11, 229–235.

Lakoff, G. & Johnson, M. (1999). Philosophy in the Flesh: The Embodied Mind and Its Challenge to Western Thought. New York: Basic Books.

Lara, A. H. & Wallis, J. D. (2015). The Role of Prefrontal Cortex in Working Memory: A Mini Review. *Frontiers in Systems Neuroscience,* 9, 173.

Lenggenhager, B., Smith, S. T., & Blanke, O. (2006). Functional and neural mechanisms of embodiment: Importance of vestibular system and the temporal parietal junction. *Reviews in Neuroscience,* 17, 641–657.

Libet, B. (1985). Unconscious cerebral initiative and the role of conscious will in voluntary action. *Behavioral and Brain Sciences,* 8, 529–566.

Lucas, G. A. (2023 3rd ed.). Minding Consciousness: How Life Urges Embody Attention. Amazon.com.

León Middleton, F. A. & Strick, P. L. (2000). Basal ganglia output and cognition: Evidence from anatomical, behavioral, and clinical studies. *Brain and Cognition,* 42, 183–200.

Munn, B.R., Müller, E.J., Wainstein, G. et al. (2021). The ascending arousal system shapes neural dynamics to mediate awareness of cognitive states. *Nature Communications,* 12, 6016.

O'Reilly, R. C. & Frank, M. J. (2006). Making working memory work: A computational model of learning in prefrontal cortex and basal ganglia. *Neural Computation*, 18, 283–328.

O'Reilly, R. C., Noellel, D. C., Braver, T. S. & Cohen, J. D. (2002). Prefrontal cortex and dynamic categorization tasks: Representational organization and neuromodulatory control. *Cerebral Cortex*, 12, 246–257.

Oswald, M.J., Han, Y., Li, H. et al. (2022). Cholinergic basal forebrain nucleus of Meynert regulates chronic pain-like behavior via modulation of the prelimbic cortex. *Nature Communications,* 13, 5014.

Petrides, M. (1994). Frontal lobes and working memory: Evidence from investigations of the effects of cortical excisions in nonhuman primates. In F. Boller & J. Grafman (Eds), *Handbook of Neuropsychology, Vol. 9,* (pp. 59–82). Amsterdam: Elsevier.

Piaget, J. (1977). The Development of Thought: Equilibrium of Cognitive Structures. New York: Viking.

Redish, A. D. (2016). Vicarious trial and error. *Nature Reviews Neuroscience*, 17, 147–159.

Reynolds, J. R. & O'Reilly, R. C. (2009). Developing PFC representations using reinforcement learning. *Cognition*, 113, 281–292.

Sherman, S.M. & Guillery, R.W. (2006). *Exploring the Thalamus and its Role in Cortical Function.* Cambridge, MA: MIT Press.

Soutschek, A., Ruff, R. C., Strombach, T., Kalenscher, T., & Tobler, T. N. (2016). Brain stimulation reveals crucial role of overcoming self-centeredness in self-control. *Science Advances*, 2(10), e1600992.

Sperling, M. & Carrasco, M. (2015). Acting without seeing: Eye movements reveal visual processing without awareness. *Trends in Neurosciences*, 38, 247–258.

Stephenson-Jones, M. Kardamakis, A.. A., Robertson, B., & Grillner, S. (2013). Independent circuits in the basal ganglia for the evaluation and selection of actions. *Proceedings of the National Academy of Sciences (USA),* 110, E3670–E3679.

Vogeley, K. & Fink, G. R. (2003). Neural correlates of the first-person perspective. *Trends in Cognitive Sciences*, 7, 38–42.

Wen, X., Yao, L., Liu, Y. & Ding, M. (2012). Causal interactions in attention networks predict behavioral performance. *Journal of Neuroscience*, 32 (4), 1284-1292.

Wimmer, R. D. et al. (2015).Thalamic control of sensory selection in divided attention. *Nature*, 526, 705–709.

Wirth, S., Baraduc, P., PlanteÂ A., Pinède S., & Duhamel J-R. (2017). Gaze-informed, task-situated representation of space in primate

hippocampus during virtual navigation. *PLoS Biol* 15(2): e2001045
Wolters, G., & Raffone, A. (2008). Coherence and recurrency: Maintenance, control and integration in working memory. *Cognitive Processing, 9*(1), 1–17.
Zhu, F., Elnozahy, S., Lawlor, J. et al. (2023). The cholinergic basal forebrain provides a parallel channel for state-dependent sensory signaling to auditory cortex. *Nature Neuroscience,* 26, 810–819.

7: ANTICIPATION, OWNERSHIP, AND MEMORY

160 Medina et al., 2002. See also Lucas, 2011, Chapters 8 and 10.
161 Guyton & Hall, 1996.
162 Fiez, 1996; Gao et al., 1996; Parsons et al. 1997; Thach, 1996.
163 Courchesne & Allen, 1997; Courchesne, Townsend, et al., 1994; Grafman et al., 1992.
164 Schmahmann & Sherman, 1998.
165 Pollack et al., 1995.
166 According to a new technique for estimating neuron counts, the cerebellum accounts for about 80 per cent of all the neurons in the human brain, while only occupying about 10 percent of brain volume. See Azevedo et al., 2009.
167 See Decety & Lamm, 2007; Lenggenhager, Smith, & Blanke, 2006; Vogeley & Fink, 2003.
168 Tsakiris et al., 2007, report body ownership is related to correlated activity in the right posterior insula and the right frontal operculum, a part of the TPJ region.
169 Guterstam, Petkova & Ehrsson, 2011.
170 See Blanke et al., 2002, 2004; Decety & Sommerville, 2003.
171 Bar & Aminoff, 2003; Davachi, Mitchell & Wagner, 2003; Fernadez et al., 2002.
172 Knierim, Lee & Hargreaves, 2006; Manns & Eichenbaum, 2006.
173 Edelman, 1989.
174 Eichenbaum et al., 1999.
175 See Arnaud et al., 2016; Rogerson et al., 2014.
176 McClelland, McNaughton & O'Reilly, 1995.
177 Shors, et al., 2012.
178 Papez, 1937
179 Thirtamara Rajamani et al., 2023.
180 Rolls, 2019.

181 Aggleton & Brown, 1999.

182 See Rogerson et al., 2014.

183 See Preston & Eichenbaum, 2013. The link between the medial PFC and the hippocampal formation is thought to involve the *reuniens* and *rhomboid* nuclei in the ventral midline thalamus, Xu & Sudhof, 2013.

184 Redish, 2016.

185 Decety & Lamm, 2007; Decety & Sommerville, 2003.

186 As noted in the previous chapter, the rostral intralaminar complex is extensively connected to the frontal cortex, the posterior cingulate, and the temporal-parietal area. These connections appear poised to play a role in the integration of cortical and striatal motor planning and an awareness of agency. See Hudetz, 2012; Saalmann, 2014. In addition, connections with both the TPJ and the posterior cingulate make this region a likely candidate for promoting self-referential activity to attention.

Aggleton, J. P. & Brown, M. W. (1999) Episodic memory, amnesia, and the hippocampal-anterior thalamic axis. *Behavioral and Brain Sciences*, 22, 425–489.

Arnaud, M., Reichinnek, S., Villette, V., Haimerl, C. & Cossart, R. (2016). Awake hippocampal reactivations project onto orthogonal neuronal assemblies. *Science*, 353, 1280–1283.

Azevedo, F., Carvalho, L., Grinberg, L., Farfel, J. R., Ferretti, R., Leite, R., Jacob Filho, W., Lent, R., and Herculano-Houzel, S. (2009). Equal numbers of neuronal and non-neuronal cells make the human brain a scaled-up primate brain. *Journal of Comparative Neurology,* 513, 532–541.

Bar, M. & Aminoff, E. (2003). Cortical analysis of visual context. *Neuron*, 38, 347–358.

Blanke, O. (2012). Multisensory brain mechanisms of bodily self-consciousness. *Nature Reviews. Neuroscience*, 13(8), 556–571.

Courchesne, E. & Allen, G. (1997). Prediction and preparation, fundamental functions of the cerebellum. *Learning & Memory*, 4, 1–35.

Courchesne, E., Townsend, J., Akshoomoff, N. A., Saitoh, O., Yeung-Courchesne, R., Lincoln, A. J., James, H. E., Haas, R. H., Schreibman, L. & Lau, L. (1994). Impairment in shifting attention in autistic and cerebellar patients. *Behavioral Neuroscience,* 108, 848–865.

Davachi, L., Mitchell, J. P. & Wagner, A. D. (2003). Multiple routes to memory: Distinct medial temporal lobe processes build item and source memories. *Proceedings of the National Academy of Sciences (USA),* 100, 2157–2162.

Decety, J. & Lamm, C. (2007). The role of the right temporoparietal junction in social interaction: How low-level computational processes contribute to meta-cognition. *Neuroscientist,* 13(6): 580–593.

Decety, J. & Sommerville. J. A. (2003). Shared representations between self and other: A social cognitive neuroscience view. *Trends in Cognitive Sciences,* 7, 527–533.

Edelman, G. M. (1989). The Remembered Present: A Biological Theory of Consciousness. New York: Basic Books.

Edelman, G. M. (2003). Naturalizing consciousness: A theoretical framework. *Proceedings of the National Academy of Sciences (USA),* 100 (9), 5520–5524.

Eichenbaum, H., Dudchenko, P., Wood, E., Shapiro, M. & Tanila, H. (1999). The hippocampus, memory, and place cells: Is it spatial memory or a memory space? *Neuron,* 23, 209–226.

Fernandez, G., Klaver, P., Fell, J., Grunwald, T. & Elger, C. E. (2002). Human declarative memory formation: Segregating rhinal and hippocampal contributions. *Hippocampus,* 12, 514–519.

Fiez, J. A. (1996). Cerebellar contributions to cognition. *Neuron,* 16, 13–15.

Gao, H. H., Parsons, L. M., Bower, J. M., Xiong, J., Li J. & Fox, P. T. (1996). Cerebellum implicated in sensory acquisition and discrimination rather than motor control. *Science,* 272, 545–547.

Grafman, J., Litvan, I., Massaquoi, S., Stewart, M., Sirigu, A. & Hallett, M. (1992) Cognitive planning deficits in patients with cerebellar atrophy. *Neurology,* 42, 1493–1496.

Guterstam, A., Petkova, V. I., & Ehrsson, H. H. (2011). The illusion of owning a third arm. *PLoS ONE,* 6(2): 1–11, e17208.

Guyton, A. C. & Hall, J. E. (1996). The Cerebellum, the Basal Ganglia, and Overall Motor Control. In: A. C. Guyton (Ed.) *Textbook of Medical Physiology, 9th edition,* (pp. 715–731). W. B. Saunders Company, Toronto.

Hudetz, A. G. (2012). General anesthesia and human brain connectivity. *Brain Connections,* 2, 291–302.

Knierim, J. J., Lee, I. & Hargreaves, E. L. (2006). Hippocampal place cells: Input streams, subregional processing, and implications for episodic memory. *Hippocampus,* 16, 755–764.

Lenggenhager, B., Smith, S. T., & Blanke, O. (2006). Functional and neural mechanisms of embodiment: Importance of vestibular system and the temporal parietal junction. *Reviews in*

Neuroscience, 17, 641–657.

Lucas, G. A. (2011). Emergence, Mind, and Consciousness: A Bio-Inspired Design for a Conscious Agent. Bloomington, IN: iUniverse.

Manns, J. R. & Eichenbaum, H. (2006). Evolution of declarative memory. *Hippocampus, 16*, 795–808.

McClelland, J. L., McNaughton, B. L. & O'Reilly, R. C. (1995). Why there are complementary learning systems in the hippocampus and neocortex: Insights from the successes and failures of connectionist models of learning and memory. *Psychological Review, 102*, 419–457.

Medina, J. F., Repa, J. C., Mauk, M. D. & LeDoux, J. E. (2002). Parallels between cerebellum and amygdala-dependent conditioning. *Nature Reviews Neuroscience, 3*, 122–131.

Papez, J. W. (1937). A proposed mechanism of emotion. *Archives of Neurology & Psychiatry, 38*, 725–743.

Parsons, L. M., Bower, J. M., Gao, J., Xiong, J., Li, J. & Fox, P. (1997). Lateral cerebellar hemispheres actively support sensory acquisition and discrimination rather than motor control. *Learning & Memory, 4*, 49–62.

Pollack, I. F., Polinko, P., Albright, A. L., Towbin, R. & Fitz, C. (1995). Mutism and pseudobulbar symptoms after resection of posterior fossa tumors in children: Incidence and pathophysiology. *Neurosurgery, 37*, 885–893.

Preston, A. R. & Eichenbaum, H. (2013). Interplay of hippocampus and prefrontal cortex in memory. *Current Biology, 23*, R764–R773.

Redish, A. D. (2016). Vicarious trial and error. *Nature Reviews Neuroscience, 17*, 147–159.

Rogerson, T. et al. (2014). Synaptic tagging during memory allocation. *Nature Reviews Neuroscience, 15*, 157–169.

Rolls, E. T. (2019). The cingulate cortex and limbic systems for emotion, action, and memory. *Brain Structure & Function, 224*(9), 3001-18.

Saalmann, Y. B. (2014). Intralaminar and medial thalamic influence on cortical synchrony, information transmission and cognition. *Frontiers in Systems Neuroscience, 8*, 83.

Schmahmann, J. D. & Sherman, J. C. (1998). The cerebellar cognitive affective syndrome. *Brain, 121*, 561–579.

Sherman, S. M. & Guillery, R. W. (2006). *Exploring the Thalamus and its Role in Cortical Function.* Cambridge, MA: MIT Press.

Shors, T. J., Anderson, M.L, Curlik II, D M., & Nokia, M. S (2012). Use it or lose it: How neurogenesis keeps the brain fit for learning.

Behavioural Brain Research, 227 (2), 450e458.

Thach, W. T. (1996). On the specific role of the cerebellum in motor learning and cognition: Clues from PET activation and lesion studies in man. *Behavioral and Brain Sciences,* 19(3), 411–431.

Thirtamara Rajamani, K., Barbier, M., Lefevre, A. et al. (2023). Oxytocin activity in the paraventricular and supramammillary nuclei of the hypothalamus is essential for social recognition memory in rats. *Molecular Psychiatry,* https://doi.org/10.1038/s41380-023-02336-0.

Tsakiris, M., Hesse, M. D., Boy, C., Haggard, P., & Fink, G. R. (2007). Neural signatures of body ownership: A sensory network for bodily self-consciousness. *Cerebral Cortex*, 17, 2235–2244.

Vogeley, K. & Fink, G. R. (2003). Neural correlates of the first-person perspective. *Trends in Cognitive Sciences*, 7, 38–42.

Xu, W. & Sudhof, T. (2013). A neural circuit for memory specificity and generalization. *Science,* 339, 1290–1295.

8: THE SOCIAL BRIDGE

187 Gallup, 1970.

188 Gallup, et al., 1995.

189 Khoda et al., 2023; Plotnik, de Waal, & Reiss, 2006; Prior, Schwarz & Güntürkün, 2008; Reiss & Marino, 2001.

190 See Decety & Lamm, 2007; Lenggenhager, Smith, & Blanke, 2006.

191 Gallese, Keysers & Rizzolatti, 2004.

192 Rizzolatti et al., 1996.

193 de Gelder, 2006; Habas, Guillevin,& Abanou, 2011.

194 Carr et al., 2003; see also Schwiedrzik, et al., 2015.

195 Soutschek et al., 2016.

196 Insel & Fernald, 2004; Insel & Young, 2000; Kosfeld et al., 2005.

197 Domes et al., 2007.

198 Zak, Stanton, & Ahmadi, 2007.

199 Depue & Morrone-Strupinsky. 2005.

200 Heinrichs, von Dawans, & Domes, 2009; Meyer-Lindenberg, Domes, Kirsch, & Heinrichs, 2011.

201 Damasio, 1994.

Carr, L., Iacoboni, M., Dubeau, M. C.,Maziotta, J. C. & Lenzi, G. L.

(2003). Neural mechanisms of empathy in humans: A relay from neural systems for imitation to limbic areas. *Proceedings of the National Academy of Sciences (USA),* 100, 5497–5502.

Damasio, A. R. (1994). Descartes' Error: Emotion, Reason, and the Human Brain. New York: Avon Press.

Damasio, A. R. & Carvalho, G. B. (2013). The nature of feelings: Evolutionary and neurobiological origins. *Nature Reviews Neuroscience,* 14, 143–152.

de Gelder, B. (2006). Towards the neurobiology of emotional body language. *Nature Reviews Neuroscience,* 7, 242–249.

Decety, J. & Lamm, C. (2007). The role of the right temporoparietal junction in social interaction: How low-level computational processes contribute to meta-cognition. *Neuroscientist,* 13(6): 580–593.

Depue, R. A. & Morrone-Strupinsky, J. V. (2005). A neurobehavioral model of affiliative bonding: Implications for conceptualizing a human trait of affiliation. *Behavioral and Brain Sciences,* 28, 313–350.

Domes, G., Heinrichs, M., Michel, A., Berger, C. & Herpertz, S. C. (2007). Oxytocin improves "mind-reading" in humans. *Biological Psychiatry,* 61, 731–733.

Gallese, V., Keysers, C. & Rizzolatti, G. (2004). A unifying view of the basis of social cognition. *Trends in Cognitive Sciences,* 8, 396–403.

Gallup, G. G. Jr. (1970). Chimpanzees: Self-recognition. *Science* 167, 86–87.

Gallup, G. G. Jr., Povinelli. D. J., Suarez, S. D., et al. (1995). Further reflections on self-recognition in primates. *Animal Behaviour,* 50, 1525–1532.

Habas, C., Guillevin, R., Abanou, A. (2011). Functional connectivity of the superior human temporal sulcus in the brain resting state at 3T. *Neuroradiology,* 53(2), 129–140.

Heinrichs, M., von Dawans, B., & Domes, G. (2009). Oxytocin, vasopressin, and human social behavior. *Frontiers in Neuroendocrinology,* 30, 548–557.

Insel, T. R. & Fernald, R. D. (2004). How the brain processes social information: Searching for the social brain. *Annual Review of Neuroscience,* 27, 697-722.

Insel, T. R. & Young, L. J. (2000). Neuropeptides and the evolution of social behaviour. *Current Opinion in Neurobiology,* 10, 788-789.

Kohda M, Bshary R, Kubo N, Awata S, Sowersby W, Kawasaka K, Kobayashi T, Sogawa S. (2023). Proceedings of the National

Academy of Sciences, 14;120(7):e2208420120.

Kosfeld, M., Heinrichs, M., Zak, P. J., Fischbacher, U. & Fehr, E. (2005). Oxytocin increases trust in humans. *Nature*, 435, 673-676.

Lenggenhager, B., Smith, S. T., & Blanke, O. (2006). Functional and neural mechanisms of embodiment: Importance of vestibular system and the temporal parietal junction. *Reviews in Neuroscience*, 17, 641–657.

Meyer-Lindenberg, A., Domes, G., Kirsch, P., & Heinrichs, M. (2011) Oxytocin and vasopressin in the human brain: Social neuropeptides for translational medicine. *Nature Reviews Neuroscience*,12(9), 524–538.

Plotnik, J. M., de Waal, F. B. M. & Reiss, D. (2006). Self-recognition in an Asian elephant. *Proceedings of the National Academy of Sciences (USA)*, 103, 17053–17057.

Prior, P., Schwarz, A. & Güntürkün, O. (2008). Mirror-induced behavior in the magpie (Pica pica): Evidence of self-recognition. *PLoS Biology*, 6(8), e202, 1642–1650.

Reiss, D. & Marino, L. (2001). Mirror self-recognition in the bottlenose dolphin: A case of cognitive convergence. *Proceedings of the National Academy of Sciences (USA)*, 98, 5937–5942.

Rizzolatti, G. & Craighero, L. (2004). The mirror-neuron system. *Annual Review of Neuroscience*, 27, 169–192.

Rizzolatti, G., Fadiga, L., Gallese, V. & Fogassi, L. (1996). Premotor cortex and the recognition of motor actions. *Cognitive Brain Research*, 3, 131–141.

Schwiedrzik, C.M., Zarco, W., Everling, S., & Freiwald, W.A. (2015). Face patch resting state networks link face processing to social cognition. *PLoS Biology*, 13(9).

Soutschek, A., Ruff, R. C., Strombach, T., Kalenscher, T., & Tobler, T. N. (2016). Brain stimulation reveals crucial role of overcoming self-centeredness in self-control. *Science Advances*, 2(10), e1600992.

Zak, P. J., Stanton, A. A. & Ahmadi, S. (2007). Oxytocin increases generosity in humans. *PLoS ONE*, 2(11), e1128.

9: SIGNS AND MINDS

202 In ethology, stimuli that trigger innate action patterns are usually called sign stimuli, although some authors call sign stimuli that act

as communication signals releasers. However, this distinction is neither consistent nor important. Further, the term releaser is never used to refer to learned communication signals. Thus, it seems more reasonable to refer to both innate and learned social communication signals as signs, noting that both innate and learned social communication signs often "release" social reactions when they are recognized.
203 See Krebs & Dawkins, 1984.
204 Seyfarth & Cheney, 1997.
205 Damasio, 1996.
206 Emoticons are facial graphics. Textual emoticons are considered to have originated in 1982 when Scott Fahlman suggested to the Carnegie Mellon University message board that :-) and :-(could be used to distinguish jokes from serious statements online. As graphics became available, graphic versions of facial emoticons gained favor. With the success of emoticons, pictographic versions of objects, actions, and settings soon appeared. These are now generally called emojis. Gestural emojis sometimes convey motives or intentions just as the gestures that accompany speech do.
207 See Kobayashi & Kohshima, 2001.
208 Cheney & Seyfarth, 1990; Seyfarth & Cheney, 1997.
209 Seyfarth & Cheney, 1997.
210 See the analysis in Schmahmann et al., 2007. See also Rilling et al., 2008.
211 Compared to other primates, what humans appear to have added to this mix are better connections between auditory analysis and vocal production regions. These presumably make vocal imitation more likely.
212 Skeide & Friederici, 2016. Much of this model is derived from work using EEG studies. The neural subsystems described by Schmahmann et al., 2007, are not used in this analysis.
213 See Skeide & Friederici, 2016, Figure 3.
214 Ding, et al., 2016; Ghitza, 2011; Martin & Doumas, 2017; Peelle & Davis, 2012.
215 Pepperberg, 1999.
216 The Guardian, 12 August 1986, cited by David Crystal in The English Language, 2002, p. 46.
217 See Phillip Anderson, 1972.

Anderson, P. W. (1972). More is different. Science, 177, 393–396.
Cheney, D. L. & Seyfarth, R. M. (1990). How Monkeys See the World.

Chicago: University of Chicago Press.

Crystal, D. (2002). The English Language: A Guided Tour of the Language (2nd edition). London, Penguin Books.

Damasio, A. R. (1996). The somatic marker hypothesis and the possible functions of the prefrontal cortex. Philosophical Transaction of the Royal Society of London. B, 351, 1413–1420.

Ding, N., Melloni, L., Zhang, H., Tian, X., & Poeppel, D. (2016). Cortical tracking of hierarchical linguistic structures in connected speech. Nature Neuroscience, 19(1), 158–164.

Ghitza, O. (2011). Linking speech perception and neurophysiology: Speech decoding guided by cascaded oscillators locked to the input rhythm. Frontiers in Psychology, 2: 130.

Iverson, J. M. & Thelen, E. (1999). Hand, mouth, and brain: The dynamic emergence of speech and gesture. Journal of Consciousness Studies, 6(11–12), 19–40.

Kobayashi, H. & Kohshima, S. (2001). Unique morphology of the human eye and its adaptive meaning: Comparative studies on external morphology of the primate eye. Journal of Human Evolution, 40(5), 419–435.

Krebs, J. R. & Dawkins, R. (1984). Animal signals: Mind-reading and manipulation, pp. 38-0402. In J. R. Krebs, & N. B. Davies, (Eds.). Behavioural Ecology: An Evolutionary Approach, (2nd Ed). Oxford: Blackwell Scientific Publications.

Martin, A .E. & Doumas, L. A. A. (2017). A mechanism for the cortical computation of hierarchical linguistic structure. PLoS Biology, 15(3): e2000663.

Peelle, J. E. & Davis, M. H. (2012). Neural oscillations carry speech rhythm through to comprehension. Frontiers in Psychology, 3: 320.

Pepperberg, I. M. (1999). The Alex Studies: Cognitive and Communicative Abilities of Grey Parrots. Cambridge, MA: Harvard University Press.

Rilling, J. K., Glasser, M. F., Preuss, T. M., Ma, X., Zhao, T., Hu, X. & Behrens, T. E. (2008). The evolution of the arcuate fasciculus revealed with comparative DTI. Nature Neuroscience, 11, 426–428.

Schmahmann, J. D., Pandya, D. N., Wang, R., Dai, G., D'Arceuil, H. E., de Crespigny, A. J. &. Wedeen, V. J. (2007). Association fibre pathways of the brain: Parallel observations from diffusion spectrum imaging and autoradiography. Brain, 130, 630–653.

Seyfarth, R. M. & Cheney, D. L. (1997). Some general features of vocal development in nonhuman primates. In: CT. Snowdon & M.

Hausberger (Eds.), Social Influences on Vocal Development, (pp. 249–273). Cambridge: Cambridge University Press.
Skeide, M. A. & Friederici, A. D. (2016). The ontogeny of the cortical language network. Nature Reviews Neuroscience, doi:10.1038/nrn.2016.23.

10: DYNAMIC FLOW

218 This table is more graded than the one first proposed in Lucas, 2011 and earlier versions of this book. It distinguishes between Planning Agency and Ownership Agency. It adds Reflective Agency to the Memory-Guided variations section. These additions emphasize that many systems which contribute to the full sense of agency. The table also expands on attention-managing strategies, and breaks the original Social Reasoning and Narrative Consciousness categories into several parts. And it now includes the sexual feelings of a gender self.

219 The neural systems identified here are first-level connections. Thus, they serve as starting points. To simplify the presentation, I have avoided identifying the many thalamic nuclei thought to be involved in supporting these connections. Further, I have avoided discussing their extensions in more complex neural hubs.

220 While the high-level categories here often appear hierarchical, as we have noted that much of the processing within levels are largely parallel and seem to resolve themselves by mutual inhibition. Thus, it would be a mistake to overemphasize the hierarchical organization of these processes.

221 See Edelman, 2003, p. 5522.

222 See Prinz, 2012, pp. 4-7 for other commonly proposed categories of consciousness.

223 Nagel, 1974.

224 Block, 1998. Note, the access consciousness concept is closely related to the global workspace model developed by Bernard Baars, 1997; 2002. As noted, I acknowledge the role that the thalamocortical architecture plays in enabling a broad array of processes to interact when they gain attention. However, attention is focused, not global. Thus, I do not consider global access to be a property of any kind of conscious experience or a requirement for feeling-bound consciousness.

225 Episodic memories for connected spatial locations or other
features that occur spontaneously seem to qualify as aspects of
core consciousness. However, later aspects of episodic
association, such as social and autobiographical memories or
those produced via extended memory searches, are generally
considered to be aspects of higher-order consciousness.
226 Damasio, 1999.
227 Edelman, 1989.
228 Clark, 2003.
229 See Damasio, 2010; Shewmon et al., 1999.
230 "Louder Than Words", lyrics by Polly Samson, music by David
Gilmour, is the last track on the Pink Floyd album The Endless
River, 2014. The lyrics were inspired by how the band members
interacted on their reunion with Roger Waters in July of 2005. As
Gilmour's wife Polly Samson noted, they didn't talk much. And
then they stepped onto a stage and musically the communication
was extraordinary. – My point: Consciousness is much more than
thought guided by words.
231 The data reported here are from a paper on observer reliability by
Hurlburt and Heavey, 2002. For a more complete overview of this
line of work and more detailed categories see the books by
Hurlburt, 1993, 2011, and Hurlburt and Heavey, 2006.
232 See Buckner et al., 2008; Schooler et al., 2011; Smallwood &
Schooler, 2015.
233 The mechanisms for cross-linking events in memory are only
partly understood. However, a simple model for how this may be
implemented and for the effects of shifting between vigilant and
reflective states of attention is presented in Lucas, 2011, Chapter
14, pp. 270–271.

Baars, B. (1997). *In the theater of consciousness: The workspace of
the mind.* New York: Oxford University Press.
Baars, B. (2002). The conscious access hypothesis: Origins and
recent evidence. *Trends in Cognitive Science,* 6 (1), 47–52.
Block, N. (1998). On a confusion about a function of consciousness.
In N. Block, O. Flanagan, & G. Guzeldere, (Eds.), The Nature of
Consciousness: Philosophical Debates, (pp. 375–415).
Cambridge, MA: MIT Press.
Buckner, R. L., Andrews-Hanna, J. R., & Schacter, D. L. (2008). The
brain's default network: Anatomy, function, and relevance to
disease. *Annals of the New York Academy of Sciences*, 1124, 1–
38.

Clark, A. (2003). Natural-Born Cyborgs: Minds, Technologies, and the Future of Human Intelligence. New York: Oxford University Press.

Damasio, A. R. (1999). The Feeling of What Happens: Body and Emotion in the Making of Consciousness. New York: Harcourt Brace & Co.

Damasio, A. R. (2010). Self Comes to Mind: Constructing the Conscious Brain. New York: Pantheon Books.

Dennett, D. C. (1992). The self as the center of narrative gravity. In F. Kessel, P. Cole, & D. L. Johnson, (Eds.), *Self and Consciousness: Multiple Perspectives,* (pp. 103–115). Hillsdale, NJ: Lawrence Erlbaum.

Edelman, G. M. (1989). The Remembered Present: A Biological Theory of Consciousness. New York: Basic Books.

Edelman, G. M. (2003). Naturalizing consciousness: A theoretical framework. *Proceedings of the National Academy of Sciences (USA),* 100 (9), 5520–5524.

Edelman, G. M. & Tononi, G. (2000). *A Universe of Consciousness: How Matter Becomes Imagination*. New York: Basic Books.Hurlburt, R. T. (1993). *Sampling inner experience in disturbed affect.* New York: Plenum Press.

Hurlburt, R. T. (2011). *Investigating pristine inner experience: Moments of truth.* Cambridge: Cambridge University Press.

Hurlburt, R. T. & Heavey, C. L. (2002). Interobserver reliability of descriptive experience sampling. *Cognitive Therapy and Research*, 26, 135–142.

Hurlburt, R. T. & Heavey, C. L. (2006). *Exploring inner experience.* Amsterdam: John Benjamins.

Lucas, G. A. (2011). Emergence, Mind, and Consciousness: A Bio-Inspired Design for a Conscious Agent. Bloomington, IN: iUniverse.

Melloni, L., Schwiedrzik, C. M., Muller, N., Rodriguez, E. & Singer, W. (2011). Expectations change the signatures and timing of electrophysiological correlates of perceptual awareness. *Journal of Neuroscience, 31*, 1386–1396.

Nagel, T. (1974). What is it like to be a bat? *Philosophical Review, 83*, 435–450.

Pepperberg, I. M. (1999). The Alex Studies: Cognitive and Communicative Abilities of Grey Parrots. Cambridge, MA: Harvard University Press.

Pitts, M. A., Metzler, S. & Hillyard, S. A. (2014). Isolating neural correlates of conscious perception from neural correlates of reporting one's perception. *Frontiers in Psychology*, 5, 1078.

Prinz, J. J. (2012). *The Conscious Brain: How Attention Engenders Experience*. Oxford: Oxford University Press.

Ray, S. & Maunsell, J. H. (2011). Network rhythms influence the relationship between spike-triggered local field potential and functional connectivity. *Journal of Neuroscience,* 31, 12674–12682.

Schooler, J. W., Smallwood, J., Christoff, K., Handy, T. C., Reichle, E. D., & Sayette, M. A. (2011). Meta-awareness, perceptual decoupling and the wandering mind. *Trends in Cognitive Sciences*, 15(7), 319–326.

Shewmon, D. A. Holmes, G. L. & Byrne, P. A. (1999). Consciousness in congenitally decorticate children: Developmental vegetative state as self-fulfilling prophecy. *Developmental Medicine and Child Neurology*, 41, 364–374.

Smallwood, J. & Schooler, J. W. (2015). The science of mind wandering: Empirically navigating the stream of consciousness. *Annual Review of Psychology*, 66, 487–518.

Tononi, G. (2004). An information integration theory of consciousness. *BMC Neuroscience*, 5:42.

Tononi, G. (2008). Consciousness as integrated information: A provisional manifesto. *Biological Bulletin*, 215, 216–242.

EPILOGUE: BEYOND *NOTHING BUTTERY*

234 Crick, 1994.

235 Arthur Koestler, Clive Staples Lewis, and Donald M. MacKay have all been credited with the phrase "nothing buttery" to describe this class of arguments.

236 See Clayton & Davies, 2006, for a number of views.

237 Chalmers, 2006.

238 Lucas, 2011. See Chapter 1, The Organization Effect.

239 Anderson, 1972, p. 393.

240 Holland, 1995.

241 See Eric Chaisson, 2001, 2004, 2005, for a wondrous introduction to *cosmic evolution*.

242 Chaisson, 2004.

243 Swenson, 2000.

244 This effect is what Gerald Edelman, 1989, called the *remembered present*.

245 This quote is from Chapter 1.
246 Jameson, Highnote, & Wasserman, 2001.
247 Voorhees, 2000, pp. 55-56.
248 Dennett, 2003, p.16-17.
249 Dennett, 2003, p. 7.
250 Baumeister, 2008, p. 14.

251 Readiness potential is the English translation of
    bereitschaftspotential from the German. Kornhuber and Deecke,
    1965, 1990, discovered this process and introduced the German
    term in 1965.
252 Libet, 1985, 1999; Libet et al., 1983.
253 See the discussion of free won't by Brass & Haggard, 2007.
254 Rigoni et al., 2015.
255 Rigoni et al., 2011.
256 Lucas, 2011, p. 77.
257 Edelman, 2006, p. 145.
258 Edelman, 2003, p. 5523.
259 As Lokhurst, 2014, notes, Descartes' thinking varied at times, and
    there are several varying interpretations of how best to
    characterize his ideas about the connection between mind and
    body. However, at times Descartes clearly suggested that mind
    and body could interact, making him an interactionist.
260 Koch, 2018, Chapter 8.
261 Tononi & Koch, 2015, see abstract.
262 Tononi, 2004, 2008; Tononi, Boly, Massimini, & Koch, 2016;
    Tononi & Koch, 2015.
263 Edelman & Tononi, 2000.
264 Tononi, Boly, Massimini, & Koch, 2016; Tononi & Koch, 2015.
265 Dehaene & Naccache, 2001.
266 Baars, 1988, 1997.
267 Baars, 2002.
268 Dehaene & Naccache, 2001.
269 Dehaene, 2014.
270 Block, 1998.
271 See Fries, 2015
272 Gollo et al., 2015.
273 Damasio, 1999.
274 Huang et al., 2020.
275 Lakoff & Johnson, 1999, p. 46. The authors describe this as an
    extension from "sensorimotor to subjective (nonsensorimotor)
    experiences." The subjective experiences are more abstract.

276 Lucas, 2011. See Chapter 16, An Incremental Storm.
277 Lakoff, 2002.
278 Gallese & Lakoff, 2005.
279 Graybiel, 1998, 2008.
280 Bjordahl, Dimyan & Weinberger, 1998; Fuller et al., 2011; Kilgard
    & Merzenich, 1998; Kilgard et al., 2002.
281 Hodas & Lerman, 2014.
282 Quote from Lucas, 2011, Chapter 19, The Stuff of
    Consciousness. I'm still trying to refine these ideas but it should
    be clear they have a long history.
283 Nagel, 1974.
284 Dennett, 1991.
285 Chalmers, 1995.
286 Graybiel, 1998, 2008.
287 Lakoff & Johnson, 1980; 1999.
288 Lakoff & Johnson, 1980; 1999.
289 Graybiel, 1998, 2008.

Anderson, P. W. (1972). More is different. *Science*, 177, 393–396.
Baars, B. J. (1988). *A Cognitive Theory of Consciousness.*
    Cambridge, MA: Cambridge University Press
Baars, B. J. (1997). *In the Theater of Consciousness.* New York, NY:
    Oxford University Press.
Baars, B. J. (2002). The conscious access hypothesis: Origins and
    recent evidence. *Trends in Cognitive Sciences*, 6 (1), 47–52.
Baumeister, R. F. (2008). Free will in scientific psychology.
    Perspectives on Psychological Science, 3, 14–19.
Bjordahl, T. S., Dimyan, M. A. & Weinberger, N. M. (1998). Induction
    of long-term receptive field plasticity in the auditory cortex of the
    waking guinea pig by stimulation of the nucleus basalis.
    Behavioral Neuroscience, 112, 467–479.
Block, N. (1998). On a confusion about a function of consciousness.
    In N. Block, O. Flanagan, & G. Guzeldere, (Eds.), *The Nature of
    Consciousness: Philosophical Debates,* (pp. 375–415).
    Cambridge, MA: MIT Press.
Brass, M. & Haggard, P. (2007). To do or not to do: The neural
    signature of self-control. *Journal of Neuroscience*, 27, 9141–9145.
Cahill, L. (2006). Why sex matters for neuroscience. *Nature Reviews
    Neuroscience*, 7, 477–484.
Chaisson, E. J. (2001). *Cosmic Evolution: The Rise of Complexity in
    Nature.* Cambridge, MA: Harvard University Press.
Chaisson, E. J. (2004). Complexity: An energetics agenda.

Complexity, Journal of the Santa Fe Institute, 9, 14–21.

Chaisson, E. J. (2005). *Epic of Evolution: Seven Ages of the Cosmos.* New York: Columbia University Press.

Chalmers, D. J. (1995). Facing up to the problem of consciousness. *Journal of Consciousness Studies*, 2(3), 200–219.

Chalmers, D. J. (1997). Moving forward on the problem of consciousness. *Journal of Consciousness Studies*, 4(1), 3–46.

Chalmers, D. J. (2006). Strong and weak emergence. In P. Clayton & P. Davies: *The Re-Emergence of Emergence: The Emergentist Hypothesis from Science to Religion,* (pp. 244–255). Oxford: Oxford University Press.

Clark, A. (2008). Supersizing the Mind: Embodiment, Action, and Associative Extension. Oxford: Oxford University Press,

Clayton, P. & Davies, P. (2006). The Re-Emergence of Emergence: The Emergentist Hypothesis from Science to Religion. Oxford: Oxford University Press.

Crick, F. (1994). The Astonishing Hypothesis: The Scientific Search For The Soul. New York: Charles Scribner's Sons.

Dawkins, R. (1989, New Edition). *The Selfish Gene.* New York: Oxford University Press.

Damasio, A. R. (1999). The Feeling of What Happens: Body and Emotion in the Making of Consciousness. New York: Harcourt Brace & Co.

Dehaene, S. (2014). Consciousness and the Brain: Deciphering How the Brain Codes Our Thoughts. City of Westminster, London: Penguin Books.

Dehaene & Naccache, (2001). Towards a cognitive neuroscience of consciousness: Basic evidence and a workspace framework. *Cognition*, 79, 1–37.

Dennett, D. C. (2003). Explaining the "magic" of consciousness. *Journal of Cultural and Evolutionary Psychology*, 1, 7–19.

Edelman, G. M. (1989). The Remembered Present: A Biological Theory of Consciousness. New York: Basic Books.

Edelman, G. M. (2003). Naturalizing consciousness: A theoretical framework. *Proceedings of the National Academy of Sciences (USA)*, 100 (9), 5520-5524.

Edelman, G. M. (2006). *Second Nature: Brain Science and Human Knowledge.* New Haven: Yale University Press.

Edelman, G. M. & Tononi, G. (2000). *A Universe of Consciousness: How Matter Becomes Imagination.* New York: Basic Books.

Fries, P. (2015). Rhythms for cognition: Communication through coherence. *Neuron*, 88, 220–235.

Fuller, P.M., Sherman, D., Pedersen, N.P., Saper, C.B & Lu, J. (2011). Reassessment of the structural basis of the ascending arousal system. *Journal of Comparative Neurology*, 519(5), 933–956.

Gallese, V. & Lakoff, G. (2005). The brain's concepts: The role of the sensory-motor system in conceptual knowledge. *Cognitive Neuropsychology*, 22, 455–479.

Gollo, L. L., Zalesky, A., Hutchison, R. M., van den Heuvel, M., & Breakspear, M. (2015). Dwelling quietly in the rich club: brain network determinants of slow cortical fluctuations. *Philosophical Transactions of the Royal Society B*, 370: 20140165.

Graybiel, A. M. (1998). The basal ganglia and chunking of action repertoires. *Neurobiology of Learning and Memory*, 70, 119–136.

Graybiel, A. M. (2008). Habits, rituals, and the evaluative brain. *Annual Review of Neuroscience*, 31, 359–387.

Hodas, N. O. & Lerman, K. (2014). The simple rules of social contagion. *Scientific Reports*, 4, 4343.

Holland, J. H. (1995). *Hidden Order: How Adaptation Builds Complexity*. Reading, MA: Perseus Books

Huang, Z., Zhang, J., Wu, J., Mashour, G. A., & Hudetz, A. G. (2020). Temporal circuit of macroscale dynamic brain activity supports human consciousness. *Science Advances*, 11: eaaz0087.

Jameson, K. A., Highnote, S. M., & Wasserman, L. M. (2001). Richer colour experience in observers with multiple photopigment opsin genes. *Psychonomic Bulletin & Review*, 8, 244–261.

Kilgard, M. P. & Merzenich, M. M. (1998). Cortical map reorganization enabled by nucleus basalis activity. *Nature Neuroscience*, 1, 727–731.

Kilgard, M. P., Pandya, P. K., Engineer, N. D. & Moucha, R. (2002). Cortical network reorganization guided by sensory input features. *Biological Cybernetics*, 87, 333–343. Koch, C. (2018). The Feeling of Life Itself. Cambridge, MA: MIT Press.

Kornhuber, H. H. & Deecke, L. (1965). Hirnpotentialanderungen bei Willkurbewegungen und passive Bewegungen des Menschen: Bereitschaftspotential und reafferente Potentiale. Pflügers Archiv für die Gesamte Physiologie des Menschen und der Tiere, 284, 1–17.

Kornhuber, H. H. & Deecke, L. (1990). Readiness for movement – The Bereitschaftspotential-Story, *Current Contents Life Sciences* 33, 14.

Lakoff, G. (1987). Women, Fire, and Dangerous Things: What Categories Reveal about the Mind. Chicago: University of Chicago

Press.

Lakoff, G. & Johnson, M. (1980). *Metaphors We Live By*. Chicago: University of Chicago Press.

Lakoff, G. & Johnson, M. (1999). Philosophy in the Flesh: The Embodied Mind and Its Challenge to Western Thought. New York: Basic Books.

Lakoff, G. (2002). *Moral Politics: How Liberals and Conservatives Think*. University of Chicago Press, 2002.

Libet, B. (1985). Unconscious cerebral initiative and the role of conscious will in voluntary action. *Behavioral and Brain Sciences, 8*, 529–566.

Libet, B. (1999). Do we have free will? *Journal of Consciousness Studies*, 6 (8–9), 11–29.

Libet, B., Gleason, C. A., Wright, E. W. & Pearl, D. K. (1983). Time of conscious intention to act in relation to onset of cerebral activity (readiness potential): The unconscious initiation of a freely voluntary act. *Brain*, 106, 623–642.

Lokhorst, G-J. (2014). Descartes and the pineal gland. In: Edward N. Zalta (Ed.), *The Stanford Encyclopedia of Philosophy* (Spring 2014 Edition), URL = <http://plato.stanford.edu/archives/spr2014/entries/pineal-gland/>.

Lucas, G. A. (2011). Emergence, Mind, and Consciousness: A Bio-Inspired Design for a Conscious Agent. Bloomington, IN: iUniverse.

Nagel, T. (1974). What is it like to be a bat? Philosophical Review, 83, 435–450.

Rigoni, D., Kühn, S., Sartori, G. & Brass, M. (2011). Inducing disbelief in free will alters brain correlates of preconscious motor preparation: The brain minds whether we believe in free will or not. *Psychological Science, 22(5), 613– 618.*

Rigoni, D., Pourtois, G. & Brass, M. (2015). 'Why should I care?' Challenging free will attenuates neural reaction to errors. *Social Cognition and Affective Neuroscience*, 10(2), 262–268.

Swenson, R. (2000). Spontaneous order, autocatakinetic closure, and the development of space-time. *Annals of the New York Academy of Sciences*, 901, 311–319.

Tononi, G. (2004). An information integration theory of consciousness. *BMC Neuroscience*, 5:42.

Tononi, G. (2008). Consciousness as integrated information: A provisional manifesto. *Biological Bulletin*, 215, 216–242.

Tononi, G., Boly, M., Massimini, M., & Koch, C. (2016). Integrated information theory: From consciousness to its physical substrate.

Nature Reviews Neuroscience, 17, 450–461.

Tononi. G. & Koch, C. (2015). Consciousness: Here, there and everywhere? *Philosophical Transactions of the Royal Society of London B*, 370, 20140167.

Voorhees, B. (2000). Dennett and the deep blue sea. *Journal of Consciousness Studies*, 7, 53–69.

APPENDIX: EVOLVING CORE CONSCIOUSNESS

290 See Descartes, 1955; Lokhorst, 2014.

291 Chalmers, 1997.

292 Lubinski & Thompson, 1993, have shown that pigeons can learn to report, via different responses, about experiential states induced by a stimulant, cocaine, a depressant, pentobarbital, or a control, saline. While we cannot be certain of exactly what subjective feelings the pigeons use for this discrimination, it seems clear that they are aware of states that as humans we would call feelings.

293 See Fujita, Blough, & Blough, 1991, for evidence that pigeons experience the Ponzo illusion.

294 Carruthers, 1996, 1998.

295 Browne, 1999.

296 Damasio, 1999, 2010, argues that consciousness involves an object-organism interaction. Note also that life urges are re-represented several times more in the cortex (see Craig, 2010). Thus, there are plenty of opportunities for higher-order object-organism interactions to gain consciousness without language.

297 Carruthers, 1989, p. 268.

298 Keijzer, 2017.

299 Berg, 2003.

300 For broader definitions of cognition and intelligence extending to protists and plants see Trewavas, 2017.

301 Elkameem et al., 2018.

302 Stopfer, 2014.

303 Klein & Barron, 2016. See also, Feinberg & Mallatt, 2016.

304 Edelman's *primary consciousness*, 1989, corresponds to what Antonio Damasio, 1999, called *core consciousness*. Both these involve states of feeling-bound awareness.

305 Damasio, 1999, p.170.

306 Llinás, 2001.

307 Trestman, 2013. p.80.

308 Parker, 2004.

309 Ginsburg & Jablonka, 2010.

310 Merker, 2005, p. 89.

311 Cabanac, 1996; Cabanac, Cabanac, & Parent. 2009.

312 Stephenson-Jones et al., 2011, 2012, 2013.

313 Butler & Hodos, 1996, p.457.

314 See Denton, 2006; Denton, McKinley, Farrell, &. Egan, 2009; Panksepp, 2005.

315 Denton, McKinley, Farrell, &. Egan, 2009, p. 500.

316 Damasio et al., 2000. See Damasio & Carvalho, 2013, for a more recent version of this argument.

317 McDougall, 1923, p. 110.

318 Damasio, 1999.

319 Clark & Squire, 1998.

320 Damasio, 1999, p. 270.

321 Panksepp, 1998, 2005.

322 Zamora-Lopez, Zhou, & Kurths, 2011.

323 Bassham & Postlethwait, 2005.

324 Lacalli, 2001; Lacalli & Kelly, 2000.

325 Wicht & Northcutt, 1998.

326 Butler and Hodos, 1996; Stephenson-Jones, Ericsson, Robertson, & Grillner, 2012.

327 Feinberg & Mallatt, 2016.

328 Butler, 2008.

329 Long et al., 2006.

330 Shubin, Dreschler, & Jenkins, 2006.

331 See Karten, 1991; Medina & Reiner, 2000; Reiner, 2002.

332 Puelles et al., 2000.

333 Durstewitz, Kröner & Güntürkün, 1999.

334 Rattenborg, Martinez-Gonzalez & Lesku, 2009.

335 Olkowicx et al., 2016.

336 Calabrese & Woolley, 2015; Güntürkün & Bugnyar, 2016.

337 Husband & Shimizu, 2001.

338 Husband & Shimizu, 2001.

339 Csillag & Montagnese, 2005.

340 Güntürkün, 2005.

341 Brown, 2015.

342 Brown, 2012.

343 Bshary, Gingins, & Vail, 2014.

344 Brown, 2015.

345 Rose, 2002; Rose et al., 2014.

346 Key, 2016. The broad consensus among reviewers of Key's article is that a laminated cortex is not essential for similar functions. See, in particular, the review by Bjorn Merker, 2016.

347 See Ritchie, 1979; Husband et al., 1995.

348 For an example see Chandroo, Yue, & Moccia, 2004.

349 Brown, 2015.

350 Sneddon, 2011.

351 Sneddon, 2003.

352 For fish, see Trinh et al., 2016. For avians see Calabrese & Woolley, 2015; Güntürkün & Bugnyar, 2016.

353 Keijzer, 2017.

Bassham, S. & Postlethwait, K. (2005). The evolutionary history of placodes: A molecular genetic investigation of the larvacean urochordate *Oikopleura dioica*. *Development*, 132(19), 4259–4272.

Berg, H. C. (2003). The rotary motor of bacterial flagella. *Annual Review of Biochemistry*, 72, 19–54.

Brown, C. (2012). Tool use in fishes. *Fish and Fisheries*, 13, 105–115.

Brown, C. (2015). Fish intelligence, sentience and ethics. *Animal Cognition*, 18(1), 1–17. http://psych.cs.monash edu. au/v4/psyche-4-03-carruthers.html

Bshary, R., Gingins, S., & Vail, A. L. (2014). Social cognition in fishes. *Trends in Cognitive Sciences*, 18(9), 465–471.

Butler, A. B. (2008). Evolution of the thalamus: A morphological and functional review. *Thalamus & Related Systems*, 4(1), 35–58.

Butler, A. B. & Hodos, W. (1996). Comparative Vertebrate Neuroanatomy: Evolution and Adaptation. New York: Wiley-Liss.

Cabanac, M. (1995). On the origin of consciousness, a postulate and its corollary. *Neuroscience and Biobehavioral Review*, 20, 33–40.

Cabanac, M., Cabanac, A. J., & Parent, A. (2009). The emergence of consciousness in phylogeny. *Behavioural Brain Research*, 198, 267–272.

Carruthers, P. (1989). Brute experience. *The Journal of Philosophy*, *86*(5), 258–269.

Carruthers, P. (1996). Language, thought and consciousness: An essay in philosophical psychology. Cambridge: Cambridge University Press.

Carruthers, P. (1998). Natural theories of consciousness. *European Journal of Philosophy, 6(2), 203–222.*

Chalmers, D. J. (1997). Facing up to the problem of consciousness. *Journal of Consciousness Studies*, 4(1), 3–46.

Chandroo, K. P., Yue, S., & Moccia, R. D. (2004). An evaluation of current perspectives on consciousness and pain in fishes. *Fish and Fisheries*, 5, 281–295.

Calabrese, A. & Woolley, S.M.N. (2015). Coding principles of the canonical cortical microcircuit in the avian brain. *Proceedings of the National Academy of Sciences (USA)*, 112, 3517–3522.

Clark, R. E. & Squire, L. R. (1998). Classical conditioning and brain systems: The role of awareness. *Science*, 280, 77–81.

Craig A. D. (2010). The sentient self. *Brain Structure and Function*, 214, 563–577.

Csillag, A. & Montagnese, C. M. (2005). Thalamotelencephalic organization in birds. *Brain Research Bulletin*, 66, 303–310.

Damasio, A. R. (1998). Investigating the biology of consciousness. Philosophical *Transaction of the Royal Society of London. B*, 353, 1879–1882.

Damasio, A. R. (1999). The Feeling of What Happens: Body and Emotion in the Making of Consciousness. New York: Harcourt Brace & Co.

Damasio, A. R. (2010). Self Comes to Mind: Constructing the Conscious Brain. New York: Pantheon Books.

Damasio, A. R. & Carvalho, G. B. (2013). The nature of feelings: Evolutionary and neurobiological origins. *Nature Reviews Neuroscience*, 14, 143–152.

Damasio, A. R., Grabowski, T. J., Bechara, A., Damasio, H., Ponto, L. I. B., Ponto, J. P., et al (2000). Subcortical and cortical brain activity during the feeling of self-generated emotions. *Nature Neuroscience*, 3, 1049–1056.

Dehaene, S. (2014). Consciousness and the Brain: Deciphering How the Brain Codes Our Thoughts. City of Westminster, London: Penguin Books.

Denton, D. A. (2006). *The primordial emotions: The dawning of consciousness*. Oxford: Oxford University Press.

Denton, D. A., McKinley, M. J., Farrell, C. M., & Egan, G. F. (2009). The role of primordial emotions in the evolutionary origin of consciousness. *Consciousness and Cognition*, 18, 500–514.

Descartes, R. (1955). *The Philosophical Works of Descartes (2 vols)*. Trans. E. S. Haldane & G. R. T. Ross. New York: Dover.

Durstewitz, D., Kröner, S., & Güntürkün, O. (1999). The dopaminergic innervation of the avian telencephalon. *Progress in Neurobiology*, 59, 161–195.

Edelman, G. M. (1989). The Remembered Present: A Biological Theory of Consciousness. New York: Basic Books.

Elhakeem, A., Markovic, D., Broberg, A., Anten, N.P.R., Ninkovic, V. (2018). Above ground mechanical stimuli affect below ground plant-plant communication. *PLoSONE* 13(5): e0195646.

Feinberg, T. E. & Mallatt, J. (2016). The nature of primary consciousness. A new synthesis. *Consciousness and Cognition*, 43, 113–127.

Fries, P. (2005). A mechanism for cognitive dynamics: Neural communication through neural coherence. *Trends in Cognitive Sciences*, 9, 474–480.

Fries, P. (2015). Rhythms for cognition: Communication through coherence. *Neuron*, 88, 220–235.

Fujita, K., Blough, D. S., & Blough, P. M. (1991). Pigeons see the Ponzo illusion. *Animal Learning & Behavior*, 19, 283–293.

Ginsburg S. & Jablonka, E. (2010). The evolution of associative learning: A factor in the Cambrian explosion. *Journal of Theoretical Biology*, 266(1), 11–20.

Güntürkün, O. (2005). The avian 'prefrontal cortex' and cognition. *Current Opinion in Neurobiology*, 15, 686–693.

Güntürkün, O. & Bugnyar, T. (2016). Cognition without cortex. *Trends in Cognitive Sciences*, 20(4), 291–303.

Husband, S. & Shimizu, T. (2001). Evolution of the avian visual system. In: R. G. Cook (Ed.) Avian Visual Cognition. Cyberbook published in cooperation with Comparative Cognition Press at: http://www.pigeon.psy.tufts.edu/avc/husband/default.htm

Karten, H. J. (1991). Homology and evolutionary origins of the 'neocortex'. *Brain Behavior & Evolution*. 38, 264–272.

Keijzer, F. A. (2017). Evolutionary convergence and biologically embodied cognition. *Interface Focus*, 7: 20160123.

Key, B. (2016). Why fish do not feel pain. *Animal Sentience* 2016.003.

Klein, C. & Barron A. B. (2016). Insects have the capacity for subjective experience. *Animal Sentience*, 9(1).

Lacalli, T. C. & Kelly, S. J. (2000). The infundibular balance organ in *Amphioxus* larvae and related aspects of cerebral vesicle organization. *Acta Zoologica,* 81, 37–47.

Lacalli T. C. (2001). Frontal eye circuitry, rostral sensory pathways and brain organization in amphioxus larvae: Evidence from 3D reconstructions. *Philosophical Transactions of the Royal Society of London, B*, 356, 1565–1572.

Llinás, R. (2001). *I of the Vortex: From Neurons to Self*. Cambridge, MA: Bradford/MIT Press.

Lokhorst, G-J. (2014). Descartes and the pineal gland. In: Edward N. Zalta (Ed.), *The Stanford Encyclopedia of Philosophy* (Spring 2014 Edition), URL = http://plato. stanford. edu/archives/spr2014/entries/pineal-gland/

Long, J. A., Young, G. C., Holland, T., Senden, T. J., & Fitzgerald, E. M. G. (2006). An exceptional Devonian fish from Australia sheds light on tetrapod origins, *Nature*, 444, 199–202.

Lubinski, D. & Thompson, T. (1993). Species and individual differences in communication based on private states. *Behavioral and Brain Sciences,* 16, 627–680.

McDougall, W. (1923). *An Outline of Psychology*. London: Charles Scribner's Sons.

Medina, L. & Reiner, A. (2000). Do birds possess homologues of mammalian primary visual, somatosensory and motor cortices? *Trends in Neurosciences,* 23, 1–12.

Merker, B. (2005). The liabilities of mobility: A selection pressure for the transition to consciousness in animal evolution. *Consciousness and Cognition*, 14, 89–114.

Merker, B. (2016). Drawing the line on pain. *Animal Sentience*, 2016.030.

Olkowicz, S. et al. (2016). Birds have primate-like numbers of neurons in the forebrain. *Proceedings of the National Academy of Sciences (USA)*, 1517131113v1-201517131.

Panksepp, J. (1998). *Affective Neuroscience.* Oxford: Oxford University Press.

Panksepp, J. (2005). On the embodied neural nature of core emotional affects. *Journal of Consciousness Studies*, 12(8–10), 158–184.

Parker, A. (2004). In The Blink Of An Eye: How Vision Sparked The Big Bang Of Evolution. Basic Books.

Puelles, L., Kuwana, E., Puelles, E., Bulfone, A., Shimamura, K., Keleher, J., Smiga, S., Rubenstein, J. L. R. (2000). Pallial and subpallial derivatives in the embryonic chick and mouse telencephalon, traced by the expression of the genes Dlx-2, Emx-1, Nkx-2. 1, Pax-6, and Tbr-1. *Journal of Comparative Neurology*, 424, 409–438.

Rattenborg, N. C., Martinez-Gonzalez, D. & Lesku, J. A. (2009). Avian sleep homeostasis: Convergent evolution of complex brains, cognition and sleep functions in mammals and birds. *Neuroscience and Biobehavioral Reviews*, 33, 253–270.

Reiner, A. (2002). Functional circuitry of the avian basal ganglia: Implications for basal ganglia organization in stem amniotes. *Brain*

Research Bulletin, 57, 513–528.

Shubin, N. H., Daeschler, E. B., & Jenkins, F. A. (2006). The pectoral fin of *Tiktaalik roseae* and the origin of the tetrapod limb. *Nature, 440,* 764–771.

Sneddon, L. U. (2003). The evidence for pain in fish: The use of morphine as an analgesic. *Applied Animal Behavior Science, 83,*153–162.

Sneddon, L. U. (2011). Pain perception in fish: Evidence and implications for the use of fish. *Journal of Consciousness Studies, 18,* 209–229.

Stephenson-Jones, M., Samuelsson, E., Ericsson, J., Robertson, B., & Grillner, S. (2011). Evolutionary conservation of the basal ganglia as a common vertebrate mechanism for action selection. *Current Biology, 21,* 1081–1091.

Stephenson-Jones, M., Ericsson, J., Robertson, B., & Grillner, S. (2012). Evolution of the basal ganglia: Dual-output pathways conserved throughout vertebrate phylogeny. *Journal of Comparative Neurology, 520,* 2957–2973.

Stephenson-Jones, M., Kardamakis, A. A., Robertson, B., & Grillner, S. (2013). Independent circuits in the basal ganglia for the evaluation and selection of actions. *Proceedings of the National Academy of Science (USA),* 110, E3670–3679.

Stopfer, M. (2014). Central processing in the mushroom bodies. *Current Opinion in Insect Science,* 6, 99–103.

Trestman, M. (2013). The Cambrian explosion and the origins of embodied cognition. *Biological Theory,* 8. 80–92.

Trewavas, A. (2017). The foundations of plant intelligence. *Interface Focus,* 7: 20160098.

Trinh, A-T., Harvey-Girard, E., Teixeira, F., & Maler, L. (2016). Cryptic laminar and columnar organization in the dorsolateral pallium of a weakly electric fish. *Journal of Comparative Neurology,* 524, 408–428.

Wicht, H. & Northcutt, R. G. (1998). Telencephalic connections in the Pacific hagfish (*Eptatretus stouti*), with special reference to the thalamopallial system. *The Journal of Comparative Neurology,* 395, 245–260.

Zamora-Lopez, G., Zhou, C., & Kurths, J. (2011). Exploring brain function from anatomical connectivity. *Frontiers in Neuroscience,* 5:83.